# UVF

## JIM CUSACK
## HENRY McDONALD

POOLBEG

Published 1997 by
Poolbeg Press Ltd
123 Baldoyle Industrial Estate
Dublin 13, Ireland

A catalogue record for this book is available from the British Library.

ISBN 1 85371 687 1

Cover design by Poolbeg Group Services Ltd
Set by Poolbeg Group Services Ltd in Stone 9.5/13.5
Printed by The Guernsey Press Ltd,
Vale, Guernsey, Channel Islands.

# CONTENTS

## ABOUT THE AUTHORS

Jim Cusack worked as a reporter for *The Irish News*, *The Belfast Telegraph* and as Northern Editor of *The Irish Times* during the height of loyalist violence in the 1970s. He is now Security Correspondent of *The Irish Times*.

Henry McDonald is Northern Ireland Correspondent for *The Sunday Times*. He is the author of *Irishbatt: The Irish Army in Lebanon* and co-author with Jack Holland of *INLA: Deadly Divisions*.

In writing this book the authors were determined never to forget the innocent victims who have been killed or maimed over the last three decades of sectarian conflict. The UVF, like other paramilitary groups, has been responsible for a series of heinous crimes against ordinary people, which have left thousands of families devastated. When attempting to understand the reasons for the existence of organisations such as the UVF, we were always mindful of the pain and suffering inflicted by such groups.

Nevertheless, it is imperative that in the spring of 1997, as the people of Northern Ireland wait to see if there will be peace or renewed ethnic war, we examine the roots of UVF and loyalist violence. Until now there has been a dearth of literature related to all the loyalist terrorist movements in the North. This may be somewhat deliberate.

According to violent nationalist ideology, the loyalists don't really exist. They are portrayed merely as "puppets of imperialism" or "death squads" under the command and control of their British masters. This is the standard line of much of the left in Ireland and Britain as well as the Provisional IRA's traditional nationalist intellectual sympathisers in the Republic. To put their case bluntly, the "Prods" are really misguided Irishmen who, when Britain decides to withdraw from Ulster, will come to their senses and integrate into a United Ireland.

This of course is fantasy politics and poor history. The existence of the UVF, in both its original and modern forms, proves that there is unbroken indigenous resistance to Irish nationalist designs. The British presence in Ireland is the million Protestants who want to remain British. The UDA and UVF are merely the most violent manifestation of Unionist opposition to republican goals.

By the time this book is published, all-party talks will be underway at Stormont. The grave danger for policy makers in Dublin and London is that in their well-intentioned desperation to get Sinn Féin into the negotiations (predicated on an IRA ceasefire) they will alienate all the unionist parties. The mandarins at the Department of Foreign Affairs and the Northern Ireland Office may be tempted to steam ahead with some kind of Anglo-Irish Agreement Mark II which might just get the support of the SDLP, Sinn Féin and small political constellations like the Women's Coalition. This however would alienate the entire unionist population and leave the UVF and its political ally the Progressive Unionist Party with no choice but to walk out of talks. Such a scenario could only lead to more loyalist violence and deeper ethnic conflict across the North, which would inevitably spill over into the Republic.

It is fair to say that thirty years after the UVF's reformation, men who emerged from that movement such as Gusty Spence, David Ervine, Billy Hutchinson, and others who prefer to remain in the shadows, seem genuinely interested in an historic compromise with nationalism. Their metamorphosis from sectarian militarism to a position more liberal than the mainstream Ulster Unionist Party has been a remarkable political journey. While preserving the union, they appear prepared to accept some form of government which would accommodate nationalist rights and fears.

Their position at present though is threatened by anti-ceasefire rejectionists. Indeed the ceasefire seems to be cracking under the strain as rebel loyalists defy the Combined

2

Loyalist Military Command's direction to hold fire. Recent attacks on republicans and the callous slaying of John Slane in front of his children in March have undermined Ervine and Co's claim that the loyalist ceasefire is still intact.

The UVF, an even older organisation than the IRA, is a product of the upheavals of the early 20th century in Ireland, from the Home Rule crisis to the carnage of the Somme. In our century across Europe millions were slaughtered in the name of a nation, a class or a creed. Grandiose designs, historic missions and national destinies have resulted in disaster. Ireland has not been immune from this disease. Today at the end of the century there are still those in the post-nationalist Republic who dream about the "unfinished business of the national revolution". Their dangerous delusions have coloured much of Irish intellectual and political life over the last 30 years. In its present guise, violent nationalism is trying to set the agenda of the Irish political establishment and push the Dublin government and its allies, the SDLP, in a more extreme direction than their own democratic instincts should allow.

The purpose of this book is to show the other side of the Irish question, to point up how trenchant, ruthless and brutal Protestant resistance towards violent nationalism's agenda has been in the past and will be in the future.

*Jim Cusack, Henry McDonald*
*April 7, 1997*

3

## One

## A DEADLY CONSPIRACY

Matilda Gould lived with her son in a small rented house in Upper Charleville Street, in the heart of the Protestant Shankill area of west Belfast. She was a 77-year-old widow and had difficulty in walking, but still managed to look after her son, Samuel, an engineering worker. He paid her £4 a week to wash his clothes, do his cooking, and clean the small house they rented from Gerard McKeown, the Catholic proprietor of the off-licence next door.

The two premises were painted similarly and, to some people, the Goulds' home was indistinguishable from the Catholic property next door. During the early spring nights of 1966 someone painted anti-Catholic slogans on the wall of Goulds' home apparently under the impression it was part of McKeown's shop. The graffiti was traditional, crude sectarian fare proclaiming: *Remember 1690. This house is owned by a Teague, and Popehead.*

At 10.40 p.m. on May 7, 1966, Mrs Gould had retired to her bed – set up in the ground floor front parlour because of her difficulty with the stairs – and, it is presumed, was sleeping. Two men, one wearing a Dexter raincoat with its collar pulled up around his face, emerged from an entry, crossed Charleville Street and threw a Molotov cocktail into the room where she lay in her bed.

The men had been seen by several people, including a schoolboy, Samuel Andrews, who said the man whose coat collar was pulled up around his face and who threw the petrol bomb appeared to be drunk.

The attack brought neighbours running and two men broke down the Goulds' front door to save whoever was inside. William McGuinness, from Upper Charleville Street, broke into the front room and turned over the bed but found no one. Outside, neighbours insisted that an elderly, crippled woman slept in the room and McGuinness and another man braved the flames a second time. They found Mrs Gould lying behind the door, still burning from the petrol which had been sprayed over her.

She was taken to the Royal Victoria Hospital and died there from her injuries seven weeks later. At her inquest, a barrister appearing for Mrs Gould's son, Samuel, observed: "I think it is clear that this woman was murdered by members of an unlawful association. This old, crippled lady lived next door to an off-licence owned by a Roman Catholic and, unfortunately, a petrol bomb was thrown into her bedroom."

The barrister, William Doyle – a Catholic who later became a judge and was himself killed by republican gunmen – sought evidence from RUC Detective James McComb. McComb said he had been given the name of a suspect, a man with a prison record, but there was not sufficient evidence to charge him. He added: "I think the act was part and parcel of the activities of an organisation known as the Ulster Volunteer Force."

Thus Matilda Gould, it can be said, was the first victim of the UVF, and although almost never recalled, the first of more than 3,000 victims of the ensuing decades of civil conflict in Northern Ireland.

Sporadic petrol bombing and vandalism aimed at Catholic property had been underway since the start of 1966, particularly in and around the Shankill Road. The petrol bomb which killed Matilda Gould had its desired effect, anyway, as the Catholic off-licence owner immediately transferred his business across the Crumlin Road to the mainly Catholic Ardoyne area.

The attempts to foment further sectarian violence included the firing of two revolver shots through the front door of the home of a local Unionist politician, Johnny McQuade, on April 16, 1966.

It was the intention of the gunmen, a group which gathered in a public house in the lower Shankill Road and who had begun to call themselves the UVF, to create the impression that republicans had come into the Shankill and attempted to kill a local political leader. This, in the minds of the gunmen, would provide some form of excuse for their coming acts of violence, such as the bungled petrol bombing of the Catholic off-licence in Upper Charleville Street.

At a subsequent compensation case brought by Mrs Gould's son, Samuel, the attack was said to be the work of the "Shankill UVF". This group was described by Justice Gibson (also, incidentally, killed later by bombers from the Catholic Irish Republican Army) as: "a seditious combination or unlawful association whose activities were directed to asserting and maintaining the Protestant ascendancy, in areas of the city where there was a predominantly Protestant majority of the local population, by overt acts of terror". An anonymous telephone caller to a Belfast newspaper later claimed the attack was not the work of the UVF. However, the local police continued to insist it was and that the man who threw the petrol bomb was later jailed for other, less serious offences.

Granting Samuel damages of £336 for the loss of his mother's care and assistance, Justice Gibson referred to police testimony that the attacks on the Shankill were the work of a group "known as the Ulster Protestant Action which later changed its name to the Ulster Volunteer Force".

While Mrs Gould was still in hospital, dying from her injuries, the UVF struck again. On the evening of May 27,

1966, a Catholic man, John Patrick Scullion, was admitted to the Royal Victoria Hospital, apparently the victim of a beating or accident.

He died fifteen days later and was buried, also without public attention, in Milltown Cemetery. It was believed he had been the victim of a fall or some other kind of accident. He had an abdominal wound which was not properly diagnosed. There was no reason, apparently, for wider concern at what had happened to Scullion, a 28-year-old Catholic engineering worker from Oranmore Street, in the Falls Road area. Belfast doctors were not accustomed to examining accident and emergency patients for gunshot wounds. It was known Scullion had been drinking the night he died and his seemed a fairly typical case of a befuddled drunk dying from a fall or a beating.

In the days after Scullion died, anonymous telephone calls to Belfast newspapers claimed that an IRA member had been shot dead in the Falls Road area. At first, there was nothing to connect Scullion to the calls. Then, three weeks after Scullion died, one telephone caller to the *Belfast Telegraph*, using the code-name Captain William Johnston, Adjutant of the 1st battalion of the Ulster Volunteer Force, identified Scullion as the victim. The body was exhumed and the undiagnosed abdominal wound was found to have been caused by a gunshot.

Then, on May 21, 1966, an anonymous telephone caller to the *Belfast Telegraph* gave the following message: "From this day we declare war against the IRA and its splinter groups. Known IRA men will be executed mercilessly and without hesitation. Less extreme measures will be taken against anyone sheltering or helping them but, if they persist in giving them aid, then more extreme measures will be adopted. Property will not be exempted in any action taken. We will not tolerate any interference from any source and we solemnly warn the authorities to make no more speeches of

8

appeasement. We are heavily armed Protestants dedicated to this cause."

The fact that a full-blown loyalist terror campaign was underway did not dawn fully on the public until the morning of Sunday, June 26, 1966.

In the early hours, Peter Ward and his three friends left work in the bar of the International Hotel in Belfast city centre and walked to Watson's Bar, in Malvern Street off the lower Shankill Road, for a late-night drink. They kept their own company as did most of the other late-night drinkers, including, in the rear lounge, a small group of off-duty policemen.

At about 2 a.m., a man climbed up the lamppost outside the bar and doused the light. Two other men stood waiting nearby and a fourth waited in a car parked around the corner in Langford Street.

As the first of the four young barmen left by a side entrance, the gunmen approached and opened fire. Richard Leppington, the 16-year-old barman who left first, was able to run off. As he rounded the corner into Brownlow Street, he heard shooting and one of his friends crying: "Don't do it. Don't do it."

Leppington ran back and found his friend Liam Doyle (19) lying on the ground bleeding from a stomach wound. One of the gunmen, who possibly failed to recognise Leppington, told him: "Let him lie there."

Leppington did not see his other friend, Peter Ward (18) who was already dead, or Andrew Kelly (27) who was shot in the stomach and critically ill.

One of the witnesses, a 17-year-old girl who lived opposite Watson's Bar, later recalled seeing the two gunmen waiting at the corner. "They seemed to have guns in their hands and were shooting down Brownlow Street. A third man with a gun in his hand was standing in the middle of Malvern Street and seemed to be shooting round him in circles. He was

9

firing an awful lot. I saw him shoot towards two fellows who were outside the pub. One man fired another bullet into a man who was lying at the pub. A fellow standing at the lamppost had his hands up. He shouted: 'What do you want to shoot me for? I never did anything.' The man with the gun fired at him and shot him in the left side. He looked as if he was going to shoot again and I started to scream and he shot at us. My sister and the other girl jumped out of the way. When I started to scream the man got all excited and he ran to a blue car parked in Langford Street. Two others ran towards the car and they drove off."

The news of the murder reached the Prime Minister of Northern Ireland, Capt. Terence O'Neill, just as he arrived in France for the Battle of the Somme 50th anniversary commemoration service. He returned to Northern Ireland immediately and announced the proscription of the UVF which he described as: "This evil thing in our midst."

Addressing the House of Commons at Stormont, O'Neill referred to his journey to commemorate the original UVF men of the 36th Division who had died at the Somme in 1916. "Let no one imagine that there is any connection whatever between the two bodies: between men who were ready to die for their country on the fields of France and a sordid conspiracy of criminals prepared to take up arms against unprotected fellow citizens."

Proscription under the Special Powers Act made membership of an illegal organisation an offence punishable by imprisonment. The UVF joined the Irish Republican Army (IRA) on the schedule of banned organisations. "I warn those who set their ends before the interest of the community that the Government, acting in the best interests of all, will move against them with rigorous severity," O'Neill said.

By the time O'Neill had spoken, the RUC already had begun making arrests. On June 28, 1966, Augustus Andrew Spence (33) – a shipyard stager and former British Army military policeman – from the Grosvenor Road, appeared in court charged with the murders of Peter Ward and John Patrick Scullion.

Hugh McClean (46) of Larne, Road, Carrickfergus, Co Antrim, and Robert Williamson (33) of Dagmar Street, Belfast, were also charged with the murder of Peter Ward as were two other men, William Millar and George McCullough.

The prosecution case rested heavily on the statements McClean made to police after his arrest. McClean had made a very full statement of admission, although he sought to minimise his own involvement in the Ward murder and other events. Spence made no statement under interrogation and, to this day, rejects McClean's confession as lies.

The Shankill UVF, the court heard, had met regularly in a back room of the Standard Bar where plots to kill IRA members were discussed over drinks. Gusty Spence, he said, chaired the meetings. Among others he named James "Rocky" Burns, Leslie Porter and Henry Hayes, a cousin of Spence's. McClean said Burns supplied the meetings with names and addresses of people he said were IRA members.

The leading target was Leo Martin, a well-known republican in the Falls area. On the evening of June 25, 1966, Spence and Robert Williamson had taken part in a demonstration by the Prince Albert Temperance Loyal Orange Lodge, on the Shankill Road. The Lodge had marched from the home of its leading figure, the MP Johnny McQuade, whose house had been fired on earlier in the year. McQuade led the demonstration down the Shankill Road. Afterwards Spence and his associates stopped at two public houses, the Four Step Inn and the Rex Bar, before moving to a UVF meeting in the back room of the Standard Bar. It was decided to kill Leo Martin. Leslie Porter was dispatched through the back streets of the Shankill across into the Falls area, to find Martin's house on the Oldpark Road. He

11

returned and then Rocky Burns and McClean were dispatched with a gun to carry out the killing. "Burns and I arranged that we would knock on Martin's door, and, if he answered the door, we would shoot him." There was no one home when the two men called. They broke into the house and set fire to it before returning to the Standard Bar.

At closing time, the party then moved to the home of Spence's sister, Cassie Currie, in Belgrave Street where there was talk of acquiring more guns for the UVF. They then set off for the Malvern Arms where it was known they could drink after hours.

McClean's statement to police said: "When we were in the bar for about an hour, four lads came in and went for a drink at the counter. The conversation came up about the religion of these fellows. Spence asked the company if they would be Catholics. Spence then went up to the bar beside the four lads to buy a drink. When he returned to our table, he said: 'I have been listening to their conversation and they are four IRA men.' We had some more drinks. Spence said: 'These are IRA men and they will have to go'."

Spence, McClean and Williamson left the bar at about midnight, armed themselves and returned to wait outside for the four barmen. After the shooting, McClean said they returned to Mrs Curry's house where Spence collected the guns from the others and said: "That's the job done" or words to that effect.

McClean's statement connected his joining the UVF with support for the Rev Ian Paisley. "I was asked did I agree with Paisley and was I prepared to follow him. I said that I was." The evening before the murder of Peter Ward the men had marched with a group from the Shankill to one of the Rev Paisley's political rallies in the Ulster Hall, in Belfast city centre.

Williamson also made what amounted to a corroborating confession of the events at Malvern Street. He told police in

Brown Square RUC station on the day after his arrest: " . . . I had quite a lot of drink that night in McDowell's. Some time after 11 p.m. I went to Watson's bar [Malvern Arms] in Malvern Street with Gusty Spence, Frank Curry, Porter, Reid, and McClean.

"Rocky Burns did not come. We had a few drinks in there and then me and Porter and Reid went out in the direction of Glengormley. Reid left the car and came back with a parcel which he put in the boot. I never saw what was in the parcel but Reid told me it was gelignite. We drove to Craven Street and I left them at the car and went to Curry's house. I was standing outside Curry's house with Henry Johnston. I don't know where the gelly went to. I went round to Watson's bar. I had a Luger gun in a shoulder-holster with me. It was loaded with six rounds of small calibre ammunition. I joined two comrades who I don't wish to name. I was told there was four IRA men in the bar.

"There was instructions given by one of my comrades to scare them. I took up my position at the corner of Malvern Street and Ariel Street. My comrades took up their own positions. The four IRA men came out of Watson's pub. I moved towards the centre of the road. I drew my gun and fired towards the men, but low. Everybody was told to fire low. I mean my comrades. My gun jammed twice, and I had to cock it and a round was ejected each time. That's how I know that I fired four rounds. We all ran down Langford Street and made our way to a certain place, where we all put our guns in a sack. I went home after that. This was not a deliberate attack. It happened on the spur of the moment. I think that the one who got away had a gun on him. I did not know that these IRA men were going to be in Watson's that night."

Spence, Williamson and McClean were found guilty and sentenced to life imprisonment with a recommendation by the judge, Lord Justice MacDermott, that they serve no less than twenty years in jail. McClean was to die in prison and Spence served eighteen years before being released on licence.

On the day Spence and the others were charged, Paisley issued a statement saying he did not know who the UVF was or who its leaders were and that any groups he was associated with were constitutional and law-abiding.

O'Neill counterblasted Paisley the next day, saying: "I have seen reports in the press that Mr Paisley stated last night in Holywood: 'I don't know what the Ulster Volunteer Force is, or who its leaders are, or what its intentions are, but evidently Captain O'Neill does.' He also said that he had never been associated with or had anything to do with this organisation. I have also received from the police a verbatim report of a speech made by Mr Paisley in the Ulster Hall, Belfast, on June 16, 1966. I should like to quote a relevant extract. Mr Paisley said, and I may add that he was well aware that police were present, 'Let me tell you this, friends, there are many ex-service men at this meeting; they are the defenders of the flag of Ulster, I have a resolution here from some of them, the ex-service men of both World Wars, now comprising four divisions of the Ulster Volunteer Force: We are solidly behind Rev Paisley and repudiate the dirty slur and the classifying of those who fought the menace of Nazism as Republican-inspired and we give him our full support'."

O'Neill added: "May I say in parenthesis here that I regard it as a slur on the body of ex-service men of Ulster to suggest that any considerable number of them would lend support to this sordid organisation.

"Going back a little further, to the Ulster Hall meeting of 17 April, 1966, Mr Paisley thanked all those who had come along and marched that day, and he specifically mentioned by name the Ulster Volunteer Force. The police also inform me that a leading member of the Ulster Volunteer Force is

14

also an important official of the so-called Ulster Constitution Defence Committee, of which Mr Paisley is the publicly-acknowledged chairman.

"Honourable Members will be able to judge for themselves the extent to which Mr Paisley can properly claim ignorance of the Ulster Volunteer Force. He is no doubt anxious to wash his hands of it now but the record clearly shows that he has hitherto received and welcomed their support."

O'Neill's comments confirm the fact that the Royal Ulster Constabulary (RUC) Special Branch officers from the Brown Square District, which covered the lower Shankill, were aware that a small terrorist group had formed in the Shankill area and that it was attending and playing a part in Paisley's rallies. O'Neill was scoring political points against the young firebrand orator who was also his most outspoken critic.

There were, in fact, still doubts, despite the three deaths, the many petrol bombings in Belfast and Carrickfergus and the arrests of Spence and his associates, that a new UVF really existed. Captain O'Neill was, however, clear and correct on the fact that a group called the UVF existed. He was also satisfied that, despite Paisley's invoking of the UVF's name and motto, the Shankill UVF was not the same as Paisley's own quasi-military organisations the UPV (Ulster Protestant Volunteers) or UCDC (Ulster Constitution Defence Committee).

While the UVF was proscribed along with the IRA, the UPV and UCDC were ignored. Although much publicity had been given to a telegram sent by one of Paisley's supporters to the moderate Unionist MP, Nat Minford, claiming to be from the UVF, the Government had no further indications that the UPV or UCDC were "contemplating physical violence".

Paisley's inflammatory oratory and his rabble-rousing activities were, however, the focus for extremists and if there was no evidence to connect him in law with illegal activities, it was widely felt he was a bad influence. O'Neill's hatred of

15

Paisley carried throughout the moderate sections of Protestant opinion.

A *Belfast Telegraph* editorial pondered whether or not the special powers legislation might not be extended to Paisley's groups. "For the moment, however," the editorial read, "The Government has done enough to make those Protestants who distrust the ecumenical movement and the North-South rapprochement consider how to express their views and with whom they should be associated in their protest.

"Their protest may be a vain one; the indications are that the majority of people in Northern Ireland welcome any easing of the tensions which have prevented a maturing of community life over many decades. If so, the will of the majority must prevail.

"Protests become no more valid by being couched in threatening language. The antics of militants only serve to pose the question: what is left of Protestantism or the British way of life when they are defended in this way?"

Spence and his associates were sent to Crumlin Road Prison and there they languished as the Twelfth of July marching season got underway without them.

There was another court sequel three years later. A Catholic man, living in the village of Eden, north of Carrickfergus on the shores of Belfast Lough, claimed compensation of £85 for damage to his house caused by shots fired into his home. During the court hearing, on March 3, 1970, an RUC officer read a written statement by Hugh McClean in which there was reference to the killing of John Scullion. McClean's statement said he was not involved in Scullion's murder. The statement claimed Spence had told him Scullion was an IRA man, and that he wasn't stabbed but had been shot. Spence, McClean said, admitted he had shot Scullion. McClean said Spence later gave him the gun in Belgrave Street and said: "This gun is red hot and I want you to use it in Eden to throw the police off the scent."

16

There was some residual speculation about the UVF in the local newspapers over the coming months, none of it seeming to be in any way informed about the make-up of the group. There were strong nationalist suspicions that the UVF was simply a cover-name for Stormont's own law and order institutions, particularly the Ulster Special Constabulary (USC). There was something in this. Many UVF members would later be found to have served in the USC and its successor, the Ulster Defence Regiment (UDR). During a debate in Stormont on the Public Order Bill, on May 29, 1966, the Nationalist MP for South Down, Michael Keogh, declared that the USC and UVF were "the one force".

There were important organic links to the group of extremists at the core of Paisley's operations, which would emerge later. At Paisley's Ulster Hall rally of April 17, 1966, he had announced the establishment of the Ulster Constitution Defence Committee which "governs in one united society" a group he called the Ulster Protestant Volunteers. The UPV he described as "Protestant patriots pledged by all lawful methods to uphold and maintain the Constitution of Northern Ireland as an integral part of the United Kingdom . . ." The UPV motto was "For God and Ulster", the same motto used by the original Ulster Volunteer Force set up in 1912 by Lord Carson and James Craig.

Paisley was appointed chairman of the UCDC which formally began life on May 2, 1966. Paisley's commitment to "lawful" methods failed to filter down to the entire UPV membership.

Paisley's UCDC and the UPV, and other groups including Ulster Protestant Action (UPA) and the UVF were all manifestations of the extremes of unionism and Ulster loyalism. Membership was, at times, interchangeable. There were counterparts on the extremes of Catholic nationalism in the form of the Catholic Action, Republican Clubs, the Wolfe Tone Associations and the IRA.

In the late summer of 1966, three UPV members were arrested by the RUC and charged with conspiracy to provide and procure explosive substances for the purposes of endangering life. Noel Doherty, the leader of the UPV group, and two others were tried and sentenced in October, 1966.

Doherty made a detailed statement to police in which he named his associates who were "of the opinion that the IRA monuments should be blown up and the IRA leaders should be shot". In his statement, Doherty said that while he agreed "to a certain extent on blowing up monuments, never could I sanction the taking of life".

Billy Mitchell, who later became a prominent UVF figure and also served a life sentence, was named as Doherty's right-hand man. Mitchell accompanied Doherty on visits to other Paisley followers in Armagh who had access to explosives and wanted to blow up monuments and IRA members.

Paisley's repeated invoking of the memory of the original UVF and the formation of his own quasi-paramilitary organisations – the first of several "third forces" he was to be associated with over the next decades – along with his close association with Doherty and others have continued to lead to claims that he was involved in the conspiracy that became the UVF.

The leaders of the UVF are adamant that he had nothing whatsoever to do with them. Several of their members, particularly in country areas, were followers of Paisley and some men who were original members of Paisley's UPV joined the UVF. But, the leaders insist, the UVF had been wary of Paisley from the outset. Theirs was a secret and deadly conspiracy and control of it was tightly guarded. Broad sympathy with his political sentiments and pronouncements would later turn into outright hostility between Paisley, the constitutional politician, and the outlawed loyalist paramilitaries.

Similarly, the UVF rejected the suggestion that they were

controlled by powerful figures from the unionist establishment, that somewhere in the shadows were "big house" unionists manipulating the men in masks. The UVF and the Ulster Unionists shared identical political aims but there, it seems, the similarities ended. The UVF themselves concur that Capt O'Neill spoke for virtually the entire Protestant population as well as his party colleagues when he denounced and banned the Ulster Volunteer Force.

Individuals did have contact – Spence's brother William was the Shankill Road electoral agent for the Unionist MP, Jim Kilfedder. Over the coming decades of trouble the unionist politicians and the loyalist paramilitaries would occasionally come close. There was "touching but no sex", as one put it. In an academic study of the formation of Spence's UVF, Roy Garland, who was himself closely involved in loyalist agitation during the 1960s and knew many of the central figures of loyalist politics and paramilitarism, surveyed the list of leading figures of Ulster unionism in the 1960s for figures who could be behind an armed conspiracy. He found almost none.

Several leading Unionists were clearly fomenting opposition to O'Neill. However, none was ever found to be pulling the strings of the UVF. "In all the interviews (of UVF suspects) I never came across any UVF member who was sitting in the background and was pulling strings," one senior RUC officer said.

Twenty-five years later, when asked if the UVF was under political control, Gusty Spence told Garland it was "under no political control". The UVF, he said was "the same as the Orange Institution in 1795. That was very dangerous to those who held power". The hierarchy in the Unionist Party did not attempt to take over the UVF. They attempted, at times, to give them political guidance. It was done in a surreptitious way.

"At the same time they used the threat: the political power

the UVF had, in order to try and extract concessions from the British Government. You know: 'If you don't talk to us you will have to talk to these armed men.'

"The UVF did respond to some of the calls being made by the Unionist hierarchy and, I suppose, they knew that they were being used but felt it incumbent upon themselves to respond to these calls" (Garland p61).

Spence maintains he was inducted into an existing UVF structure, about which he knew little, in 1965 by two people, one of whom he says was a Unionist politician. Spence says he was driven to a farm outside Pomeroy, a predominantly Catholic village in Co Tyrone, for the swearing-in ceremony which he recollects was performed by an ex-British Army colonel.

There were, he says, maybe forty people in the building, including four other men from Belfast who had to be sworn in with him. Spence still maintains he knew little of who was behind this ceremony or exactly what it signified.

The RUC view was that Spence was one of the founders of the new reborn UVF and that the trip to Tyrone may have been the formalising of links between the Belfast militants and their rural counterparts from the Mid-Ulster area. Spence had been involved in loyalist activity in one form or another from at least 1959 when he took part in a protest march to Belfast City Hall to protest at anti-loyalist comments by the west Belfast Republican Labour candidate, Gerry Fitt. Spence also attended Paisley rallies in the Ulster Hall, in Belfast. Spence was, in Belfast terminology, a "hard man", an ex-military police sergeant who came from a tradition of loyalism who revered "old UVF gunmen" from the Shankill. The names of these men, such as George Scott, "Snatch" McCracken and Robert Moore, live on in the lore of Shankill loyalists. Spence was also a street fighter and occasionally brawled with Catholics who could claim a similar political pedigree on the republican side.

While remaining silent about the organisational aspect of the UVF, Spence speaks freely about the circumstances leading to its decision to resort to violence. Commenting on the climate in Belfast prior to the 1966 Easter Rising republican demonstrations, he says: "The whole of the UVF was stood to and they were armed and on duty at interface areas. I remember going up to visit two men down Cupar Street. There were two men at the top of Denmark Street and there were men on duty on the Springfield Road and at the corner of Cupar Street, the top end and at the bottom end. There were about eight or ten men in a house to be drafted in. There was a fair bit of tension."

The UVF killings stopped after Spence's imprisonment. He passed on the reins of the organisation to Samuel "Bo" McClelland, a friend and also a former British soldier who had seen action in Korea, just as Spence had seen action in Cyprus. McClelland, described by another Shankill UVF man as a tough disciplinarian, set about quietly following in Spence's footsteps. McClelland's job was to maintain discipline among the handful of UVF members who stayed on after the Malvern Street case, recruit suitable new members and mark time. This he did.

Meanwhile, loyalist anger at O'Neill and the perceived "sell-out" of Unionism's bedrock principles did not disappear with the revulsion and public denunciations of the Shankill extremists. On June 26, 1966, the First Londonderry Division of the UPV called for O'Neill's resignation and questioned "the loyalism of our fellow Protestant and leader of a Protestant Party and Protestant Ulster, Captain Terence O'Neill." In July 1966 the UPV South Antrim Division issued a statement calling for the resignation of Captain O'Neill. Simultaneously Paisley launched his campaign against O'Neill.

Spence's actions had, however, caught the imagination of the many loyalists who felt the threat of encroaching Irish nationalism and the weakening of its traditional unionist leadership. The UVF had already become an invisible but potent force in Northern Ireland. The initials appeared on gable walls and on Catholic property across Northern Ireland. Its name was used, often by other loyalists with no connection with the organisation, as a device to scare opponents of loyalism but bore no other public manifestation. On July 13, after making a programme exposing discrimination against Catholics in Northern Ireland, the BBC reporter Cliff Michelmore received a telephone death threat from someone purporting to represent the UVF. It was, he said, a "vicious example of the extremism now at work in Northern Ireland".

In November 1966, republicans in Derry City began receiving UVF death threats through the post. "What happened in Malvern Street can just as easily happen in Rossville Street," warned one of the letters which named seven republicans in the city. Graffiti like "Up the UVF" and "Up Paisley" appeared on factory walls in Derry. Republicans in east Tyrone also began receiving similar threats in letters and telephone calls.

Catholic families in the Glenbryn estate in north west Belfast began receiving threatening notices to quit in letters purporting to come from the UVF. The issue was raised with the then Minister of Home Affairs, William Craig, by Harry Diamond, the Republican Labour MP for Falls. Anti-Catholic slogans were daubed on walls. Graffiti such as "Fenians get out" and "Fenians go back to the South" was accompanied by anonymous letters saying: "Your windows will be next. Up the UVF."

The years 1967 and 1968 were to be the last period of calm before storms broke again over Ulster. The Government banned a republican demonstration to commemorate the 1867 Fenian Uprising but allowed the annual 1916 Rising commemoration for Easter, 1967. Queen Elizabeth visited

Belfast on July 4, 1967, and her car was hit by a brick thrown by a Catholic workman from a building site in the city centre. On December 11, 1967, the new Dublin Prime Minister, Jack Lynch, paid a courtesy call to Captain O'Neill at Stormont. Only Ian Paisley and a few of his stalwarts turned out to protest. Paisley and his friends threw snowballs at Lynch's car as it left the gates of Stormont.

Things had calmed sufficiently by February 1968 for an attempt by the unionist MP for Willowfield in Belfast, William Hinds, to attempt to have the proscription order on the UVF lifted. His attempt to raise the issue during a Stormont debate was politely turned down by Bill Craig who said if it was raised on an appropriate occasion he would give it appropriate consideration. The nationalist MP, Austin Currie, pointed out that if the UVF ban was lifted, he would seek the lifting of the ban on the Republican Clubs, the IRA's political front, which had also been banned by O'Neill.

By early spring 1968, however, the perennial issue of controversial marches rose again. That January the Northern Ireland Civil Rights Association (NICRA) had been formed on an anti-discrimination agenda based on a charter similar to that of the National Council of Civil Liberties in Britain. NICRA organised and gathered support throughout the coming year. It defied a ban placed on demonstrations in Armagh, in April 1968. On April 27, 1968, about 3,000 nationalists attended a NICRA demonstration in Armagh to protest against the Stormont ban on parades. Calls were made to "nationally-minded people" to withdraw co-operation in the forthcoming civic week in the town.

Simultaneously, loyalist pressure on O'Neill was growing. Some 500 loyalists jeered and heckled him as he left a Unionist Association in the Shankill area on May 20 1968. Catholic civil rights agitation also grew. The Nationalist MP for East Tyrone, Austin Currie, "squatted" in a house which the local unionist council had allocated to a single Protestant

23

woman ahead of large Catholic families on the local authority's waiting list.

An uneasy but relatively peaceable Orange marching season passed by in 1968. At the end of August, however, there were confrontations between NICRA marchers and loyalists after a civil rights march from Coalisland to Dungannon, Co Tyrone. NICRA had been agitating about gerrymandering and discriminatory housing policy in Derry and gave notice of a public demonstration on October 5th. The Apprentice Boys of Derry, an off-shoot of the Orange Order, gave notice of its intention to hold an "annual initiation ceremony" on the same day. Craig issued an order banning both demonstrations.

The NICRA executive announced its defiance of the banning order and went ahead with the demonstration. By Northern Ireland standards, what ensued was little more than the norm for such events. Some eighty-eight people, seventy-seven civilians and eleven police were injured. What had changed was that such a set-piece event was, for the first time in history, recorded by television. The televised depiction of events gave the impression of brutal policing methods being deployed against peaceful civil rights demonstrators, casting the demonstrators in something of the mould of the black civil rights demonstrators in the southern states of America. Four days of rioting in the Catholic Bogside of Derry followed. The under-resourced RUC (it had only 2,500 members at the time) and its incompetent auxiliary force, the "B" Specials, were cast in the role of villain of the piece.

O'Neill shuttled between Stormont and Downing Street and on November 22, 1968, announced a five-point reform programme for Northern Ireland which met most of the NICRA demands. The British Labour Party Prime Minister, Harold Wilson, broke the tradition of the previous fifty-six years and began openly intervening in Northern Ireland's

24

internal affairs, supporting O'Neill's programme of liberal reform.

This incensed loyalist opinion. On November 30, 1968, loyalists descended on Armagh where permission had been given for a NICRA demonstration. The RUC intercepted thirty cars driven by loyalists and seized two revolvers, 220 cudgels and other weapons.

The threat to Captain O'Neill's liberal unionist stance grew, as much within his own party as on the streets of Northern Ireland. His Minister for Home Affairs, Mr Craig, publicly criticised O'Neill's concessions to the NICRA demonstrators and adopted a hectoring, angry stance, addressing angry public meetings of loyalists. O'Neill was eventually pulled back by the Ulster Unionist Council which exacted an assurance from him that he would make "no further changes" without prior consultation. O'Neill appealed for public support in a public broadcast on December 9 in which he uttered the prophetic words that "Ulster stands at the crossroads". Despite substantial public outpouring of support in newspapers and broadcasting media, the disorder continued.

On New Year's Eve Paisley's lieutenant, Major Ronald Bunting, the self-styled commandant of the Loyalist Citizens of Ulster, called on all "dedicated" people to take action against the march by a NICRA off-shoot called People's Democracy (PD) from Belfast to Derry, which was set to begin the next morning.

About 40 PD demonstrators set off on New Year's Day, 1969. Just hours before they did so, a bomb planted by UVF members in mid-Ulster destroyed a republican memorial on the marchers' route at Toomebridge, Co Antrim. Despite further harrying by loyalists, the march to Derry picked up support until about seventy arrived at the bridge at Burntollet outside Derry on Saturday, January 4. There, more than 1,000 loyalists overpowered police and stoned and bludgeoned the marchers. Thirteen marchers had to receive hospital treatment in Derry.

After the attack on the marchers, rioting broke out in nationalist areas of Derry. A week later another PD demonstration in Newry, Co Down, precipitated further rioting. A statement was issued by the UVF in south Down saying: "We will not permit any brand of rebel anarchists to parade through the Protestant sections of Newry." Some twenty-eight civilians and ten police were injured in the riot in Newry, on January 11.

O'Neill's problems were growing. The Minister of Health and Social Services, William Morgan, resigned from the Government. In his letter of resignation, Morgan said he felt a change of leadership would be in the best interests of Northern Ireland. Four days later, on January 30, a group of twelve dissident Unionist MPs, including Desmond Boal, William Craig, Capt John Brooke, Harry West and John Taylor, signed a letter calling for O'Neill's resignation. William Morgan and another front bench party member, Brian Faulkner, declined to contribute to a debate in Stormont which was designed as a confidence motion in O'Neill.

Large loyalist demonstrations gathered at Crumlin Road Jail when Paisley and Bunting were imprisoned after they refused to pay small fines for their part in the disturbances the previous November, in Armagh.

On Monday, February 3, O'Neill decided to call everyone's bluff, dissolved the Parliament at Stormont and called a general election on February 24.

He almost succeeded. Of 36 official Unionists elected only 12 were intransigent opponents. But the loyalty of half of the remainder was questionable.

Embarrassingly, however, Paisley had come close to unseating the Prime Minister in his North Antrim constituency, which had not been contested for a generation.

26

O'Neill survived on a humiliating minority vote, polling 7,745 votes to Paisley's 6,331 and the People's Democracy candidate, Michael Farrell's 2,310. Four of the other five Protestant Unionists took second place and only Bunting, who was beaten to second place by Labour, failed to poll a spectacular total for the Paisleyites. Paisley achieved his legitimate constitutional goal the following year when he won the April by-election caused by O'Neill's resignation and his decision to take a seat in the House of Lords.

The crucial blow to O'Neill came at 3:55 on the morning of Sunday, March 30, 1969. Four bomb explosions wrecked the electricity sub-station at Castlereagh in the suburbs of Belfast, cutting off electricity to a large part of south and east Belfast. The explosions were widely believed to be the work of the IRA. It had already been anticipated in both British and Irish intelligence assessments of the time that a republican bombing campaign was the natural progression of the civil rights public agitation. Unionist MPs blamed O'Neill for allowing this security crisis to develop and began rapidly to withdraw from him.

The Castlereagh explosions occurred on the eve of the crucial Unionist Party Standing Committee meeting convened to discuss the leadership. There were other blasts: on the main Belfast water supply pipe from Lough Neagh, at Dunadry, Co Antrim on April 4; two on the night of April 20, at the Silent Valley reservoir in Co Down and at an electricity pylon in Kilmore, Co Armagh; another at the Lough Neagh water pipe line on April 24; and at the main water pipe line in Annalong, Co Down, on Friday, April 25. All immediately preceded internal Unionist Party meetings which were crucial to O'Neill.

Simultaneously, republican violence was also growing. On the night of April 20-21 republicans petrol-bombed eleven post offices.

It was clear there was a conspiracy to create pressure on

O'Neill. No group was accepting responsibility for the attacks but loyalist opponents of O'Neill's, some of whom knew the source of the bombings, were pointing the finger at the IRA.

The local media was also loath to confront the fact that there could be a loyalist conspiracy and to recognise that bombings were clearly aimed at bringing O'Neill down. The Nationalist MP Austin Currie, however, hit the mark when he publicly voiced the private suspicions of a growing number by suggesting the blasts were the work of Protestant extremists who intended to force a crisis which would so undermine confidence in O'Neill's ability to maintain law and order that he would be obliged to resign.

On April 28, two days after the last explosion, O'Neill resigned. "Either we live in peace or we have no life worth living," he told the party. A week earlier Major Chichester-Clark had withdrawn his support for O'Neill in protest at the O'Neillites' endorsement, at last, of one-man-one-vote. "I fear that our supporters will lose all faith in the determination of the present government," he told O'Neill. That was precisely the response the bombers had sought. O'Neill later wrote that he had been "literally blown out of office". Bonfires were lit on the Shankill Road in celebration of O'Neill's defeat.

The UVF had achieved their object of destroying O'Neill through the subterfuge of simulating an IRA bombing campaign. Gusty Spence later recalled that, once it had achieved this object, the UVF briefly went into decline and lost direction. Over the coming year or two it engaged in only minor and increasingly sectarian acts of violence.

During early 1969, UVF graffiti appeared on Catholic businesses and houses in the sectarian flash-points in Belfast. Little else was known about the organisation, even by the young men from the Protestant working classes who sought to join. Only those who were picked could join.

The newspapers continued to carry reports of threats to

Catholic families living in mainly Protestant areas, threats purporting to come from the UVF in east Antrim. Families living in the Craigyhill area of Larne received threats purporting to come from the UVF.

On September 1, 1969, another statement was issued to the Belfast newspapers saying: "Battalions of the UVF are ready for action and new battalions are being formed." It also warned Catholics to remove the barricades which had been erected around their areas. There was, however, relatively little action.

For several months there was no firm indication of who was responsible for the explosions which had preceded O'Neill's resignation. A UPV booklet repeated the charge that the blasts were "a skilfully executed plot, undoubtedly the work of the IRA".

Then on the night of Sunday, October 19, the true answer emerged in the unlikely setting of the Electricity Supply Board sub-station at Ballyshannon, across the Border in Co Donegal.

The bombers who had conspired to blow Terence O'Neill out of office now had a new agenda. With the slide into widespread disturbances and riots in the North – ten people had been killed in the summer rioting and the British Army had been called in to assist the RUC – the Irish Government had begun to show an interest in the North, criticising the Stormont Government and the RUC and sending battalions of soldiers to the Border. The Irish Prime Minister, Jack Lynch, effectively drew his country into the conflict with the words: "The Irish Government can no longer stand by and see innocent people injured and perhaps worse". It was now the turn of the Republic to receive the attentions of the UVF's leading bomber.

Thomas Campbell McDowell was known around his home in south Down as a follower of Ian Paisley. He was a member of the Mourne Free Presbyterian Church and, on the morning of the Ballyshannon blast, had attended a service in the church with his wife and eight children. He had joined the Ulster Protestant Volunteers.

"Tommy", as he was known, was also an experienced quarry man and explosives expert who had carried out work, including well-drilling and blasting, for farmers on both sides of the Border. In September 1968 his work had brought him to Donegal where he carried out drilling work on a farm outside Letterkenny. He later returned, bringing associates, two men and a woman in her early 20s, back to Donegal to pick a suitable bomb target, according to the local Garda Special Branch detectives.

In the week before the attack on the electricity sub-station, McDowell and two other men had stayed in bed-and-breakfast accommodation in Ballyshannon, posing as anglers from Northern Ireland. The police believe one of these men, a loyalist from Portadown, Co Armagh, accompanied McDowell to Ballyshannon on the night of the attack along with the young woman and another man.

McDowell and the young woman drove from Co Down carrying explosives to Moy, outside Portadown, where they were met by their accomplices and went from there on to the sub-station.

At the Ballyshannon sub-station McDowell set about his work in a thorough way. He planted 181 lbs of gelignite capable of destroying the sub-station and almost anything else in a 300-yard radius, according to an Irish Army ordnance officer. McDowell was close to completing his work when a car rounded the corner above the station, shining its headlights towards him. As he ducked for cover, he grabbed one of the bushings carrying 5,600 volts of electricity from the top of the transformer. The flash lit up the Donegal sky.

The driver of the car turned back to Ballyshannon and raised the alarm. McDowell was literally cooked by the electricity surge. His clothing, with the exception of his shirt collar and tie, had been blown off his body but he was still alive. He had burns to 80 per cent of his body surface and to all his internal organs. The gardai, not knowing if the man they had found was a republican or loyalist bomber, called the local Catholic parish priest, Canon Deeny, who administered the last rites of the Catholic Church, anointing a man who had given his life to fighting Roman Catholicism and Irish nationalism and who probably believed Ian Paisley when he called the Pope the Anti-Christ.

Two Garda detectives, called to the scene, found his coat nearby. In the pockets along with a .32 pistol was a blue armlet with the letters UVF, in red imitation leather, sewn on to it. The officers remembered that the electrical shock was so great that it had fired off the round in the barrel of the pistol.

He survived for three days in Ballyshannon hospital, drifting in and out of consciousness, before he died of renal failure, a result of the burns to his kidneys.

RUC enquiries into McDowell's death led them to a close associate of McDowell, Samuel Stevenson, a 46-year-old unemployed driver and a former "B" Special from Newtownards, Co Down. In the February general election, Major Bunting had appointed him manager of his election campaign and, for a time he was secretary of Donegal Pass UPV in south Belfast, until removed for failing to attend meetings.

Stevenson told police he was involved in the explosions that had preceded O'Neill's downfall earlier in the year. He also implicated a number of other men, including McDowell who, he said, had planted the explosives. Stevenson also led police to the door of John McKeague, self-styled leader of the Shankill Defence Association, a group which had carried out counter-demonstrations against Catholic civil rights demonstrations and, during 1969, had started rioting and other sectarian trouble in Belfast.

Altogether Stevenson's confessions led to four separate conspiracy trials which alleged the involvement of loyalists in the bombs which brought down Capt O'Neill's premiership.

In the first trial Paisley's name arose in Stephenson's testimony. He said: "I first came into contact with the Rev Paisley by attending his services at the Ulster Hall on Sunday nights about 18 months to two years ago. I got a job at the Protestant Unionist headquarters at Shaftesbury Square helping in the election.

"During this time I met Frank Mallon from Holywood, who I later discovered was the treasurer of the UCDC. For some time there was nothing doing and then Dr Paisley commenced his campaign against O'Neill.

"As this had not the desired effect, I was approached by Frank Mallon who made several suggestions to cause disturbance in the country to have O'Neill overthrown. Among these suggestions was that some installations should be destroyed. He said that this would cause confusion in the country and bring about O'Neill's downfall, which was what Dr Paisley wanted. He said that as the Attorney-General lived at Castlereagh district that would be a good place to hit.

"Mallon said he would finance the operation and gave me about £30 or £40. He approached me again a few days later to make sure that this job would be done. I think he gave me £25 on this occasion. I then arranged to have the electricity transformer at Castlereagh destroyed.

"A few days later Frank Mallon came to my house and congratulated me on the Castlereagh job. He suggested that if similar jobs here and there were done it would be in the bag. He suggested that I should do something to cause further confusion and mentioned: 'We will do something about the water supply'. From then on Mallon was a constant caller at my house. He gave me money on numerous occasions and on other occasions when I was not there he left money in an envelope with my wife. On two or three occasions my wife opened the envelope and counted the money before handing it over to me when I came home. Altogether I got approximately £200 from Mallon. This was payment for Castlereagh, the pylon at Kilmore and the pipeline at Dunadry (Templepatrick). Frank Mallon saw me after each of these outrages and said: 'Good job, good job,' several times."

The trial began on February 16, 1970. Charges of conspiracy with Stevenson and McDowell to cause the Templepatrick explosion were also put to five other men: McKeague, the 39-year-old salesman and prominent loyalist agitator; William Owens, a 19-year-old from Ballymoney, Co Antrim who was said in court to share a flat with McKeague; Derek Elwood (21) from Rosebank Street, in Belfast; Trevor Gracey (26) also from Belfast; and Francis Mallon (48) a technical representative, from Holywood, Co Down.

McKeague, the court heard, attended Paisley's Martyrs Memorial Free Presbyterian Church in south Belfast and was a member of Willowfield UPV until May 1969. He had taken part in Council elections in Belfast, standing as a Protestant Unionist, but had failed to be elected.

Frank Mallon was treasurer of the UCDC. Derek Elwood was a B-Special and a UPV member. Trevor Gracey was circulation manager of the Protestant *Telegraph* and his brother, Hercules, had taken over the secretaryship from Noel Doherty. Owens was one of McKeague's camp followers.

On February 18, 1970, the trial was interrupted by a small explosion in the corridor outside the courtroom which followed another small explosion at the perimeter of Crumlin Road Prison, across the road from the Court House. A statement purporting to be from the UVF Brigade headquarters said the prison explosion was "a token protest blast". The second UVF statement, a week later, admitted the blast in the corridor outside the courtroom where the five defendants were being tried.

At the re-convened trial, on March 3, similar charges were heard against the five men in respect of the Kilmore pylon explosion. Mallon was again one of the accused and the others were William Gracey (no relation of the Trevor Gracey involved in the previous case) and three Portadown members of the UPV, John Love (a sergeant in the "B" Specials), David McNally and Robert Murdoch (another "B" Special), who had been cleared of an explosives charge in the UVF trials of 1966.

Stevenson was again crown witness and he repeated his charges against Mallon, alleging he had proposed the explosion and provided money for gelignite. He also alleged that Mallon had suggested Murdoch as a suitable assistant, since Kilmore was not far from his home in Portadown.

Stevenson said he had contacted Murdoch, who contacted McDowell and, with Love and McNally, they together brought a quantity of explosives from McDowell's house to Murdoch's home where it was "prepared". McDowell showed them how to fire the gelignite and Stevenson then drove with the five accused to Kilmore where he and Gracey stayed in the car while Murdoch, Love and McNally, he said, put the gelignite in place and lit the fuse.

Sgt George Jackson, explosives inspector for the Portadown district, gave evidence that, having examined the scene of the explosion on April 22, he went to a Portadown quarry where he found a car he knew belonged to Mr McDowell, the foreman in charge of drilling and blasting. In the car he found keys which belonged to the quarry magazine. There he found 313 lbs of gelignite of a type not used in quarry work, plus detonators, connections, fuse wire and ignition cord. McDowell's access to explosives was understandable. But the storage in the quarry magazine of non-quarry types of gelignite was never explained.

The gelignite was British National Coal Board stock which had been smuggled out of Scottish pits. It was part of a substantial consignment sent by Protestant miners sympathetic to the loyalist cause in Northern Ireland and which had reached McDowell.

Murdoch was said by Sgt James McKinney to have denied all knowledge of the explosion when first questioned about it. But after further questioning, he was alleged by police to have said: "Just after Dungiven Orange Hall was burnt in July, Stevenson and McDowell came to my house with about 40 lbs of gelignite. McDowell showed me how to make a bomb and told me to use it to blow up William Street Catholic chapel. After a day or two I wrote to McDowell and told him to come and take the stuff away. He came in his car and took it away."

Evidence was called which brought into question Stevenson's character and role in the affair. It was constantly suggested he was an agent provocateur or liar. Another Crown witness, Cyril McBride, whose testimony purported to substantiate Stevenson's evidence, was found to have an extensive police record. On March 4, the jury found all five defendants not guilty.

The last trial, on March 6, was brief. Mallon and Robert Campbell of Kilkeel were accused of conspiring with Stevenson and McDowell to cause the Castlereagh explosion. Stevenson was the only crown witness and no new evidence of substance was produced. Mallon and Campbell were both acquitted. Stevenson returned to jail to begin his twelve-year sentence alone.

Two days after the final acquittal, the home in Donaghmore, Co Tyrone of Austin Currie, who had first suggested the explosions were the work of the UVF, was badly damaged by a UVF bomb.

Although not acknowledged at the time, McDowell's is the first name in the UVF's role of honour. In 1972, Gusty Spence issued a statement from his prison cell praising the "hallowed memory of Tommy McDowell, killed in action with the Ulster Volunteer Force".

## Two

## ULSTER'S RESISTANCE

There are two UVFs, separated in time by the middle fifty years of the 20th century. They shared a common aim, the defence of the Union with Great Britain. Both also emerged from a tradition of sectarian and political conflict in the north eastern part of Ireland which has its roots in the 17th century "Plantation" of Ulster. The two organisations are dissimilar only in that the first force was led by Northern Ireland's Protestant aristocracy and business classes. The second UVF was almost entirely a working-class organisation whose members were reviled as "terrorists", denounced and imprisoned by the same Ulster establishment which had recruited, trained and led its predecessors.

The links with the past, however, were important to the second UVF. When on October 14, 1994, Augustus Andrew "Gusty" Spence, the founder and figurehead of the second UVF, announced a loyalist ceasefire, he chose to do so at a press conference at Fernhill House, in the Ballygomartin area of west Belfast. Fernhill was the home of a prominent Protestant business family, the Knox-Cunninghams, who made their money during the 19th century industrial boom in Belfast. Like other rich Ulster Protestant unionists, the family had allowed their stables and wooded gardens, in the Forthriver Valley looking over the Protestant working-class slums of west Belfast, to be used to store guns for the Ulster Protestant's citizen army, the original Ulster Volunteer Force.

The Protestant upper and middle classes of the early century were prepared, at least, to back the fight against forced integration of Protestant land and culture into an independent Ireland where a southern Catholic majority would hold a dominant position. The Ulster Protestants, through the original UVF, were also prepared, if necessary, to fight British forces if an attempt was made to forcibly integrate them in a Catholic-dominated state.

The leader of Ulster's resistance, Edward Carson, may well have dined at Fernhill, attended by servants from the sprawling slums around the Shankill Road in west Belfast which provided the core of the citizen army.

Spence and his predecessors came from these same Victorian slums beneath Fernhill. His father served with the original UVF. Spence grew up on the Shankill and, apart from a period of service with the British Army and eighteen years in prison, has lived there all his life.

Carson was a top London lawyer, who had prosecuted Oscar Wilde and had links to the very top of Britain's right-wing aristocracy. He had the ear of the leaders of the Conservative Party.

Along with Sir James Craig, Carson enlisted the help of a radical and dedicated UVF officer cadre which created in the first Ulster Volunteer Force a modern army, possibly 100,000 strong, which would have taken even the British Imperial army years and rivers of blood to defeat.

Carson was able to achieve his object without a fight. The UVF provided sufficient clout for its political leaders to bring about the partition of Ireland and the creation of the six-county Northern Ireland state within the United Kingdom. Unlike the twenty-six-county Republic of Ireland, it had a Protestant majority and the Roman Catholic Church held very little sway in its Government.

The members of the first UVF were officially stood down at the end of the First World War, after having fought and died in great numbers – side by side with Catholic Irish soldiers – in the trenches of France.

Many of the original UVF were enlisted into the security forces of the new Northern Ireland state. Its officer class returned to their professions or businesses. These were the men and women of the "proud", unsullied tradition of Ulster loyalism.

Spence and his army were men of a different sort. Theirs was an army which fought a bloody terrorist campaign against equally brutal working class republican terrorists. The officer classes had no stomach for and played little or no part in Spence's war. The "Establishment" had set its face against Spence's UVF from the outset and the reputation of Spence's UVF could hardly be lower. Its men were placed outside the honourable tradition, and firmly in the terrorist mould. His army was harried and imprisoned by the very security forces which had sprung from the original UVF.

However, the modern UVF regards itself as an honourable institution and the true inheritor of its predecessor's mantle. Constitutional unionist politicians have, only when the occasion demanded, associated with its members. But, for the most part of the conflict after 1966, the UVF was an illegal organisation. Thousands of its members served prison sentences or were interned without trial.

The second UVF and its actions must also be set against the backcloth of almost 400 years of ethnic-religious violence in the northeastern area of the island of Ireland. There is a monotonous rhythm to the outbreaks of ethnic, sectarian violence in the northeast counties of Ireland from the late 18th century.

Surveying the history of north-eastern Ireland from the beginning of the last century to the eve of the new Millennium, it is difficult to argue with the sentiments Winston Churchill expressed on surveying the national boundary and political changes in Europe after World War One. Turning to the North of Ireland, he wrote: "The whole map of Europe has been changed. The mode and thought of men, the whole outlook on affairs, the grouping of parties, all have encountered violent and tremendous changes in the deluge of the world but, as the deluge and the waters fall, we see the dreary steeples of Fermanagh and Tyrone emerging once again. The integrity of their quarrel is one of the few institutions that have been left unaltered in the cataclysm which has swept the world."

The "dreary steeples" analogy has been often repeated and is by now a cliche but it is nonetheless true. In the late 1980s and early 1990s, as the map of Europe from the Adriatic to the Baltic was again changing, the conflict in Northern Ireland was still unchanged.

The origins of the modern conflict are often seen as going back to the agrarian disputes of the 18th and 19th centuries. In 1795, amid Catholic and Protestant faction fighting in north Armagh, the local Protestant mob – known as the "Peep O' Day Boys" because of their predilection for launching attacks on Catholic homesteads just before dawn – formed the Orange Order.

Sectarian violence, nasty but on a small scale, carried on in the north Armagh area for the following years into the early 19th century. There were riots at a row of Catholic cottages when the newly-formed Orangemen marched on the road between Portadown and the Church of Ireland parish at Drumcree. Exactly 200 years later, in the gloriously hot summer of 1995, Orangemen were still rallying in large numbers to march past the small Catholic housing estate that had replaced the 18th century cabins at Drumcree.

In 1995, a relatively junior Ulster Unionist MP, David Trimble, struck the pose of so many successful loyalist leaders and led thousands of Orangemen in a determined stand-off with police who had barred their route past the Catholic estate. Later that year, Trimble was swept into power in the Unionist party with the support of the Orange brethren. A similarly astute and aspiring leader of the Protestant loyalists might have made the same move, in the same place, had he been seeking position in Unionist office any time in the previous two centuries.

The Protestant Peep O' Day Boys who carried out dawn raids on Catholic homes and in September, 1795, had created the Orange Order after a skirmish with the Catholic "Defenders" group at the Diamond, not far from Portadown in north Armagh, also had their counterparts in the last quarter of the 20th century. Catholics living in the most troubled parts of Northern Ireland – in north and west Belfast, north Armagh and east Tyrone – felt unsafe in their beds at night for fear of the Protestant gunmen bursting into their homes in the early hours.

The agrarian disputes and violence of earlier centuries simply transferred to an urban setting when Belfast began to grow into a city around the ship-building and linen industries. Militant urban unionism grew alongside militant 19th century Irish nationalism. Long before it received its charter as a city in 1888, Belfast had developed sectarian enclaves which would become familiar to the television news viewers of the 1970s onwards. The Catholic quarters such as the Falls, Ballymacarrett and St Matthew's grew around and between the larger Protestant areas of the Shankill, Shore Road and Sandy Row.

Electoral reform, in particular the Great Reform Bill of 1832, brought the first sectarian riots to the growing town. Many Catholics supported the Whig reformers. In Belfast Catholic support went against the Tory grandees, Lord Arthur Chichester and JE Tennent, and for the Whig reformers, Dr Robert J Tennent and William Sharman Crawford.

However, with strong Protestant and Orange Order support, Chichester and Tennent won both Parliamentary seats for Belfast with votes of 848 and 737 votes respectively – only owners or tenants of property worth £10 a year or more

40

could vote. Immediately after the election, the Orange supporters of Chichester and Tennent gathered in the town centre and began parading past the Catholic butcher shops in Hercules Street (now Royal Avenue) inciting a riot, much as their Armagh cousins would have done a decade or so earlier. The town police intervened and four people were killed.

Affrays of this sort became a fixture of political life in Belfast. The Protestant Tory supporters of 1832 were led by Orangemen and bands playing party tunes like "The Boyne Water" and "The Protestant Boys". Violence associated with the Orange 12th of July demonstrations and attacks on property and people for sectarian reasons became an indelible part of the city's life. Even after the paramilitary ceasefires of 1994 – and amid a great desire for peace and harmony among the two communities – the Orangemen's demonstrations provided an annual occasion for confrontation. The first violence in the aftermath of the ceasefire surrounded the Orange demonstrations past Drumcree and the Catholic enclave in the Lower Ormeau area of south Belfast.

A commission of inquiry in 1833 referred to the "melancholy particulars" of the previous year's election riots and the regular affray surrounding the Twelfth celebrations.

Catholic emancipation and the campaign for the repeal of the Act of Union heightened Protestant fears about what would happen to them in a Catholic-dominated Ireland. The visit to Belfast in January 1841 of Daniel O'Connell, therefore, served as another occasion for violence. A hostile crowd attacked the homes and businesses of O'Connell's Belfast supporters.

Belfast and the rural Protestant heartlands became the centre of opposition to the Home Rule Movement in the second half of the century. Mass Orange demonstrations took place. An estimated 35,000 people attended a rally in Botanic Gardens, Belfast in 1859.

Serious rioting broke out between the Catholic

communities around St Malachy's church (the Markets) and Sandy Row and between the Pound (Lower Falls) and Brown Street (lower Shankill) again in August, 1864. This trouble was sparked by an attack on supporters of O'Connell returning from a demonstration in Dublin.

The August 1864 riots included features which were to become familiar enough in the following century in Belfast. The initial exchanges of stoning were followed by sniping. Rumour spread among the Protestant population that trains were carrying supporters from Dublin for the Catholics. Protestant shipwrights left work and marched into the city, arming themselves with stolen guns and whatever tools they could lay their hands on. Catholics attacked the Protestant Brown Square school and Protestants attacked the Catholic national school in Hamill Street.

Police attempting to intervene between the mobs were fired on and retaliated. A Sandy Row man, John McConnell, was shot dead. A Catholic, Neal Fagan, was killed by a blow from a shipwright's adze, a heavy wood-hacking tool much used in sectarian riots over the coming years.

A company of Hussars, half an artillery battery, and an infantry regiment were called out in support of the town police. The police, backed by soldiers, searched entire streets of houses. Funerals – about 15 people were killed – became political processions and the occasion for more riots.

The use of terror by elements within both communities, the developing clandestine elements within the Catholic and Protestant working-class enclaves, alleged partiality on the part of the local police, and the authorities' recurrent need to call in the Army at times of heightened political and communal tensions were all becoming features that would be familiar to the people of Belfast and its rural hinterland through to the final days of the 20th century.

The presence of rabble-rousing clerics has also been a common feature of both centuries. After a relatively peaceful

Twelfth of July in 1872, the Rev Hugh Hanna chose the occasion of the first nationalist demonstrations in Belfast on August 15 to claim a Catholic conspiracy to burn down his church, St Enoch's, at Carlisle Circus.

As the nationalists marched to Hannastown, on the western outskirts of the city, the Protestant shipwrights again left their work and marched to Carlisle Circus, to defend the church. The shipwrights clashed with the police and by evening were engaged in a pitched battle with the returning nationalist demonstrators at the Brickfields between the Shankill and Falls.

The August 1872 rioting was immediately followed by the first outbreak of mass intimidation as hundreds of Catholics were evicted from Protestant areas and vice versa. Pathetic, miserable evicted families drifted across the city's sectarian front lines.

The greatest period of threat to the principle of Irish unionism and the crucible from which was forged modern, militant loyalism, however, lay in the Home Rule period which began in the 1880s.

The general election of 1885, the first under secret voting and near universal franchise, had returned eighty-five Irish nationalist MPs – members of the Irish Parliamentary Party – and only sixteen Irish Conservatives to Parliament. The nationalist MPs, led by Charles Stewart Parnell, held the balance of power at Westminster. They put a Tory Government out and a Liberal Government under William Gladstone into power. In return, Gladstone announced the introduction of the Home Rule Bill to grant an all-Ireland Parliament in Dublin. The nationalist victory was met by celebrations in Belfast's Catholic areas.

On losing office, the Conservative Lord Randolph Churchill immediately sought to rally support against Gladstone and the Home Rule Bill, beginning in Belfast on February 22, 1886, where he was met by a massive demonstration of Protestant support.

In that month, the sectarian clashes which had been a feature of life in Belfast each summer for many years erupted with a new ferocity. Five days before the Parliamentary vote on the Home Rule Bill, the issue led to a fist fight between two navvies, a Catholic named Murphy and a Protestant, Robert Bleakley, at Queen's Island shipyard. Murphy had brought proceedings to a close by threatening Bleakley with a spade and warning him: "none of the Orange sort would get leave to work or earn a loaf of bread in Belfast", according to an account given at the trial of four Protestant workmen at Down Assizes.

News of the contretemps and the remarks spread. The Belfast shipyards were a live political issue, as it was widely believed in the city that the Belfast shipbuilders would transfer to the Clyde if Irish Home Rule was introduced, and the Protestant working class population of Belfast would have to leave with them.

On June 4, 1886, an estimated 300 Protestant navvies descended on the small group of Catholics working at Queen's Island. The only route of escape was into the River Lagan. Ten Catholics were caught and beaten terribly. Others took to the water. James Curran, the frail 18-year-old son of a widow from Ballymacarrett, took to the water but was unable to swim. He drowned in front of a hostile crowd, none of whom, the commissioners found, made any attempt to save him. (This process of intimidating Catholics from Belfast's largest industrial enterprise was another common feature of the latest conflict. Through necessity Catholics continued to return to the yards for work and, up to the 1990s, were inevitably intimidated out, and on occasion killed.)

Curran's death became the focus needed for the city's latest round of bloodletting. Rioting broke out and seven people were killed, mostly as a result of police and soldiers firing on rioters and looters. Two more people were killed in riots between Sandy Row and the Falls Road on the night of

July thirteen. Another 13 people were killed in riots on the weekend of July 13th-14th when Protestant processions, returning from Sunday School outings, marched through the city and were attacked by Catholic mobs.

The remaining Catholics working in the shipyard were driven out by August 7, 1886. There was more rioting on the Shankill Road and police shot dead three men. Rioting continued until the next weekend, when another thirteen people were killed.

The riots continued until September when wet autumn weather brought the worst of the outdoor hostilities to an end.

The 600-page report of the Belfast Riots Commissioners, published in early 1887, recorded details of the fifty deaths and hundreds of injuries, the 442 people arrested, the 31 public houses burned down, and the widespread intimidation and acts of vandalism. The 371 town police had been supplemented by 1,000 infantry, 200 cavalry and a further 1,000 Royal Irish Constabulary, drawn from all over Ireland. The riots were the worst episode of violence in Ireland during the 19th century.

The first Home Rule Bill was defeated on June 8, 1886, with the defection of ninety-three Liberal MPs causing the collapse of Gladstone's government. The resumption of Conservative rule temporarily eased Home Rule fever until 1892, when Salisbury's government collapsed and Gladstone returned with a new, second Bill.

The Ulster Liberal and Conservative politicians buried their differences in opposing the new Home Rule Bill and held a mass Ulster Unionist Convention at Stranmillis, in Belfast on June 17, 1892, to show the strength of organised opposition to the Bill. Speeches were directed strongly against the legislation but avoided the use of sectarian remarks, as the evolving unionist leadership strove to distance itself from the tainted images of the 1886 riots.

By the end of the 19th century, the Ulster Protestant

45

gentry and officer class were fully behind the anti-Home Rule campaign and dedicated to the proper organisation of the loyalist masses. The adze was, temporarily, out of fashion as the Ulster gentry sought to make friends and influence people at Westminster.

Lord Cushendun, in his book *Ulster's Stand for Union*, said the Orange institutions which had "fallen into disrepute" prior to 1886 were now infused with "large numbers of country gentlemen, clergymen of all Protestant denominations, business and professional men, farmers and the better class of artisans in Belfast and other towns".

With the management of the loyalist movement in "capable hands" the movement was "completely and rapidly transformed. Instead of being a somewhat disreputable and obsolete survivor of earlier times, it became a highly respectable as well as an exceedingly powerful political organisation".

This show of respectable and stalwart unionism was not, however, sufficient to prevent Gladstone's return to power.

As Gladstone was redrafting a new Home Rule bill in 1892, Fred Crawford, a young engineer in Belfast, formed a secret society called Young Ulster. A condition of membership was possession of a revolver, a Martini-Henry rifle or a Winchester carbine.

This was the model on which a new Ulster loyalist citizen army was to be founded. Crawford was to become a leading figure in the new movement as well as the most successful arms smuggler in Irish history.

The notion of a properly-armed conspiracy had been in the air for some time. On May 11, 1886, a half-serious advertisement appeared in the *Belfast News Letter* stating: "Rifles: Tenders required for 20,000 Sniders in good order, with bayonets or swords, to be delivered, carriage paid, on or before June 1 in lots at certain railway stations on the Northern Counties Railway, as may be required by the purchaser. Address: Vigilance Committee, 8335, Office of this paper."

The Second Home Rule Bill passed through the House of Commons on April 21, 1893, but was rejected by the House of Lords. The Conservatives returned to power in 1895 and, for the next decade or so, the union with Great Britain was somewhat assured.

The marshalling of disciplined unionist militancy did not quell the tendency to sectarian riots and acts of terrorism. There were further disturbances in Belfast in September 1893, when loyalists attacked trade unionists attending the Trade Union Congress because of Labour support for Home Rule. Catholic workmen were again driven from the shipyards. There were riots in the city again in 1898 when Catholic commemorations of the United Irishmen's rising led to riots between the Shankill and Falls and the expulsion of large numbers of Catholics from the shipyards and linen mills.

The implacable opposition of northeastern Protestants to the majority Catholic nationalist opinion on the island of Ireland, combined with Belfast's phenomenal industrial growth in the 19th century, provided the engine for unionist opposition to Home Rule.

The city's architectural historian, Sir Charles Brett, commented: "Rightly or wrongly, the dominant majority in Belfast felt itself more and more threatened and beleaguered by the dominant majority of Ireland as a whole. The uneducated might express their views by rioting, but the Belfast Chamber of Commerce sent a deputation to wait on Mr Gladstone and point out to him that its members were poorer by thousands of pounds owing to the fall in Irish stocks consequent upon the introduction of his second Home Rule Bill. From 1886 onwards, Protestant Belfast was on the defensive; but it came to have a new sense of its separate identity. No longer was Belfast content to be the second city of Ireland; subjectively it saw itself both as a great industrial centre and as the religious and political capital of the Protestant and Unionist North-East."

In the opening years of the 20th century, the Ulster unionists broke ranks with the unionist MPs in the south of Ireland who had begun contemplating a limited form of devolution. The Ulster MPs joined together as the Ulster Unionist Council on March 30, 1905.

The following year, the Liberals returned to government, and without the need for Irish Parliamentary Party support for a majority in the House of Commons. However, Lloyd George set about destroying the House of Lords veto which had rejected his People's Budget of 1909. The House of Lords veto on bills from the Commons was duly curtailed to a maximum of two years.

However, in the two general elections of 1910 the Liberal majority was worn down to the point where Lloyd George needed the support of the Irish Parliamentary Party once more. A third Home Rule Bill was the price.

By June 1911 Ulster loyalists were organising and preparing to fight. Some 50,000 men assembled outside Craigavon, the home of Sir James Craig in east Belfast, to be addressed by their new leader, Sir Edward Carson.

The newest Home Rule Bill was reintroduced to Parliament by the Liberal Government of Herbert Asquith and passed through the Commons in January 1912. The House of Lords rejected the Bill but it was destined to become law in two years.

This was Ulster unionism's lowest moment. The first vote on the third Home Rule Bill came as the news of the sinking of the Belfast-built *Titanic* reached the city. The liner was built at the Harland and Wolff yard, hailed as the largest and greatest ship afloat and a symbol of the manufacturing greatness of Belfast shipyards. Too hastily prepared for its maiden voyage by its owners, the White Star Line, it struck an iceberg in the north Atlantic shortly before midnight on April 14, 1912 and sank two hours and forty minutes later with the loss of some 1,500 passengers and crew.

In Ulster, a series of unionist shows of strength, including a march of 100,000 before the Conservative leader, Bonar Law, in Belfast on Easter Tuesday, 1912 led to Covenant Day, September 28, 1912, when 471,414 signed the Solemn League and Covenant to "stand by one another in defending for ourselves and our children our cherished position of equal citizenship in the United Kingdom and, in using all means which may be found necessary, to defeat the present conspiracy to set up a Home Rule Parliament in Ireland".

Throughout that period, the unionist citizen army had been drilling in the demesnes of Ulster's titled families: at Springhill House, at Moneymore, Co Derry; Castle Hume, on Lough Erne; Killyleagh Castle; Donard Park, above Newcastle; Baronscourt, Co Tyrone; Shane's Castle, Antrim; Tobar Mhuire, at Crossgar, Co Down, and Fernhill, in west Belfast.

In January 1913 the Ulster Unionist Council inaugurated the Ulster Volunteer Force, an army of 100,000 men led by General Sir George Richardson, the British Army veteran of the Boxer Rising in China. The UVF drew together into one organisation the diverse militias and paramilitary organisations that had grown in the face of Home Rule and which spanned the area from Belfast to Donegal.

One of the most dedicated and elitist elements was an organisation of around 2,000 young Belfast loyalists known as the Young Citizen Volunteers (YCV). They had been inaugurated in September 1912 by the then Belfast Lord Mayor, Robert McMordie, and were led by Fred Crawford. The YCV's stated objects were "to cultivate, by means of modified military and police drill, a manly physique, with habits of self-control, self-respect and chivalry . . . to assist as an organisation when called upon, the civil power in the maintenance of peace." The YCV joined the UVF en masse and formed a battalion in the Belfast regiment.

The UVF was established along county divisions, regiments and battalions. It was to be the military wing of a unionist provisional government, plans for which were simultaneously drawn up.

By the early months of 1914, the UVF was prepared for a full-scale coup d'etat in the predominantly Protestant areas of northeastern Ireland. The UVF set about stockpiling food to offset the effects of a British blockade.

Aside from the Home Rule threat there were other sources of discord in Ulster. Catholic-Protestant divisions in Ulster were hardening. The suspicion that Home Rule equalled Rome Rule was underlined by the fact that Roman Catholicism was undergoing one of its extreme evangelistic lurches in the opening years of the new century. The March 1912 issue of the *Catholic Bulletin* announced "the time for action has arrived . . . to bring into the bosom of the Holy Church the million of our separated brethren". Ulster Protestants were scandalised when a Belfast Catholic, Alexander McCann, apparently under the influence of a priest, left his Protestant wife and took his children with him after the Catholic hierarchy produced its *Ne Temere* ruling. This declared marriages between Catholics and Protestants null and void unless they had taken place in a Catholic church and the children were brought up Catholics.

Catholic hierarchy members also became closely associated with the Home Rule movement. The Catholic Bishop of Derry, Charles McHugh, proposed a mass nationalist demonstration in March 1914 to "strengthen the hands of Mr Redmond and the Irish Party".

Asquith's government sought compromise and the nationalist leader, John Redmond, agreed to the temporary partitioning of Ireland despite opposition by northern nationalists who did not relish the thought of separation under the Protestant unionist government. Carson, however, declined the offer of a temporary arrangement saying Protestants would settle for nothing less than permanent partition.

In the face of unionist intransigence and the threat to set up a provisional government in Ulster, Asquith sent two Royal Navy light cruisers to Belfast Lough and directed seven battle ships and the Third Battle Squadron back from the mid-Atlantic to sit ready across the North Channel in the Clyde.

Sixty officers in the Curragh Camp in Kildare, including its commanding officer, Sir Hubert Gough, were asked by the Commander-in-Chief of the British Army in Ireland if they would move against the UVF if directed to do so or resign. They said they would resign. This constituted the Curragh Mutiny of March, 1914. However, it provided sufficient impetus for the British Government capitulation, and it withdrew directives for military action.

The unionist preparations for civil war continued, however. The leading UVF organiser, Fred Crawford, had made contact with a German arms dealer, Bruno Spiro, who acquired 20,000 rifles and two million rounds of ammunition which were transported from Hamburg to Larne, Co Antrim in April, 1914.

Under Crawford's direction, the UVF mounted a remarkable logistics operation. Weapons landed at Larne aboard the *MV Clyde Valley* were collected and distributed by an estimated 500 motor cars and lorries. Two smaller boats transhipped guns down the coast to Belfast and Donaghadee.

Civil war now loomed. In response to the arming of the Protestant militias, nationalists responded to their own calls-to-arms. By mid-1914 more than 100,000 had enrolled in the Irish Volunteers. Many Belfast Catholics joined the Irish Volunteers in response to the sight of Protestants drilling openly in the city. There was, however, no nationalist plan as advanced as the UVF's for seizing and holding power.

Three months after the landing of the *Clyde Valley*, on July 26, 1914, the Irish Volunteers were engaged in similar business at the fishing port of Howth, north of Dublin. A yacht, *The Asgard*, delivered 1,500 rifles to the nationalists who fought skirmishes with British soldiers on the road back into Dublin.

A week later, on Tuesday, August 4, 1914, Britain declared war on Germany. The declaration of war transformed affairs in Ireland. Carson deferred to the greater threat to the Union and agreed not to press for an amending bill to the Home Rule Act when it went on to the Statute Book on September, 18, 1914. John Redmond also agreed that Home Rule should immediately be suspended for twelve months or until the War ended.

But the impending war in Europe and mass enlistment of both Redmond's renamed National Volunteers and Carson's Ulster Volunteers dissipated the growing threat of all-out civil war between Protestants and Catholics in Ireland. Two citizen armies, opposed to each other but both prepared to fight against British soldiers, were suddenly joined together before a common foe. In parts of the north of Ireland, Catholic National Volunteers and Protestant Ulster Volunteers paraded together as the first contingents of enlisted men set off for the War.

The Ulster Volunteers, a large force already disciplined and trained by British Army officers, became the object of the attentions of Secretary of State for War, Lord Kitchener. He sent for Col TE Hickman, president of the British League for the Defence of Ulster, and declared: "I want the Ulster Volunteers".

Hickman arranged a meeting with Carson and Craig who agreed to commit the Ulster Volunteers on the basis of an amendment to the Home Rule Bill accommodating the unionist demands for partition. On September 3, 1914, Carson announced the formation of the 36th (Ulster) Division.

In fact, Redmond's National Volunteers joined in the war effort in greater numbers. By the end of 1915, an estimated 55,000 Irish men had enlisted, with at least 27,000 of these members of Redmond's National Volunteers, many of whom joined the 16th Division – although 13,000 of Redmond's 150,000 Irish Volunteers broke away to become the Irish Republican Army.

Figures for Irish war losses remain a point of debate, but it is probable that of the 50,000 Irish soldiers killed in the 1914–1918 War, about 40,000 were from the twenty-six counties of Ireland which became the Republic and around 10,000 were from the area which became Northern Ireland. Irish Protestants and Catholics died in roughly equal ratios.

There was some reluctance among loyalists, particularly in Belfast, about committing such large numbers of their volunteers to the British war effort. The question was put in letters to newspapers among other places: what would happen to an Ulster deprived of its fighting men?

Captain Frank Percy Crozier, a former British officer and adventurer from an Anglo-Irish family who had rallied to the Ulster cause and been put in charge of raising 300 members from the Shankill Road area of Belfast for the UVF's Special Service Section, had some initial difficulties in convincing his men to join up. The members, he wrote, "found it difficult to set themselves free from insular and parochial associations". Many of Crozier's men were the fathers and grandfathers of the Belfast men and women of the UVF's second coming. His Special Service Section was also to be the model and heroic frame within which the second UVF moulded itself.

In 1914, the UVF, reconstituted as the 36th Division, underwent retraining. Men encamped at Brownlow House, Lurgan had an ominous foretaste of what lay ahead when they spent the month before Christmas, 1914 digging trenches at Lurgan Park.

At noon on May 7, 1915, the 17,000 troops of the 36th Division assembled in the parkland at Malone, in the south of Belfast, for a parade through the city. They were embarked for camps in England before the Orange parading began for that year's Twelfth celebrations. Within three months many of the men were in the trenches of the Western Front. In March, 1916 the 36th Division moved its line from between the River Ancre and Mailly-Maillet-Serre Road to Thiepval Wood. The men began preparing for the "big push" across the Somme that summer. The 36th Division's object was to cross into German lines opposite the Wood at Schwaben Redoubt at "Zero Hour", 7.30 a.m. on July 1, 1916. All along the Somme, after months of advertising the intention, the Allied forces, almost an entire generation of young men, climbed up out of trenches and began walking, then charging towards German lines. The Ulster Volunteers were among the few units which managed to break through the German lines.

The Redoubt was seized by the Ulster men within two hours. But with no reinforcements and under pressure from reinforced German lines, the ground was surrendered. Within the opening hours of battle, hundreds were killed or left dying in no-man's land. Along the Somme the British Army suffered 20,000 dead and 35,000 injured during that day. The 600 Armagh and Cavan Volunteers who crossed the trenches recorded 532 dead and wounded by the end of the day. Only seventy members of Captain Crozier's West Belfast Battalion survived to the next day. The 36th Division suffered some 2,000 dead and 3,000 injured.

The 36th Division was moved back, and reassembled to fight alongside members of Redmond's National Volunteers at Messines in June 1917. There, the Ulster Division suffered a further 1,129 casualties. That August in the mud of Ypres the Division suffered another 3,441 casualties. Its ranks were filled up with fresh recruits from England. In November 1917, the remnants of the Division took up position east of Arras and in January 1918, it moved back to the Somme, at Sphinx Wood. There the 36th Division encountered the full force of the final German Big Push at the Somme where it suffered a further 7,252 dead or injured. On August 22, 1918, the Division took part in the final advance on German lines, suffering a further 3,000 casualties before the War ended on November 11. Most of the volunteers remained in France until the 36th Division was disbanded and written off the register, in July, 1919. They then returned home.

The UVF had served its purpose in the trenches of France. The only official legacy of the original UVF and the 36th (Ulster) Division was the UVF Hospital, opened by Carson in a building opposite Queen's University and later moved to east Belfast, for the treatment and care of men injured in the War.

The war had a profound impact on Ulster. The normal Orange celebrations were postponed and at noon on July 12, 1916, instead of Belfast and the North's provincial towns resounding to the marching bands, all work and movement came to a halt to mark the losses at the Somme.

At Easter, 1916, the splinter Irish Volunteer and Irish Republican Brotherhood groups launched their Rising in Dublin. There was some hope within the group for German aid to overthrow British rule in Ireland. It never came.

The Rising was seen as the ultimate act of treachery in London. It helped to secure the unionist position, however, as Asquith set his face against coercing Ulster out of the Union.

Naturally, the events of Easter and July, 1916, had the most profound effect on Belfast and the northeastern part of Ireland. As nationalists (Belfast had one of the most active elements of the Irish Republican Brotherhood) set their sights on separation from Britain, the unionists viewed events in Dublin as a wanton act of treachery committed in Dublin while Ulster's sons gave their lives for King and Country at the Somme.

The fact that more Catholics than Protestants gave their lives in the war was overlooked by both extremes at home in Ireland and remains, to this day, one of the forgotten facts of both nationalist and unionist histories.

In the general election of November 1918, Sinn Féin swept aside the Irish Parliamentary Party. The Sinn Féin MPs declined to take their seats in Westminster, set up the first Dail Éireann and declared their Irish Republic on January 21, 1919.

The IRA's "war of independence" began. Two Royal Irish Constabulary constables escorting a cartload of explosives in Co Tipperary were shot dead by the IRA. As the country's government apparatus began to disintegrate, with the announcement of a new Parliament by Sinn Féin, the south and west of Ireland plunged into full-scale guerrilla warfare.

The War of Independence in the south precipitated the worst violence yet in the northeastern six counties. The first outbreak of serious violence was in the centre of Londonderry in April 1920. The local head of the RIC Special Branch, and a Catholic ex-serviceman who had been gassed and wounded in the trenches, were shot dead by the IRA. UVF men seized control of the Diamond and Guildhall Square and began firing from the city's walls into the Catholic Bogside. The IRA counter-attacked. In two months of skirmishing, forty people were killed, mostly by gunfire, in the city. The Army arrived and imposed a curfew, and directed machine-gun fire at IRA snipers in the Bogside.

"A striking feature of the army's intervention in Derry was its close co-operation with the local UVF, thereby aligning itself with one side in a sectarian conflict generations old," Jonathan Bardon comments in *A History of Ulster*.

The British Army was badly stretched in conflicts around the Empire and there was an obvious tendency to "draw on the strength" of the friendly UVF.

The outbreak of full scale guerrilla war in the south tipped the entire country over into a security crisis. The RIC withdrew to central barracks. More than 500 outlying stations and tax offices were attacked and burned by the IRA. Loyalists in rural areas of Ulster where the IRA was operating felt under siege.

On June 25, 1920, the Ulster Unionist Council had decided to revive the UVF under the charge of Lt Col Wilfrid Spender in response to the growing security crisis on the island.

Spender sent Col George Moore Irvine to Derry, to liaise with and assist the British Army. Fred Crawford noted that Moore Irvine "so impressed the (British Army) GOC (General Officer Commanding) with the object and aims of the UVF that the latter now refers everything to him. Irvine says he is virtually the governor of Derry. The GOC recognises that the UVF are for King and country and that the rebels are simply for all the British enemy and to kick free from the British Empire."

The largely Catholic constabulary in the RIC were mistrusted and their policing and intelligence gathering role was usurped in Fermanagh, Tyrone and Derry by the revived UVF vigilantes.

The Twelfth of July, 1920, was more like the old days. Carson, addressing the British Government at the field where the march ended in south Belfast, warned: "We tell you this: that if, having offered you our help, you are yourselves unable to protect us from the machinations of Sinn Féin and you won't take our help, well then, we tell you that we will take the matter into our own hands. We will reorganise". He added that Ulster "will tolerate no Sinn Féin: no Sinn Féin organisation, no Sinn Féin methods".

Immediately on their return from the "Twelfth week" holiday, notices were posted at the shipyard gates for attendance at a rally of "Protestant and Unionist workers". The meeting endorsed a call to drive out "disloyal" workers. Hundreds of Catholics and socialist trade union activists were ejected from the shipyards. Similar acts of mass intimidation took place at engineering works in the city. A Catholic Church committee estimated that 1,000 Catholic workers were forced from their jobs.

That evening, trams carrying Protestant shipyard workers from work were stoned as they passed the Catholic Short Strand area. Five days of intense rioting ensued in which twenty people died. After a lull, the violence broke out again in August after republican gunmen shot dead a police inspector in Lisburn. A further twenty-seven people were killed. The violence intensified in late August and in September another twenty people were killed. Another nine people died in sporadic violence before the year ended. Hundreds of people, the majority of them Catholics, were intimidated from their homes. A curfew, from 10.30 p.m. to 5 a.m., was placed on the city and continued until 1924.

On July 21, 1920, in Cork, the IRA shot dead the RIC divisional commissioner, Col GF Smyth, of Banbridge, Co Down. In the aftermath of his funeral, Catholic businesses and homes were attacked and destroyed in Banbridge and Dromore, Co Down.

The traditional loyalist reaction in Belfast began. Catholics were ejected from the shipyards. Rioting broke out around the Catholic Short Strand enclave in east Belfast – the nearest Catholic community to the shipyards and the one most frequently afflicted by sectarian violence. In three days of violence thirteen people were killed.

On August 22, 1920, another senior RIC officer was shot dead in Lisburn, Co Antrim. Within days, sixty Catholic businesses and homes were destroyed in the town. All but a few of the Catholic residents of Lisburn were forced to flee. The Banbridge and Lisburn pogroms were carried out by local UVF men.

Col Fred Crawford, the UVF arms runner, helped rearm and reorganise the UVF to defend Protestant areas. He organised the manufacture of improvised grenades and distributed ammunition from the store he kept at his bleach works in the lower Shankill Road area.

The routine of sectarian conflict in the city was becoming

58

established again. Repeated attempts were made to drive the Catholics from east Belfast and Short Strand was besieged almost nightly. The loyalist attacks on the isolated Catholic areas like Short Strand brought criticism in British newspapers. Stimulated by the criticism and the deteriorating security situation in Ulster, Craig sent a memorandum to Westminster in September 1920 saying: " . . . the situation is becoming so desperate that unless the Government will take immediate action, it may be advisable for them to see what steps can be taken towards a system of organised reprisals . . . partly to restrain their own followers . . . unless urgent action is taken, civil war on a very large scale is inevitable".

On October 22, 1920, the decision was taken at Government level to create the Ulster Special Constabulary. The USC had three categories. It was to operate only in the six northeastern counties of Ireland, Armagh, Down, Tyrone, Derry, Fermanagh and Antrim. The Government's intention was to free British soldiers to counteract the growing rebellion in the south of Ireland. The deployment of the USC in only six counties was also a clear indication that the British Government was about to partition Ulster. It did so, establishing the six-county area of Northern Ireland, with its own parliament, in December, 1920.

The "A" Specials consisted of 2,000 full-time constables, uniformed and mobile and paid like the RIC. The largest part of the USC was the "B" Specials, part-time, uniformed and unpaid and serving in their local areas. In addition there was an irregular force of "C" Specials who were unpaid, identified only by caps and armlets and who were to be called out in emergencies only. The USC was under the control of the new RIC Divisional commissioner in the North, Lt Col Charles Wickham. The USC structure was similar to the UVF and whole units of the UVF enlisted together. Catholics were excluded by order and there was fear of trouble between the new Force and Catholic members of the RIC.

Home Rule was finally granted, for twenty-six counties of Ireland at least, in December 1920. The six counties of Northern Ireland received their own Parliament and continued to be represented in the British House of Commons with thirteen MPs.

Men who had served in the UVF, and particularly the remnants of Crozier's Special Services Section, from the Shankill Road area, were active in the violence in Belfast. In Fermanagh, the local UVF was revived by Sir Basil Brooke to protect isolated Protestant villages and townlands. However, the UVF was no longer a centrally led and disciplined force. It was entirely irregular and led, if at all, in Belfast from within its own ranks or by sympathetic local political figures.

The terms of the Anglo-Irish Treaty, granting dominion status to the twenty-six counties, deeply unsettled the unionists. The violence in Belfast escalated during November and December 1920 as the Treaty negotiations reached its conclusion.

In January 1921 the IRA launched an offensive against the police and army in Ulster.

An IRA killing of two constables at a hotel in Townhall Street, Belfast, on January 26, restarted the violence. Later that night three men forced their way into a house in Bray Street and shot dead a 23-year-old Catholic man, Michael Garvey. Garvey's landlady gave evidence that one of the killers was dressed as a policeman. The first policeman to arrive at the house after the killing was District Inspector John William Nixon, from Cavan, who was stationed at Brown Square, in the Shankill area. It was widely suspected among nationalists that Nixon, along with other police officers from Brown Square station, was engaging in a campaign of assassination against suspected republicans. Rioting, intimidation and shootings escalated. Thirty-one people were killed in four days of intense violence between February 12 and 16.

After the assassination of another constable by the IRA in April 1921 another two young Catholic men were shot dead at their home in Clonard Gardens, on the Falls Road. Again, Nixon was widely suspected of leading the reprisals. The fighting continued through 1921 and by March the following year some 300 people had died.

The violence reached its climax in March 1922, despite a pact signed between Michael Collins and James Craig under which Collins undertook to withdraw IRA units and Craig undertook to induce Catholics into the Special Constabulary and to recover jobs for those Catholics intimidated from their workplaces. In the violence in Belfast, sixty-one people were killed that month.

Possibly the ugliest acts of violence occurred at this time. On the morning of March 24, 1922 a group of men – again, reputedly organised by Nixon – burst into the home at Kinnaird Terrace, off the lower Antrim Road, of Owen McMahon, a well-known Belfast bar owner.

Owen McMahon, his sons Thomas (15), Frank (24) and Patrick (22) and a barman, Edward McKinney (25), were roused from their beds, lined up, given five minutes to pray and then shot dead. Two other sons, John (21) and Bernard (26) were badly injured. Bernard died a week later in hospital from his injuries. John recovered.

According to accounts at the time, a night watchman at a building site in Carlisle Circus reported that two policemen approached him and took a sledgehammer from the site shortly before the attack on the McMahon home a few hundred yards away.

Rioting, intimidation and shootings escalated. Thirty-one people were killed in four days of intense violence between February 12 and 16.

The violence continued. On May 22, 1922, the Unionist MP for West Belfast, WJ Twaddell, was shot dead on his way to open his outfitters' shop in the city centre. Altogether sixty-six people were killed in May 1922.

The death toll for the violence in Belfast from July 1920 to July 1922 was 453. This included 257 Catholics, 157 Protestants, two people of uncertain religious affiliation and 37 members of the security forces. As many as 10,000 Catholics had been forced out of their jobs and Catholic relief organisations estimated that 23,000 Catholics had been intimidated out of their homes, mostly from the religiously mixed streets between the main sectarian enclaves in the city.

The bulk of organised loyalist violence was attributed to a group called the Ulster Protestant Association, the first of many guises adopted by the men from the UVF. A concerted response from the reconstituted police force culminating in the arrest of several prominent gunmen in late 1922 helped to restore peace to the city.

On April 5, 1922, the Royal Ulster Constabulary was set up to replace the Royal Irish Constabulary serving in the new state of Northern Ireland. More than 50,000 regular and part-time constables, almost all Protestant, were recruited to the new force. Northern Ireland's first emergency law, the Civil Authorities (Special Powers) Bill, was introduced two days later.

The formal decommissioning of the UVF and the recruitment of the majority of its members into the new auxiliary police forces, the "A" and "B" Specials contributed towards preventing the new State from being submerged in sectarian butchery.

The sectarian violence was largely confined to Belfast and was brought to an end within two years when the new police and the court system drew themselves together and began rounding up and imprisoning the gunmen from both communities. In early 1923, a succession of court cases and convictions for murder and other serious crimes was accompanied by a swift decline in the city's nocturnal violence.

Nixon, who later stood as a successful loyalist candidate in the Shankill area, was again the suspected ring-leader of the assassins. A report to Michael Collins' secret police in Dublin Castle – probably from agents within the RIC in Belfast – named Nixon, his superior County Inspector Harrison and ten other RIC members from Brown Square as being responsible for the McMahon and other assassinations.

Inspector Nixon was finally suspended from the RUC in February, 1924, after making a sectarian speech at Clifton Street Orange Hall. He became the object of loyalist adulation and was given a standing ovation at a rally on his behalf in April 1924. He stood as an independent loyalist candidate in the 1925 Council elections and was elected by a majority of almost 3,000 over a Labour candidate.

The "B" Specials, as the USC was better known, served the new State and the cause of unionism well enough. But, outside the official ranks, there remained small groups which adhered to the belief that insurrection by a secret guerrilla army like the IRA was, as in the past, best countered by like tactics.

Meanwhile, in the new Free State in the south, an almost identical assimilation into legitimate state forces eventually took place in respect of the IRA. The elements which supported de Valera were inducted into the Free State's police force in the early 1930s and became known by the nickname Broy Harriers.

However, the purist anti-treaty element of the IRA, although defeated by a determined use of force by the new Irish state in a brief civil war, retreated into the shadows remaining outside mainstream constitutional political life in Northern Ireland until almost the end of the century.

Nixon continued to be elected in the Shankill constituency during the mid-century, standing as an

Independent Unionist. He continued to be closely associated with violent loyalism. He was a founder of the Ulster Protestant League in 1931, whose object was to safeguard Protestant jobs or, in other words, deny employment to Catholics. He was also associated with a group known as the Ulster Protestant Association. This included a hard core of loyalist gunmen who carried out assassinations of Catholics in Belfast during the mid-1930s.

After the terrorism and horrors of the 1920s, there followed a long period free of violence. But there was no sign of a liberalising influence in either Irish nationalism or Ulster unionism. The 1930s saw a resurgence of Irish Catholic evangelising, supported by the Dublin Government. The accession to power in Dublin of Fianna Fail, in 1932, saw an increased emphasis on Irish nationalism. The Fianna Fail leader announced, in a radio broadcast on St Patrick's Day, 1935, that Ireland had been a Christian and Catholic country since St Patrick's time and "she remains a Catholic nation". He used subsequent broadcasts to attack partition and the British Government. He later pledged himself "never to rest until that land which the Almighty so clearly designed as one shall belong undivided to the Irish people".

In the same year that de Valera assumed power in Dublin, the Ulster Unionist leadership voiced its Protestant, anti-nationalist agenda. At the Twelfth of July Orange demonstration in Poyntzpass, Co Armagh, Sir James Craig stated: "Ours is a Protestant government and I am an Orangeman". In July 1933, Sir Basil Brooke, speaking to Orangemen in Newtownbutler, Co Fermanagh, urged loyalists "wherever possible, to employ Protestant lads and lassies".

Predictably, sectarian tensions grew, breaking out into renewed conflict in early 1935. The threat of serious violence during the marching period of 1935 led the Northern Ireland government to ban all processions, sparking strong opposition from the Orange Order which resulted in the ban being lifted. The violence broke out after the Twelfth demonstration, with thirteen people being killed during the ensuing riots and forced evictions. Nixon's UPA gunmen, some of whom were to become household names in working-class loyalist areas, were probably responsible for some of the assassinations of this period.

One loyalist gunman of the time, known as Buck Alex, was blamed for, but never convicted of, killing Catholics in the 1930s. He later became a well-known character in the city, and allegedly kept a lion in the backyard of his home off York Road. He was also a minor gangster figure and, by several accounts, later became a police informer. But, even during his life, he became a figure of dark legend to the nationalist population. Up to the 1960s, Catholic children in Belfast were warned by mothers that if they did not behave Buck Alex would come at night and take them away.

The sectarian violence of the 1930s also followed in the wake of the protests and riots over the levels of unemployment and poverty in the city. By the mid-1930s, 78,000 people were unemployed and virtually starving in Belfast. There was rioting, with the unemployed from both communities confronting the police.

While unemployed Protestants and Catholics marched and rioted alongside each other during the "Outdoor Relief" protests, the city's sectarian characteristics were still near the surface. In 1932, Catholics returning from the Eucharistic Congress, a large evangelical rally in Dublin, were stoned by crowds from Sandy Row as they arrived at Great Victoria Station.

The building of a Catholic church in Willowfield in east Belfast in 1935 was accompanied by attacks on Catholic homes and businesses, and a Catholic man was shot dead in his shop in Great George's Street. Another 40 houses were attacked and damaged in June 1935 and twenty-six people injured during rioting. The Stormont Government made an unsuccessful attempt to cancel that year's Twelfth demonstrations. Predictably, rioting broke out on the Twelfth evening. Mobs gathered and shots were exchanged between the Catholic New Lodge and Protestant Tiger's Bay areas of north Belfast.

Altogether thirteen people were killed and hundreds injured in the five weeks of rioting that ensued. As before, large-scale sectarian intimidation accompanied the riots. More than 500 families were forced out of the York Street area and had to find refuge in the Ardoyne and Falls Road Catholic enclaves. Although about 90 per cent of the families intimidated from the area were Catholic, Protestants were also intimidated from the streets between York Street and the New Lodge.

Buck Alex and others who had led the armed loyalist gangs were not figures who achieved any status in the official histories of Northern Ireland. Only among the working-class Catholics of Belfast and its hinterland were their names and reputations known and feared for what they were.

Lately, the UVF has begun to renounce the activities of the mid-century UVF men who engaged in sectarian assassinations during a period when there had been Protestant and Catholic consensus on basic socialist ideals. Buck Alex is now derided as an assassin in the hire of certain unionist politicians, who remained out of prison by becoming an RUC informant.

There were other directions being pursued by working-class Protestants in Belfast during the mid-century. They were in league with working-class Catholics during the Outdoor Relief protests of the time. Old UVF weapons were also sent to Spain to help the war against Franco's fascists.

Nixon's Ulster Protestant League reappeared briefly in the 1950s under the Ulster Protestant Action title. UPA members of the time included a militant figure called Noel Doherty and the young evangelist street preacher, Ian Paisley.

Doherty, later leader of Paisley's Ulster Constitution Defence Committee (UCDC), was linked to one of the first loyalist arms conspiracies of the 1960s. Referred to in court as a link between Paisley's UCDC and the UVF, Doherty was one of the best-known figures in the loyalist underground of Belfast. He was also one of the leaders of the UCDC's quasi-paramilitary wing, the Ulster Protestant Volunteers. He was not, the UVF insist, one of its members.

Doherty firmly believed there was an international conspiracy, involving communism, the IRA, the Vatican, the ecumenical movement, the British and Irish Government, most mainstream Protestant churches and liberal elements of the Ulster Unionist party, to undermine the union with Britain and force Rome Rule on the Protestants of Ulster. His beliefs were shared by some other extreme right-wing loyalists, such as Billy McGrath, a British secret service informant and leader of a clandestine though unarmed group called TARA, and Johnny McKeague, founder and leader of a succession of loyalist vigilante and paramilitary groups.

These men were the active element of underground loyalism during the early 1960s. They preached that Protestants had to prepare for the coming onslaught on their culture and lives from the combined forces of the above. One TARA member recollected the somewhat prescient slogan painted on the side of the Iron Hall, in Templemore Avenue: "Prepare: conflict is coming – TARA".

There had, however, been no concerted loyalist paramilitary response to the IRA campaign which broke out in December 1956 and lasted until 1962, and resulted in six RUC officers being killed and thirty-four people injured. The IRA campaign was confined to the Border areas. The Republic and Northern Ireland Governments simultaneously introduced internment for republicans. The IRA campaign was as easily quashed as the previous attempt at insurgency in the Second World War years when the Irish Government had introduced martial law and executed IRA leaders.

In 1963, Terence O'Neill, the son of one of the original land-owning founders of the UVF, succeeded Lord Brookeborough as Prime Minister of Northern Ireland. O'Neill promised to "transform the face of Ulster" and during the early years of his premiership Northern Ireland's working and middle classes emerged from the mid-century of depression and post-war austerity period into a period of economic boom. The boom, however, had little effect on improving the standard of life in Belfast's poorest working-class areas. Unemployment remained at high levels in Catholic parts of Belfast and provincial towns like Derry, Dungannon and Newry. On the Protestant Shankill and east Belfast, the decline in the heavy industries of ship-building and engineering, slum clearance and the movement to new housing estates on the outskirts of the city were also biting into the communal fabric.

Sectarian tension in Belfast re-emerged in the middle of the 1960s. In September 1964, during a general election campaign, the RUC raided the Divis Street offices of the Republican Clubs, the political wing of the IRA, and removed an Irish tricolour which had been on display on the first floor window. Four nights of violent rioting followed between nationalists and the RUC, causing fifty injuries.

The seizure of the tricolour, on the orders of the Minister for Home Affairs, Mr Brian McConnell, followed rallies and agitation by loyalists whose figurehead became the street preacher, Paisley.

Paisley was despised by the Ulster Unionist grandees and Stormont administration. His fundamentalist Protestantism and his atavistic political positioning stood at odds with their desire for modernisation and political accommodation. In January 1965, Captain O'Neill invited the Republic's Prime Minister, Mr Sean Lemass, to Stormont Castle, the first such meeting between a Dublin and a Northern Ireland premier at Stormont. Lemass was overseeing the economic regeneration of the Republic and both saw the meeting as an opportunity to discuss areas of mutual economic benefit and as an attempt to bury the ghosts that their predecessors had continued to invoke. The meeting was not to discuss constitutional or political issues, O'Neill stated.

However, the O'Neill-Lemass meeting stirred grass-roots loyalism like a foreboding breeze. The inevitable move to violence started innocuously enough. The Ulster Unionist headquarters in Glengall Street was petrol-bombed on February 18, 1966, during a meeting of the party's Westminster MPs. No one was injured. Two days later a petrol bomb was thrown at a Catholic school, in west Belfast.

The arson attacks continued in Belfast. A petrol bomb was thrown at the Catholic Holy Cross girls' secondary school in Ardoyne on April 6, 1966, two days before Captain O'Neill was to address a conference on reconciliation attended by Protestant and Catholic clergy and laity. UVF members acknowledge their members were engaged in this type of activity but will not, 30 years later, comment on individual attacks.

An editorial which appeared in Paisley's *Protestant Telegraph* in 1968 summed up the mood: "When this hideous policy of sell-out became known to certain people, secret meetings were called throughout the Province. From these clandestine assemblies the feelings of Ulster loyalists were made known to those who would compromise our Faith and Freedom. Contacts were established and many renewed, with sympathisers in the major cities throughout the British Isles . . . friends of Ulster in Britain were kept up to date with the latest news as further information became available . . . As never before Ulster's Loyalists should prepare themselves – spiritually and in other ways – for a test of their patriotism and devotion. The threats of Wilson and Lynch may be fulfilled sooner than we think."

The expected outbreak of violence surrounding the 50th anniversary celebrations of the Dublin Rising did not materialise. A republican demonstration and a counter-demonstration, led by Paisley in Belfast on April 17, 1966, passed within 200 yards or so of each other but no fighting ensued.

However, in parallel with the growing militancy among loyalists, the Catholic gunmen and bombers of the IRA were reverting to form.

On the evening of March 1, 1966, a "Molotov cocktail" was thrown into the home of the British military attaché to the Republic of Ireland, Brigadier RN Thicknesse, on Eglinton Road, in the elegant south Dublin suburb of Donnybrook. The device caused a fire but no injuries.

Seven days later the petrol bombers moved up a scale and bombed Nelson Pillar, in O'Connell Street, blowing it in half and toppling the statue of Lord Nelson and tons of masonry into the capital's main thoroughfare. But the destruction of Nelson's Pillar, long a target of abuse in the Republic, and even the attack on the unfortunately-named military attaché, caused no physical injury and were treated with a sense of mirth rather than alarm by the media and a broad section of the Republic's population.

The Republic of Ireland was emerging, or trying to emerge, from a 50-year infancy of poverty and Roman Catholic church-domination. The newspapers reflected the same interests in fashion and consumerism as other European countries emerging from the post-Second World War austerity. The mad stare of the republican incendiarists and bombers was avoided as Dublin society sought its places alongside the other civilised capitals of Europe.

In one respect, Ireland was experiencing the same political turmoil that other western European countries were encountering in the late 1960s. Student revolt was in the air across the western World.

Across Europe and even just across the Irish Sea, other disaffected groups were resorting to the tactics displayed by the IRA and UVF. On the night before Nelson's Pillar was demolished, Welsh nationalists attempted to blow up a dam in Montgomeryshire in order to draw attention to England's use of Welsh valleys as reservoirs to water their cities and industries.

Few of the insurgent nationalist or revolutionary student movements were, however, able to exploit such a rich vein of nationalist and religious hostility as existed in Northern Ireland.

In the summer of 1969, the mixture of Catholic Irish nationalism on one side and Ulster loyalism on the other again ignited. It was a return to the violent summer marching seasons of the past. During July and August 1969, ten peole were killed and 900 injured, including 154 by gunshot wounds; sixteen factories burned down, 170 houses were destroyed by arson and a further 417 damaged by fire. In Belfast sixty Catholic-owned licensed premises were attacked and twenty-four destroyed. Intimidation led to 1,820 families fleeing their homes, 1,505 of them Catholics.

An orchestrated campaign of rioting in nationalist towns across Northern Ireland had stretched the RUC to the limit. On August 16, after it became clear the RUC could no longer hold out, the British Government dispatched the 2nd Battalion of the Queen's Regiment, followed a week later by the Royal Regiment of Wales. The troops' arrival, followed by a visit to the Bogside by the British Prime Minister, James Callaghan, cooled the situation and there was no further serious violence from nationalists that autumn.

It was the turn of loyalists to vent their fury when it was announced, on October 10 that the Ulster Special Constabulary was to be disbanded. Rioting and gunfire broke out on the Shankill Road. Constable Victor Arbuckle was shot dead by a UVF sniper while on duty on the lower Shankill Road. The Army was sent in and engaged the gunmen, shooting two Shankill Road men dead.

However, the IRA had begun to split, with the emergence of the unreconstructed men of violence that became the Provisional IRA. With the help of £100,000 donated by the Dublin government for the relief of nationalist areas, the Provisionals were able to acquire their first arms shipment.

The "honeymoon period" for the British Army, during which they were welcomed by the Catholic community, ended, almost predictably, when a controversial demonstration by junior Orangemen was allowed along the Springfield Road near Ballymurphy housing estate on Easter Tuesday, March 31, 1970.

The inevitable sequel occured on June 2 when another Orange demonstration was stopped from marching past the Catholic Ardoyne area, precipitating two nights of loyalist rioting. When another Orange demonstration was allowed past Ardoyne weeks later, Catholic rioting erupted and during a gunbattle the Army shot dead three gunmen. Simultaneously, loyalists attempted to invade the Catholic enclave at Short Strand in east Belfast, only to be repulsed by IRA gunmen who shot dead four of the loyalists.

In July, after a curfew was imposed on the Falls Road area during Army arms searches, further rioting erupted and three people were shot dead.

The real IRA bombing campaign finally began in the autumn of 1969 with attacks on Newry bus depot, electricity sub-stations, a customs post in Armagh and the destruction of the Elsinore Hotel in Belfast and the homes of Lord Justice Curran and the Unionist MP, the Rev Martin Smyth. The real "Troubles" were under way.

## Three

# RISING SONS OF ULSTER

Article Two of the Irish Republic's Constitution states: "the national territory consists of the island of Ireland, its islands and territorial seas".

From mid-1969 there was a renewed nationalist campaign, spearheaded by the Irish Republican Army and supported by some people in the Republic of Ireland, to overthrow the British-backed government of Northern Ireland. Their aim was, effectively, the fulfilment of the Irish constitutional prerogative to reunify the island of Ireland. For militant loyalists, there was one very obvious way of striking back in order to fulfil their commitment to the Union with Great Britain: bomb the Republic. Having helped to depose O'Neill, the UVF bombers found a new target.

The idea of a bombing campaign in the Republic was prompted almost solely, UVF figures recall, by the Irish Government's decision to move troops to the Border in the summer of 1969 and the ill-judged remarks of the Irish Prime Minister, Jack Lynch, that his Government would not "stand by" over the assaults on the Catholic, nationalist community in the North.

The loyalist bombers – mostly ex-servicemen – who crossed the unprotected Border into the Irish Republic decided to seek out the type of targets that military commando units would choose when seeking to destabilise any state from within. They would attack communications, energy and transport installations, the same type of targets they had destroyed inside Northern Ireland in the period before O'Neill's resignation. In their initial attacks on the Republic, it might be noted, the UVF bombers chose to avoid civilian collateral damage.

Two months before Thomas McDowell blew himself up at the electricity station in Donegal, a small explosion damaged the headquarters of Radio Telefís Éireann (RTE), the Irish state-controlled broadcasting company in Donnybrook, Dublin. At first it had been thought this was the work of some extreme republican element who might have a gripe against RTE. An admission of responsibility for the RTE attack eventually emerged in a UVF statement issued in Belfast on October 24, 1969. In the same statement responsibility for the Ballyshannon attack in which McDowell had died was acknowledged.

The Ballyshannon raid was "executed in protest against the Éire Army units still massed on the border in Co Donegal". The statement added: "So long as the threats from Éire continue, so long will the volunteers of Ulster's people's army strike at targets in southern Ireland".

An accompanying story in the *Belfast Telegraph* reported unnamed police sources as saying the UVF "may not number more than twenty-five in all though their supporters may run into thousands". The UVF statement, carried in the *Belfast Telegraph*, said the Ballyshannon bombing was in retaliation for the activities of the Glenties (Co Donegal) IRA unit "whose leader and eight other members were killed in the Belfast riots of August 14-15". This appears to have resulted from a misunderstanding arising from a local newspaper report about a ceremony commemorating IRA men from the 1920s.

At around 5 a.m. on Halloween, Friday, October 31, 1969 another explosion occurred, this time at the grave in Co Kildare of the 18th century United Irishmen leader, Wolfe Tone.

The blast shattered one of two headstones on Tone's grave.

By coincidence, on the same night a boiler exploded at the railway works at Inchicore, in Dublin. As it was Halloween the blasts were disguised as the sound of fireworks filled the night air. Adding further to a pervading sense of unease during the evening, lights went out across south Dublin as an electricity sub-station innocently malfunctioned. The next day's newspapers carried confused and foreboding accounts of the events.

The letter of admission from "Capt Johnston" of the UVF cited the blast at the grave of the "traitor Wolfe Tone" (he was a Protestant) as the work of two active service units.

The UVF was clearly aware of the symbolic nature of the bombing of Wolfe Tone's grave. All the Republic's parties, including Sinn Féin, traditionally visited the gravesite outside the village of Sallins each year to renew their republican vows and to use the occasion as a platform for speeches on political policy. The bomb was a warning to the Republic's government, whose army had been sent to the Border, mainly to erect field camps for the Catholic refugees who had been flowing out of Belfast to escape the sectarian violence.

A statement issued to Belfast newspapers said: "Further installations in Éire will be demolished so long as the puny Irish Army continues to keep its soldiers on the border of our beloved Ulster. Our volunteers have proved and will prove that the spirit of Londonderry, the Diamond and the Somme is still in the hearts and minds of loyal Ulster men and will continue so."

The "desecration" of Wolfe Tone's grave at last brought home the message that loyalists were intent on striking south, holding the Republic responsible for the nationalist assault on Northern Ireland's status within the United Kingdom. The attack was condemned by Jack Lynch as "a measure of the evil intent of those who perpetrated the outrage and the extent to which they will go to perpetuate hatred and bigotry".

He insisted that it had never been the Irish government's intention "of using troops to intervene in the North . . . but to guard the peace and security of this State". He added by way of a rejoinder: "Recent incidents fully justify the steps taken by the Government in recent months towards that end. We have known for a long time that arms were being imported illegally into the North by the Ulster Volunteer Force."

The Dublin government told journalists that the gardaí had indications that the UVF was smuggling weapons into the North through the fishing port in Kilkeel, Co Down. Instructions were issued to gardaí in Southern ports to keep an eye on any northern fishing boats.

Immediately after the Bodenstown blast, the Irish government announced that a "cordon operation" was being put in place at the Border "to prevent saboteurs crossing". Police were transferred from Dublin to stand guard on vulnerable electricity, water and rail installations in the Border area. The exercise was an entirely futile one. Like the RUC, the gardaí was completely unprepared and understrength to deal with a serious terrorist threat. Gardaí who at the time of writing are in their fifties recall being sent to stand alone on hillsides beside electricity or water installations along the Border.

The Irish Defence Forces, which had no regular army bases north of Gormanstown, twenty miles north of Dublin in Co Meath, began establishing posts along the Border. Five new camps were established at Dundalk, Castleblayney, Cavan, Finner and Dunree, Co Donegal. Eventually two Battalions, the 27th and 29th, and a cavalry squadron based in Longford, were permanently established at the Border.

The next attack was in Dublin. Shortly after 4.30 a.m. on the morning of December 26, 1969, a 10 lb gelignite bomb exploded behind one of the four cast-iron angels at the foot of the O'Connell monument at the southern end of

O'Connell Street. The explosions blew one of the angels off its granite pedestal and shattered windows along the street.

Later the same day, the gardaí recovered an IRA rifle and 2,000 rounds of ammunition at Inchicore, in south west Dublin, adding further to the concerns about growing insurrection. The ammunition had been stolen from an Irish Army base in Cork in 1968 by republicans and had nothing to do with the loyalist attacks. A general state of alert was issued in the Dublin metropolitan area with all police leave cancelled.

On February 18, 1970, the same day that John McKeague and his associates were acquitted of bomb conspiracy charges in Belfast, another explosion damaged the 240-foot radio mast on Mongary Hill, near Raphoe, Co Donegal which had been erected to broadcast radio signals from the Irish state radio company, Radio Éireann, into Northern Ireland. The explosion put the transmitter out of action and the mast was left leaning at an angle, held by its support cables. The next day, the UVF admitted the attack, saying: "a company from Co Tyrone dealt with the Telefís Éireann mast at Raphoe, Co Donegal".

The panic over fears of a loyalist bomb attack on Dublin led to an embarrassing incident in which gardaí intercepted a hearse belonging to a firm of undertakers from Letterkenny, Co Donegal, on the evening of February, 6, 1970. Gardaí had received a report that the vehicle was carrying explosives into Dublin on behalf of the UVF. The hearse was stopped and brought to Mountjoy Garda Station where the coffin it was carrying was removed and opened to reveal, naturally enough, a body. The undertakers, who had collected the remains from a Dublin hospital for burial in Donegal, carried on.

At around 5 a.m. on March 26, 1970, an electricity sub-station at Greenhills Road, Tallaght, on the south-western outskirts of Dublin, was damaged by an explosion. An anonymous typewritten statement delivered to the *Belfast*

*Telegraph* claimed the bomb was the work of the UVF and a retaliation for the IRA's bombing of the Rev Hugh Hanna's statue on Carlisle Circus in Belfast on March 1. On July 2, a bomb explosion damaged the main Dublin to Belfast railway line at Baldoyle, in north Dublin. After examining the track, the gardaí said it believed the blast to have been the work of the UVF.

There was speculation that some of the bombs in the Republic were the work of Saor Éire, an extreme republican paramilitary faction which had decided to contribute to the general sense of unease by planting bombs and issuing claims on behalf of the UVF (taking a leaf out of the UVF's book on false claims). Saor Éire had little or no presence inside Northern Ireland but was also clearly intent on attempting to destabilise the Republic. In April, 1970 its members shot dead Garda Richard Fallon, the first member of the gardaí to be killed in the line of duty since World War Two. Saor Éire was also responsible for throwing a grenade at the Garda Special Branch offices in Dublin Castle, on July 5, 1970.

Clear evidence of Saor Éire's activities came on October 14, 1970 when one of its members, Liam Walsh, killed himself while trying to plant a bomb at the perimeter of the Irish Army's Eastern Command Headquarters, at McKee Barracks in north Dublin.

The UVF bombings in the Republic continued sporadically into 1971. On January 17, 1971 a small bomb damaged the Daniel O'Connell monument at Glasnevin Cemetery, another place of homage for Irish nationalists. A statue of Wolfe Tone, in St Stephen's Green in the centre of Dublin, was damaged by a bomb on February 8.

Within Northern Ireland, where serious communal conflict had been edging towards civil war, there was less certain motive in the UVF's actions from 1969. The organisation was still too small to have any significant impact on events. In

August 1969, the sectarian tensions had erupted into the worst communal violence ever to take place in Belfast and Derry. Intense rioting in Derry, following the Apprentice Boys demonstration on August 8, spread to the Catholic areas of Belfast. During the fortnight of violence that followed, public order collapsed and the British Army took to the streets to intervene in the worsening pitched battles.

In the late autumn, the street violence subsided. As had been the case in the past when communal violence had broken out, a magisterial inquiry – this time under a senior British judge, Lord Hunt – was set up to examine events and make recommendations. The inquiry included a "working party", a 1960s name for inquiry, into the role of the police, chaired by Lord Hunt. It reported in December 1969, recommending the disarming of the (mainly Protestant) RUC and the disbandment of the (entirely Protestant) Ulster Special Constabulary.

Loyalist areas erupted and rioting broke out on the Shankill Road and in east Belfast. During a night of intense rioting on December 12, 1969 gunmen came out on to the Shankill Road and opened fire on a police cordon. Constable Victor Arbuckle (29) was shot dead. He was the first member of the Force to be killed in the troubles and the UVF was, probably rightly, blamed. Three men were charged but subsequently acquitted of charges relating to his murder.

By November 1969, reports of widespread recruitment to the UVF were sufficient to raise alarm in Westminster. The Northern Ireland Prime Minister, Major Chichester-Clarke, flew to Downing Street to address questions from the British Labour Prime Minister, James Callaghan, on the issue. As he left on November 19, there were reports that the UVF had begun recruiting in Coleraine, Co Derry. There were also reports of UVF activity in Portadown, Co Armagh; Larne, Co Antrim; and in the mainly Protestant Waterside, of Derry city.

The British Government decision to abolish the USC and

replace it with a new militia force, the Ulster Defence Regiment, which would be under the control of the Regular British Army but recruited locally was to have a further destabilising effect on the relationship between the loyalist community and the security forces. Loyalists interpreted the dissolution of the USC/"B" Specials, a force which had been established from the ranks of the original UVF, as an assault on the Union. The move failed also to assuage Irish nationalism. The establishment of the UDR was accompanied by nationalist warnings that it would be a simple replacement of the USC.

During late 1969 there were persistent reports of the UVF holding training exercises in the Northern Ireland countryside. The South Armagh Nationalist Party MP, Paddy O'Hanlon, said he had received a list of twenty such training centres, naming one as an Orange Hall near Kilkeel not far from Thomas McDowell's home. His claims were not treated seriously by the unionist media in Northern Ireland.

Then on September 23, 1969, *World In Action*, an investigative documentary programme on British television, at last showed film footage of loyalists training at a centre said only to be "somewhere about fifty miles from Belfast". The programme was banned from being shown in Northern Ireland. An inquiry was launched but in October, the RUC reported it had been unable to find any of the reputed training camps.

Meanwhile, the old pattern of nocturnal disorder and sectarian attacks on commercial premises, mainly shops and pubs, in working-class areas of Belfast was setting in. During November, 1969 Catholic publicans with premises in Protestant areas reported intimidation by men claiming to be from the UVF. There were also reports of the UVF circulating calls for a boycott of Catholic businesses and goods from the Republic.

In the spring of 1970, as the initial Orange demonstrations

of the year began, violence erupted again in the city. In March an Orange demonstration on the Springfield Road was stoned by Catholics from the Ballymurphy area who then turned on the British soldiers sent to separate the mobs, throwing stones and petrol bombs. The British Army threatened to shoot petrol bombers and the IRA threatened to shoot British soldiers. The UVF threatened to shoot Catholics if the IRA shot any soldiers.

The corporation housing estates of New Barnsley, Ballymurphy and Springmartin, which had rehoused families moved during the slum clearances of west Belfast, had been religiously mixed until the street violence of 1969–1970. They were now segregated. Unlike other parts of Belfast, it was mainly Protestants who lost out on territory and housing here. The State-run Vere Forster Primary School and its adjoining Henry Taggart Memorial community hall, on the Springfield Road, which had been largely attended by Protestants, were abandoned, and then wrecked by local Catholics in 1970. The buildings were eventually taken over by the British Army and RUC as a base.

In June 1970 the IRA opened fire on an Orange demonstration on the Crumlin Road and serious rioting broke out on the Shankill, with the loyalist gunmen firing on the British Army. The soldiers shot dead two Protestant snipers. There were gun battles between IRA and UVF gunmen in and around the Catholic Short Strand enclave in east Belfast, during which the UVF claimed to have shot dead one IRA gunman and wounded another leading IRA figure, Billy McKee. Two Protestants were shot dead during the rioting at Short Strand.

The following Monday, 500 Catholics working in Harland and Wolff shipyard were "advised" to leave for their own safety by Protestant shop stewards. The company replied by saying it would instantly dismiss anyone found intimidating other workers. Nevertheless, many Catholics decided to stay away.

On April 30, 1970, the USC was formally stood down and replaced by the UDR. On May 10, 1970, during rioting in Tiger's Bay and the Shore Road, a Catholic bar was attacked and damaged. On June 4-5 the Army searched houses in the Shankill area for arms but found none.

The UVF was still intent on targeting institutions connected with the Irish Republic. On Friday, September 11, 1970, an explosion wrecked the Belfast offices of Bórd Bainne, the Republic's State-run milk board.

The persistence of the nightly rioting in Belfast, particularly in Hooker Street where the Catholic Ardoyne met the Protestant Shankill, led the government to direct that public houses close at 8.30 p.m. All the paramilitary organisations quickly established shebeens to replaced the proper licensed pubs.

In September 1970, rioters on the Shankill Road besieged the Army base in the old Milanda Bakery for three days and tore down the regimental flag flying over the temporary base in the former bakery. The culprit, on this occasion, was "Billy", a junior member of the west Belfast UVF, who was rising to a position of prominence despite his youth. He scaled the outside of the three-storey building and then the flagstaff to capture the "colours", which he then threw to the appreciative mob three storeys below.

The loss of the colours, a traditional signal of defeat or surrender, was a serious indignity to inflict on a regiment. Shortly afterwards, the infantry regiment was replaced with one of the "spearhead" Parachute Regiment battalions.

Billy was 14 and still at school yet had become a ring-leader of a large group of youths who had taken part in riots first at Unity Flats and later after the disbandment of the "B" Specials the previous year.

During the "The Battle of Milanda" he recounted, with some mirth, how another leading loyalist figure from the Shankill known as "Joker" had hijacked a bus. "He came over to me and said 'set fire to the bus'. So we did and the bus goes up and he was still in it when we were setting fire to it."

He went on: "The King's Own Regiment. They were from Liverpool and were up in Fort Milanda. They were kicking people up the Shankill. Everybody was trying to get in and they were sending out snatch squads. I climbed up the front of the Fort and scaled up and took down the Regimental flag and set fire to it. The Paras came then and took over after they had lost their colours.

"The riots lasted three days. They were mad nights. It was about 1970 and I was still going to school. I left school in 1971. I remember I got the bus in Tennent Street and was sitting on the bus and the next thing the Peelers and Army were there and trailed me off and they were beating the crap out of me. They accused me of climbing the wall and I was brought to the Juvenile Court. I got off over my age."

However, aside from the deaths resulting from the riots in 1970 there were no other killings that can be ascribed to the UVF. The O'Neillite tendency within Unionism was still unforgiven and a bomb damaged the offices of his sympathisers in the New Ulster Movement, in Belfast on February 3.

In early 1970, the UVF sporadically targeted the perceived political opponents of militant loyalist, particularly those within the unionist community who sought to continue Lord O'Neill's policies of agreement, "appeasement" and conciliation. A bomb exploded at the home of Miss Sheelagh Murnaghan, the former Liberal MP for Belfast, on Sunday, February 8, 1970. Miss Murnaghan had been critical of the extreme loyalists. The UVF later issued a statement saying it was not responsible, although there was an inevitable suspicion that it was responsible.

The home of the Nationalist Party MP, Austin Currie, a founder of the civil rights movement and an outspoken critic of militant loyalism, was again one of the targets in this campaign. His home was damaged by the bomb on March 7, 1970, and Currie, his wife and young children were the subject of a gun attack four months later, on July 2. Shots were fired through the livingroom window but the family again escaped injury. These two attacks in 1970 were the first of a succession of increasingly ugly attacks on Currie and his family by the UVF element in the Armagh/Tyrone area over the following decade.

Richard Ferguson, a young Unionist MP from Fermanagh and one of O'Neill's faithful followers, had his home bombed on April 28. Ferguson, one of the brightest of the new generation of unionist politicians, subsequently backed out of political life and devoted himself to a successful legal career. He eventually left Northern Ireland and became one of the leading criminal advocates in the English Bar.

Another outspoken supporter of O'Neill and critic of Paisleyism and extreme loyalism, Miss Anne Dickson, was also singled out for attack. A pipe bomb was thrown at her home in Belfast, on August 10, 1970. Two other explosions at the beginning of February 1970 were widely believed to be the work of the UVF. One was at the Belfast offices of the New Ulster Movement, the group set up to continue O'Neill's policies, and another at a Catholic church in Drumaness, near Ballynahinch, Co Down.

The old tradition of attacking targets obviously connected with the religious, political or cultural ethos of the opposite community was well under way again by the spring of 1970. The UVF was blamed for an explosion at St Thomas Aquinas Hall, the Catholic students' hostel at Queens' University, on March 7.

During 1970 the UVF carried out an estimated twenty-seven bomb attacks in Northern Ireland, mainly involving pipe bombs, small devices of a few pounds of explosive packed into a metal tube, a foot or so in length. The UVF bombs were small compared to many of the estimated 130 landmines and bombs planted in Northern Ireland the same year by the IRA.

During the early hours of January 13, 1970 a small explosion broke windows and caused other minor damage to a row of shops fronting on to the Crumlin Road from the Catholic Ardoyne area.

The UVF bombed the Catholic-owned Eagle Taxi depot, in Agnes Street, off the Shankill Road on January 26, 1970, causing considerable damage but no injuries. This was followed by a UVF statement saying it was its intention to "remove republican elements from loyalist areas and from reaping financial benefit therefrom". Not surprisingly perhaps, the UVF shortly afterwards set up its own taxi operation in Protestant areas and the IRA did the same in Catholic west Belfast.

The RUC belief is that only a small number of men were involved in the initial phase of UVF bombings in Belfast and, to a degree, this is confirmed by UVF sources. The RUC say that three of the original Belfast UVF bombing unit subsequently appeared in court in 1971 on charges arising out of a post office robbery. Another figure whom the RUC cited as a UVF bomber was Tommy Winchester, who fell through a roof and was killed while being chased by police during a burglary in Belfast city centre in early 1971. The loyalists say Winchester was just a criminal who may have been "useful" to the cause at one point or another. Winchester was an associate of the man who threw the petrol bomb into Matilda Gould's house.

During 1970, forty-two Catholic-owned licensed premises in Protestant areas were bombed, mainly, it is believed, by the UVF.

Rioting and sectarian attacks continued into 1971. Attacks in early 1971 attributed to loyalists included the bombing of a Catholic church at Whitehouse, Co Antrim, on January 15;

an explosion on March 27 at St Malachy's college on the Antrim Road in Belfast and another at the school's old boys' club on Crumlin Road the following day.

In conjunction with the bombing campaigns in the Republic and Northern Ireland, by November 1969 the UVF had announced an "economic war" on Catholic businesses and a boycott of Irish-made goods and currency. The boycott was effective in some Protestant neighbourhoods where Catholic businesses quickly reported a drop in takings. To emphasise the point, vigilante groups, claiming to be UVF, visited Catholic-owned pubs in the Lower York Street area to check if any Protestants were breaking the boycott. Retaliatory action was reported by republicans who visited Protestant premises on similar grounds.

From early on in the conflict, the UVF, like all other paramilitary groups, was engaging in "fund-raising" activities, a terrorist euphemism for robbery and extortion. Some large robberies took place and some that were the work of the UVF, but the habit of making an anonymous claim to a robbery on someone else's behalf was commonplace. On December 1, 1969, a statement purporting to be from the UVF admitted responsibility for a £20,000 mailbag robbery on the train between Armagh and Belfast. The "3rd Armagh Battalion, of the UVF" claimed the money would "be used for the purpose of defending Ulster against its enemies, external and internal . . ." The letter was signed Maj John Crawford. In the eighteen months to May, 1970 some £40,000 had been stolen in ten armed robberies, all the work of paramilitaries.

From the autumn of 1969 onwards, the UVF in Belfast had begun to select recruits from the gangs of youths who were at the front ranks of the Protestant working-class rioters. Recruitment was discreet and selective. "Billy", later to serve a life prison sentence, was recruited at this time and later recollected how, at the start, he believed he was the only member of a gang of fifteen or so friends from the Springmartin area who had been sworn into the UVF. He subsequently found himself in the same unit as three or four of his old chums and eventually came across almost the entire gang of old schoolfriends in other UVF units or in prison.

The UVF themselves are hazy about the direction they were heading in at this stage, which seemed to be dictated by events. Spence was separated by prison walls from the day-to-day conflict and was in communication mainly through the visits from the UVF Officer Commander, "Bo" McClelland. There is little clear recollection of what was actually happening in terms of loyalist paramilitary strategy at this time. Only a few local journalists appeared to have any insight into the secret life of the growing loyalist paramilitary organisation. One reporter, Andrew Hamilton, who grew up among the Protestant loyalists of Co Tyrone, wrote in *The Irish Times* in November 1969 that the Belfast UVF had very few members and had difficulty in contacting their fellow units in isolated Border areas. As well as organisational difficulties, Hamilton noted, the UVF "still hasn't made up its mind yet on its exact purpose or role". He went on: "The fact that there has been no clear statement of intent has put the force at a disadvantage from a recruitment point of view". The Tyrone UVF, he said, had been highly critical of the water pipe and electricity installation bombings inside Northern Ireland. The organisation's unspoken objectives, Hamilton wrote, were: "to defy a British government takeover (ie: the imposition of direct rule from Westminster); to defy the British military presence; to terrorise and attack the homes and property of Catholics; and to embark on a terrorist campaign in the Republic." A bombing campaign in the Republic, he wrote, had the strongest appeal.

Spence's recollections of this period tend to support Hamilton's view. Speaking to Roy Garland for his work, *The UVF, A Negotiating History*, he recalled: "After the arrests of

1966, for whatever reason, for security reasons, a certain amount of fear, all types of messages were coming to me. 'You won't be saying anything about such and such?' 'No I won't.' Never anything came from me, never, in no shape or form. Special Branch? I was a hardened soldier, Special Branch could have pushed me from now until doomsday.

"You see the three old platoons, I call them the legion of the Rearguard, I'm talking about Bo and that crowd who later came forward to the leadership of the UVF. In the countryside, I'm led to believe that quite a few of them went into the UDR. There was quite a few of them already in the B Specials. They always had this dual membership and quite a few of them said, 'Well now, we'll go into the UDR and do exactly the same thing and there's no danger of being arrested.' That type of thing, so it sundered whatever there was and I'm not sure what there was in rural areas. Whatever command structure there was, I had no knowledge of it. Very, very secretive that way but I had constant communication with my own people. They were questioning certain things and slowly they were to become the leadership of the UVF. The colonel that swore me in just seemed to vanish into thin air, invisible."

Asked if he lost contact altogether, Spence said: "Oh yes, it made it easy for me being in jail in 1966, everybody ran for cover type of thing. I was in contact with a politician who knew the overall structure."

The UVF was not yet into its stride. Of the twenty-five people recorded killed in 1970, none is attributed by security force sources to loyalists.

The security situation worsened yet further in early 1971. On February 6 the Provisional IRA shot dead Gunner Robert Curtis, the first British soldier to be killed in riots since the foundation of the state. Then on March 10, the Provisionals lured three teenage British soldiers to an isolated lane above Ligoniel in north Belfast and there shot each of them in the back of the head. This particularly callous murder angered loyalists, many of whom who had served in the British army.

There were two days of loyalist rioting on the Newtownards Road at the end of March 1971 after an absence of street violence in loyalist areas for almost three months. Protestant anger had risen at the Government's seeming inability to counter IRA violence. McKeague was orchestrating Protestant dissent against Faulkner from his shop in east Belfast where he printed *Protestant News*.

In the first press interview with a UVF leader, Robert Chesshyre of the *Observer* was told that outside the city, the UVF had country units of "no more than five or six members, usually made up of ex-B Specials. In Belfast the force is organised on a street basis with up to 30 men in any one defence committee, Many UVF men are ex-service men and highly trained. They keep their eye in at rifle clubs and out in the fields.

"We could mobilise perhaps 200 men in a matter of hours. There may be 5,000 in all and another 5,000 who would come out when it counts. These men are no mugs." Chesshyre said his interviewee had a "total fascination with weapons and a paranoid hatred of Catholics". He told Chesshyre that it was not correct to assume that because the UVF did not engage the IRA when it had fired on loyalists, this meant it had no weapons. Chesshyre noted: "UVF members have an elitist mentality born largely of their service backgrounds and often kept themselves aloof from rioters whom they regard as rabble, corner-boys and hooligans."

The UVF man conceded he would be "a bit happier" if the loyalists had more weapons. He was opposed to that year's proposal to curtail controversial Orange demonstrations and warned: "People have seen the disbanding of the Specials, the disarming of the police, the fragmentation of the Unionist Party and the usurpation of Stormont's powers. The last strong link is the Orange Institution."

Figures published in May, 1971 showed there had been 314 explosions caused by gelignite since 1969, 136 since the beginning of the year. Twenty-seven people died before the end of July. Twelve of these were members of the security forces. Fifteen civilians were killed, five in one IRA explosion, and two were assassinated by the IRA. Four people were shot by the security forces. One death was that of a Protestant woman, Kathleen Irvine, who was shot dead accidentally by a UVF sniper. Seventeen loyalist bombs in 1971 occurred before the end of April 1971.

The security forces, beset mainly by even more intense republican violence, were also beginning to uncover loyalist arms dumps. A store of UVF gelignite was found at Nutt's Corner outside Belfast on May 2, 1971. Twelve guns and 5,000 rounds of ammunition were found at Hillsborough, Co Down on July 10.

The real escalation of republican violence began in August 1971, after the new Stormont Prime Minister, Brian Faulkner, who had replaced the hapless Chichester-Clark, took the decision to introduce internment for suspected IRA members. In an operation which began on the morning of August 9, 1971, 342 men, all from the nationalist community, were arrested and taken to holding centres in Magilligan, Co Derry, Girdwood Barracks in north Belfast and Ballykinler, Co Down. No loyalists were arrested. The following day, intense rioting broke out in Catholic areas and eleven people were killed. The remaining Protestant families in Ardoyne pulled out of the area and as they did so 240 houses were burned. In the three weeks that followed almost two per cent of the 45,000 Catholic families in Belfast and 0.5 per cent of the 135,000 Protestant households were displaced. This was the biggest population displacement in Europe since the Second World War.

In August 1971 there were 131 bomb attacks in Northern Ireland, mostly the work of the IRA. There were a further 196 in September and 117 in October. The IRA bombings were increasingly wanton acts, designed to inflict greater injury.

The initial introduction of internment failed in almost every respect to stem the violence. Before August 9, four soldiers and four civilians had died. In the four months that followed internment, seventy-three civilians, thirty soldiers and eleven policemen were killed.

That same year an increasingly serious war of tit-for-tat pub bombings broke out in Belfast, and to a lesser degree, in Armagh and the Derry area. Nine people were injured in an IRA bomb attack on a Hollywood, Co Down public house which was frequented by off-duty British soldiers on February 17. Two Catholic churches, St Matthew's in the Markets area of the city and St Patrick's on Donegal Street, were damaged by loyalist bombs in April and May. A few days later another pub, the Squire's Hill Tavern, near the place where three Scottish soldiers had been shot by the IRA in March, was bombed. Another pub, the Dunadry Inn, at Templepatrick, Co Antrim was bombed in June. On the eve of the Twelfth demonstrations in Belfast, ten explosions occurred at business premises along the processional route. Another seven bars were attacked a week later. The attacks continued through August and on September 8, the North was shocked by a no-warning bomb attack on the Northern Ireland Electricity Service offices on the Malone Road in south Belfast in which dozens of clerical staff, mainly young women, were terribly injured.

In September 1971, the Bluebell Bar in Sandy Row was bombed by the IRA. Twenty-five people were injured. Two people were killed and twenty injured in another IRA bomb at the Four Step Inn on the Shankill Road. In retaliation, the Fiddler's House in the Catholic Durham Street area was bombed by the UVF and one patron was killed. The pub bombings continued into October when the mainly Catholic Red Lion on the Ormeau Road was bombed, killing two and injuring twenty-six. Another Protestant bar, the Toddle Inn on York Street, was bombed on November 9 without causing any injuries. An IRA unit of nine members, who were making bombs at a house in the Short Strand, was wiped out when their bomb detonated prematurely on November 27, 1971.

The pub bombing campaign came to an awful climax on December 4, 1971 when Robert Campbell, a UVF man from the upper Shankill area, left a bomb in a gas cylinder at the entrance to McGurk's Bar, a Catholic family-owned public house on North Queen Street. The explosion blew out the retaining wall of the Victorian brick building, starting a blaze and bringing the roof down on the patrons and the McGurk family. Fifteen people died. Campbell, an innocuous man with a drink problem, had perpetrated the worst single outrage in the north of Ireland to date in the 20th century. The next day television news broadcasts and newspapers were filled with pictures of local people, British soldiers, and RUC officers scrabbling through a smouldering pile of bricks and mortar in a vain attempt to recover survivors. It was an image to recocur in the ensuing 20-year nightmare in Northern Ireland. Ashamed of the outrage, the UVF could only manage a claim on behalf of an invented organisation, the "Empire Loyalists". A British Army press liaison officer erroneously suggested that the bomb might have been left for collection by an IRA bomber and gone off prematurely. Almost seven years later, Campbell admitted planting the bomb while being questioned about other terrorist activities. He received sixteen life terms of imprisonment on September 6, 1978.

A week after the bombing of McGurk's bar, the IRA retaliated by detonating a car bomb without warning on the busiest shopping area of the Shankill Road. The bomb killed two adults, Hugh Bruce (50) and Harold King (20) and two infants, Tracy Munn (2) and Colin Nichols (seven months). Many Shankill men who subsequently joined the paramilitary ranks say they were in the vicinity and most of them recount the same story: of a dead child still in its buggy and a headless infant corpse.

The following Friday, the UVF retaliated, bombing Murtagh's Bar on the Springfield Road and killing a 16-year-old youth, James McCollum.

Rather than marking a watershed from which the violence might abate, McGurk's and the Shankill Road bombings were merely preludes to the impending political crisis in unionism and loyalism as it began become clear that the British government was considering the closure of Stormont and introduction of direct rule from Westminster.

The violence escalated in early 1972 after paratroopers shot dead thirteen protesters during a large civil rights demonstration in Derry, on "Bloody Sunday", January 30. On February 2 a huge crowd marched on the British Embassy in Merrion Square in Dublin and burned it down. The Official IRA retaliated by bombing the Paratroop Regiment's headquarters, at Aldershot on February 22, killing five women cleaners. The Provisional IRA planted a bomb in a crowded Belfast city centre restaurant, The Abercorn, killing two young women and injuring 130 others. Four of the injured lost both legs in the explosion.

Between August 9, 1971, the end of March, 1972, 146 people were killed (forty-seven security forces and ninety-nine civilians) and 729 explosions occurred.

The IRA onslaught and nightly rioting and arson emanating largely from Catholic districts, combined with the Hunt recommendation to dismantle the traditional unionist security apparatus, led to the proliferation of Protestant vigilante groups.

In the winter of 1971-1972, these groups of Protestant vigilantes, which had been organised in local "defence associations", combined to create the Ulster Defence Association (UDA) at meetings in west Belfast and at

Monkstown, in southeast Antrim. The UVF attended the meetings and wearily watched the development of a huge, new loyalist paramilitary organisation outside its control.

From the outset the UVF leadership shied away from the public nature of the new UDA. Keeping a watching eye on the new loyalist paramilitary juggernaut, the UVF sought instead to stay in the shadows and mark time. The UDA provided a platform for mass loyalist agitation, setting up barricaded "no-go areas" in Protestant working-class areas and parading in massed ranks. The UVF, adopting the old Second World War adage, called them "Japs – because they came at you in waves . . ." There was now, however, organised competition to the UVF within the loyalist community.

The emerging loyalist paramilitary leaders were also rapidly tiring of John McKeague, who from his release from prison the previous year had become even more of a wild card, forming organisations, precipitating riots and encouraging intimidation without recourse to any of the other loyalist associations. There were also deep personal animosities against McKeague, who was a promiscuous homosexual with a liking for teenage partners. The world of loyalist paramilitarism was then and still is one of strident heterosexuality.

The east Belfast UDA threw a petrol bomb into the east Belfast home of John McKeague's mother, resulting in her death on May 8, 1971. The killing of Mrs McKeague was initially passed off as the work of Catholics but the loyalists eventually agreed they were responsible. McKeague's dream of leading the reborn Ulster Volunteers was over and he began to move away from the mainstream of loyalist paramilitarism, setting up a group which he called the Red Hand, which later became the Red Hand Commando (RHC). He recruited and trained young men in east Belfast and north Down, the most able of whom would later move to the UVF.

So, too TARA, the background core of 1960s loyalist conspiracy and resistance to O'Neillism, was facing infiltration and eradication by the new underground core in the UVF. Still short of weapons and seeking political direction, the Shankill UVF gravitated towards TARA which, under various guises, hired Orange halls to discuss the threat to Ulster from republicanism, communism or the weakness of the Unionist government at Stormont.

A number of senior UVF members recollect attending TARA meetings and listening to talks by its leader, William McGrath, particularly at the Clifton Street Orange hall. McGrath, it has since emerged, had contacts with British Intelligence and, like McKeague, was a secret homosexual. These things became known to the UVF, they say, in 1971 and all members of the UVF withdrew from TARA.

The UVF says its relationship with TARA was motivated purely to see if McGrath's followers had any guns which they could use. TARA appears to have been a hollow vessel, however, and there was little use in maintaining links for the UVF.

In mid-1971 the UVF leader Sam McClelland confronted McGrath about his homosexuality and all the UVF members left. A former TARA member, Roy Garland, recollects the UVF men leaving after burning the ledger with their names kept by McGrath. A UVF figure has confirmed that the younger UVF probably did supply their names and addresses to McGrath. "Prods are very trusting like that, particularly young ones."

The UVF disputes that TARA was ever a significant paramilitary organisation or that its relationship with it was, ultimately, for any other reason than to procure guns.

During the period of association with TARA, however, all UVF sergeants were also commissioned TARA sergeants by William McGrath.

Former TARA members confirm that the UVF retained its own structure throughout, and TARA platoons were virtually left to their own devices. One platoon did not know what the other platoons were doing or even who their members were.

McClelland allowed himself to be "commissioned" into TARA, something which greatly amused other Shankill UVF members. Former TARA members say some of them were aware of McClelland's position as leader of the UVF. In TARA, McGrath created a bizarre mixture of loyalist and Gaelic imagery, naming the organisation after the hill in Co Meath where the high kings of Ireland were reputed to have had their seat. He drew together a number of the quasi-historical and cultural beliefs that exist on the outskirts of Protestant-loyalist thinking in Northern Ireland. He was, however, a persuasive speaker and may have convinced the UVF for a time that there was substance behind his claims about setting up a "Doomsday organisation" to rescue Ulster loyalism in its greatest hour of need.

The emphasis on Gaelic as well as Ulster loyalist culture in TARA caused concern for most of the UVF but others accepted it, and rumours circulated that some UVF men were learning the Irish language. According to former TARA figures, the UVF kept most of their thinking and activities to themselves but they were occasionally addressed by TARA officers who were aware of their "separate" existence.

Eventually McClelland was contacted by people concerned at McGrath's use of his organisation to pick up young men for sex. McGrath was aware of the complaints against him and tried to direct the UVF people who attended TARA meetings to kill one disillusioned member of TARA who had begun to speak out openly against McGrath. McClelland is also believed to have received warnings about McGrath from other sources including, it is said, one senior Unionist politician. McClelland confronted McGrath and withdrew his men in the summer of 1971.

From McClelland's point of view, the infiltration of TARA was no longer worth the time or effort. What little weaponry TARA was known to have was moved to the UVF's armoury. McGrath and TARA would have been consigned to only a minuscule mention in the history of Ulster loyalism if it were not for the notoriety he later achieved when he was exposed as having raped and sexually abused orphan boys in his care at the Kincora Boys' Home in east Belfast. The revelation of his activities at the home led to a re-examination of his past and with it the disinterring of TARA.

Associates of McGrath later confirm that he was the author of many of the "doomsday" statements issuing from named and unnamed loyalist groups in the late 1960s and early 1970s. After his conviction in 1980 for sexually abusing boys at Kincora, McGrath withdrew to a Co Down village and died there in 1992 without ever commenting on his role in the loyalist underground movement.

The former Stormont Home Affairs Minister, Bill Craig, now tried to seize control of Ulster loyalism in a fashion not seen since the days of Carson and Sir James Craig (no relation to Bill).

Craig's Vanguard political party and Vanguard Volunteer movement struck a chord. Thousands attended the first of a series of open-air rallies in Lisburn, Co Antrim, on February 12, 1972. By March 28 his rally at Ormeau Park in Belfast attracted more than than 50,000. At this rally Craig used the term "liquidate the enemy". In the midst of Craig's rallies and the increasing anxiety among unionists the IRA stepped up its no-warning bombings. On March 20 a car bomb killed six people and injured 100, nineteen of them seriously, in Donegall Street.

On March 24, 1972, Brian Faulkner was summoned to Downing Street and told by Edward Heath that Stormont was to be prorogued and control of Northern Ireland's affairs transferred to Westminster; that he was appointing a Secretary of State to run the North; that he intended to end internment, and transfer control of the RUC to the new Secretary of State. Faulkner and his Cabinet resigned the next day.

On the last day that the Northern Ireland Parliament convened, March 28, a crowd of 100,000 descended on Stormont, filling its mile-long avenue. There were widespread rumours of a coup by Craig's Vanguard movement which included a military wing known as the Vanguard Service Corps. This did not materialise.

The proroguing of Stormont encouraged the Provisional IRA to step up its bombing. In one day, April 14, thirty IRA bombs exploded in Northern Ireland. A total of forty people were killed in the month of May. "No-go" areas were established across Protestant working-class communities of Belfast. Barricades, manned by UDA members in combat fatigues, were erected at Woodvale on May 15, 1972, and at Willowfield on May 20. A further 160 barricades were erected in Protestant areas between June 9 and 11, 1972. The UDA also embarked on a campaign of sectarian assassination, including torture and murders, in an attempt to terrorise the Catholic community away from supporting the IRA. Virtually none of the UDA's randomly-selected victims had any connections with the IRA. Many were stabbed or hacked to death with hatchets after being kidnapped and taken to UDA drinking dens.

The UVF was also now beginning to come together into a cohesive force. The youths who had been recruited during the riots of the previous years were now trained young soldiers. UVF members were involved in a gun battle on April 27, 1972, in the Oldpark area of north Belfast, from which a number of Protestant families had been evicted. The UVF pulled back as British Army reinforcements moved between them and IRA gunmen. According to a UVF member involved in the exchange, individual British soldiers came across armed UVF men but allowed them to move away with their arms. It was a significant point, at which regular British soldiers and disciplined loyalists recognised they were no threat to each other but were both fighting the IRA.

The young UVF man, Billy, recollected: "The Greenjackets

took about eight casualties in 1972. They were under severe pressure. One night our unit took position to defend a small Protestant area near Ardoyne called Wheatfield. We took over a local school. We were armed with archaic rifles like German Mausers. On that day the soldiers allowed us to occupy the building. That was the only time I witnessed on the ground collusion between us. We opened on Ardoyne and one of our volunteers hit a guy wearing a yellow T-shirt. He was wounded and ironically, some time after one of our lads ended up sharing a cell with the fellow in the Crumlin Road."

The west Belfast UVF finally had their chance at action on Friday May 12, 1972, when the nightly clashes between the Protestant Springmartin area and the Catholic Ballymurphy area turned more serious. During the night UVF gunmen took up position along the second floor of an abandoned row of maisonettes looking out over Ballymurphy. Rifles, mostly from Second World War and earlier stock, were moved up from hide-outs in the Shankill. The shooting began on the following afternoon after a bomb exploded at Kelly's Bar, at the junction of the Springfield Road and Whiterock Road in Ballymurphy. Immediately after the explosion, the IRA shot dead a soldier and then began exchanging shots with the UVF snipers in Springmartin.

During the day four people were shot dead, three on the Catholic side and one, a 17-year-old youth, on the Protestant side. By Saturday night the shooting had turned into the most intensive gun battle to date in the Troubles. British soldiers were moved into the ground floor of the flats while the UVF snipers continued firing from the flats above them. The soldiers and UVF were firing into Ballymurphy, initially unaware of each other. The IRA unit in Ballymurphy was returning fire at an equal rate and some 400 strike marks were later counted on the Springmartin flats.

The only UVF casualty was a member, who has since died, who was standing beside a water boiler which was hit by a round. He suffered a shrapnel injury, "Billy" recollected: "There was the whole bit about real soldiering, sleeping on the floor. There was an occasion when he was moving guns from the flats when he was confronted by an army foot patrol and he threw the bag in a bin. The young officer asked him what he had put in the bin and he said it was rubbish. The squaddie went over and looked in the bin, then winked at him and told the officer it was rubbish.

"It depends on your interpretation of collusion. We were just as nervous as they were. I know of occasions when they done something similar with republicans. Our fingers were put against the walls as well. They took over Springmartin School and I could not move."

Two of the young gunmen operating from Springmartin on the night of May 13 were arrested by the RUC. James Trevor King (19), who was later to rise to the leadership of the UVF, and William Graham (21), later to serve a life sentence, were arrested by RUC men who found them working with a rifle bolt in the back yard of a house in Blackmountain Pass. In a bedroom the police found three old Steyr rifles and a bag of ammunition. One of the rifles was jammed and the young men had been working with its bolt to free it. The police also found illuminating flares. Under cross-examination from Desmond Boal, the policeman confirmed there had been firing from the Ballymurphy area and the "military were returning fire from the Springmartin area".

When he was arraigned before the Recorder's Court, King announced: "I refuse to recognise this court, as an instrument of an illegal and undemocratic regime. Also, I would like to make it clear Graham is innocent of all charges."

Graham was released and King imprisoned. King was eventually shot dead by a republican gunman as he stood talking to friends on the Shankill Road in 1994. Graham was later convicted on other offences and served a lengthy term of imprisonment.

## Four

# BOMBS IN THE REPUBLIC

## THE CARNAGE COMES SOUTH

The blooding of the young west Belfast units of the UVF during the May 1972 gun battle at Springmartin was followed by another event which helped to further forge the Belfast UVF into a proper fighting machine. On July 2, 1972, Gusty Spence was allowed six hours parole to attend his daughter's wedding. He was being driven back to prison by his nephew when the car was surrounded by masked men, his nephew rough-handled and Spence taken away in another car. The incident took place almost within sight of Crumlin Road Prison.

At first it was unclear what had happened, then the UVF announced it had "abducted" him. The organisation had regained its figurehead. A few days after his "abduction" he was posed for press pictures, in a west Belfast UVF club, seated between armed and masked young UVF members, one of whom was the young man who had pulled down the regimental flag during the Battle of Milanda. Spence said he was being held against his will but happy to be out of prison.

A few days before the Twelfth of July, 1972, *World In Action* broadcast an interview with Spence. He denied killing Peter Ward, saying the evidence against him was fabricated and that he still anticipated a retrial.

Spence immediately began preaching a policy of anti-sectarianism. An interview with Spence was published in the

*Sunday Telegraph* on September 17 in which he denounced what he described as the "terrorism" of random assassinations which were almost entirely the work of the UDA. He also admitted that the UVF was having trouble engaging the IRA.

Spence had realised that the entire loyalist response to the IRA campaign was ineffective. There had been almost two years of disturbances and rioting in Protestant areas of Belfast where the loyalists were dissipating their strength against security forces, when the loyalists should actually have been helping them to fight the IRA. He was keen to get his message across to as wide an audience as possible. "Often we have fought the IRA at long range. I'd like to get a wee bit closer. Unfortunately we can't. To get at these IRA people you have to go through British lines. As 80 per cent of our members are ex-servicemen they would never dream of firing on a British soldier. The British army are, to a large degree, holding us back."

He added: "We could go out tonight if we were really disposed to and create a civil war. But we have no such intention. It's too awful to contemplate." He said the UVF had around 1,500 members in three battalions, preferring to recruit ex-servicemen. He denied it was involved in sectarian shootings.

In the absence of any proper means of determining responsibility for loyalist killings the UVF was being blamed for all loyalist killings including random assassinations and torture murders of Catholics that were almost entirely the work of the UDA.

In response to a statement by the Official Sinn Féin leader, Tomás MacGiolla, in October 1972, calling on the UVF to condemn sectarian killings, the following statement was issued by the UVF: "Of course we condemn sectarian killings. Our own people have suffered every bit as much as anyone else through these hideous crimes but are not these acts a positive result of the bigoted actions of the IRA? Has it not been the IRA who have created the strife and the alienation among all the working-class people? Has it not been the activities of the IRA which have resulted in the formation of the UDA and the enormous recruitment to the ranks of the Ulster Volunteer Force?

"Where was MacGiolla's condemnation of the murders at the Four Step Inn and the Balmoral showrooms, or the killings of Ranger Best, Senator Barnhill or Marcus McCausland (all killed by the Official IRA)? So MacGiolla get your priorities right. You are no more interested in the working-class Protestant than the man in the moon."

UVF members speak of Spence's period of liberty as a time when the organisation reshaped itself and grew in size and confidence. The UVF again had a figure of strength and repute in the loyalist community at its head. He was jealously guarded from recapture by the young west Belfast units. Rioting broke out on the Shankill Road when an army patrol unsuccessfully attempted to grab him in a social club two months after his disappearance.

Spence was out at a time when loyalists were becoming truly incensed about the continuing IRA bombings and killings. There was also a deep sense of frustration about the continued political drift in unionist politics. Rioting continued in loyalist areas of west and east Belfast. Spence's UVF, conscious of the fact that many of its members were ex-army, issued a statement on September 17, 1972 denying it had opened fire on the army during the riots earlier in which two people had been killed in the Shankill. The former UVF spokesman and city Councillor Hugh Smyth, who later became Lord Mayor, said there was "prima facie evidence" that the army had killed the two men in the Shankill.

Despite the denials both UVF and UDA men were involved in shooting at the army. Amid growing anger within the loyalist community, Spence eventually warned that the UVF would operate as "a paramilitary organisation in close association with the UDA" to "resist" the army if action was not taken against the IRA. After intense rioting and gun battles in the Shankill in September, the UDA had to admit it was responsible for the exchange of fire with the paratroopers. Two Shankill men who were shot by the army, Robert McKinney (49) and Robert Johnstone (50), were claimed as UDA members.

Within a few weeks, however, Spence again began to push the line that the security forces and loyalists were on the same side.

He was finally rearrested after being recognised by soldiers near his home in Springmartin. He was in a stolen car at the time and made no attempt to escape. He was on the run for four months during which time, it was reported, he had held the post of deputy commander of the UVF. After he had been rearrested on November 4, 1972, the UVF directed there would be no rioting and none occurred.

Despite a reasonably clear idea about its objectives and a good supply of recruits, the UVF also badly needed weapons if it was to engage the IRA in a serious way. This led them to the British military depot in Lurgan, Co Armagh on October 23, 1972. A total of 104 weapons – SLR rifles and sub-machineguns – were stolen from the Ulster Defence Regiment and Territorial army (TA) Depot in Lurgan, the biggest raid on a military arsenal in Northern Ireland since an IRA raid on Gough Barracks in Armagh in 1956.

The UVF raid began at around 4 a.m. Four men in army uniform approached the TA sentry and overpowered him. Another ten men arrived overpowering a further eight off-duty soldiers in the guardroom. The armourer locked himself in, but relented after the UVF men threatened to shoot his colleagues.

The UVF men loaded the weapons on to two Land Rovers and drove off, dropping one sub-machinegun on the road.

Later the same morning the RUC recovered sixty-eight rifles and sub-machineguns and one of the Land Rovers near Portadown Golf Course. The vehicle had been parked in a wooded area and an unsuccessful attempt made to camouflage it with branches.

The UVF later said that they had had to abandon the Land Rover after it developed "technical trouble" but they succeeded in escaping with twenty-four guns and 500 rounds of ammunition. "We would stress that these weapons are solely for the defence of loyal Ulster men and women and will not be turned on any of the security forces."

More organised arms training took place with the new weapons. One UVF figure said: "We had places in the country (for training). There were quite a few trained. There was ex-army guys who did the training. It was all done in Northern Ireland as it was impossible to travel. We did rifle work in fields."

Some UVF units also "acquired" weapons which came from the UDA. The UVF in north Belfast discovered an IRA arms dump complete with IRA armlet in a house on the Cliftonville Road.

By mid-1972, the UVF may have had as many 2,000 members, all of whom had received firearms training. Some were instructed in the manufacture of bombs. The organisation, at this stage, had a fairly steady supply of gelignite and detonators from sympathisers in the Scottish mines. It was also developing home-made explosives from ammonium nitrate and sugar.

The UDA had an estimated 20,000 to 30,000 members, relatively few of whom had any experience with guns. The average UDA member at this stage was characterised as a corner-boy by the UVF. Aside from the huge vigilante movement of the UDA, one of the few loyalist groups which could claim to be a serious paramilitary organisation was the Orange Volunteers. Formed in 1972, it had between 200 and

500 members, mostly in east Belfast and Sandy Row, with more members in north Down and east Antrim. It was set up by militant Orangemen, including one or two figures later to become prominent in unionist politics. The majority of its members were ex-Special Constabulary members. It was never active and within a year or so of its foundation some members were closely associated with the UVF. According to a Special Branch assessment, Orange Volunteers were "operating closely" with the UVF during the early 1970s, but it later died out. Individual members were accepted into the UVF. Others stayed legal.

The core of the UVF had also remained unimpressed by Bill Craig's apocalyptic rhetoric and had not rallied to his Vanguard movement which, by mid-1972, had set up some fifty Ulster Vanguard Clubs across Northern Ireland. These recruited a mainly urban lower middle-class and rural membership and former members of the Ulster Special Constabulary were encouraged to join. The Vanguard Service Corps, directly answerable to Vanguard Command, was encouraged to refrain from violent or criminal activity. The UVF infiltrated some of these corps. However, once they realised that Vanguard offered no source of weapons or good quality recruits, the UVF quickly lost interest in Craig and Vanguard. Craig gradually led his Vanguard movement back towards politics, and by 1973 had formed the Vanguard Unionist Party, allowing his more military-minded followers to drift off either into retirement or the other loyalist paramilitary organisations.

A small and highly militant group did exist within Vanguard which called itself the Vanguard Volunteers, according to Special Branch reports from this time. This was led by a man who was a brigadier, in what became known as the Vanguard Service Corps. This group emerged a few years later involved with another group known as the Loyalist Defence Volunteers, but were reported by the RUC to have collapsed as an organisation by 1974. This internal Vanguard organisation appears to have had links with other minor loyalist groups such as the Orange Volunteers, Ulster Special Constabulary Association, Down Orange Welfare.

John McKeague spent much of the period 1970-1975 interned in prison but managed to build a small organisation which became the Red Hand Commando. It has continued a separate existence, although affiliated to and probably under the direction of the UVF.

The UDA had developed much stronger links with the Vanguard and other loyalist associations forming, in 1972, an association known as the United Loyalist Council (ULC).

The UDA, Vanguard and the other associations in the ULC claimed a composite membership of 60,000. This included the Loyalist Association of Workers (LAW), led by loyalist trade unionists like the shipyard shop steward and Shankill man, Billy Hull, and Glen Bar, from Derry. This movement was emerging as the most important strategic directing force within unionist and loyalist politics.

The UVF, still a highly secretive and militaristic organisation, again held back from associating with the new loyalist mass movements. By the end of 1973 angry words were being exchanged between the ULC/LAW/UDA leaders and the UVF.

Some insight into the hidden life of the UVF of this time was afforded by evidence given in a court case following an RUC raid on a UVF club in east Antrim in September 1972. Sixteen members of the east Antrim UVF were arrested in the raid, on a disused farmhouse beneath Carnmoney Hill which had been turned into a shebeen. Police recovered five rifles, three revolvers, a sub-machinegun, bombs, explosives, detonators and cordtex. They also found a large quantity of stolen furniture and, strangely, medical supplies taken from a hijacked lorry.

The police also found an 11-page document which

detailed the command structure of the organisation, its financial arrangements, training and disciplinary procedures and how to make bombs. They also found UVF membership forms. The sixteen men were playing cards or drinking when arrested.

The UVF in east Antrim was undeterred by the arrests and while their associates were still awaiting trial, masked UVF members armed with handguns, some of the stolen army rifles and a machine gun, posed for photographs for the local newspaper. The accompanying interview, with a UVF member of "colonel" rank, revealed some of the militaristic culture of the UVF. The East Antrim Battalion spokesman explained recruiting, training and disciplinary procedures thus: "A potential member is discussed at platoon level before he is approached. One adverse vote in ten excludes him from further consideration but if the platoon is satisfied the man is then approached. The final decision rests with the Provost Marshall on battalion staff and the applicant's past and political views are investigated. Once in the Force, a volunteer cannot leave at least until the present emergency is over. If a volunteer is a genuine conscientious objector to using weapons he can put in a request for transfer to a non-combatant unit. No one has yet made a request for discharge."

The UVF's main task was to "train, prepare and equip a military force to protect the heritage of the Ulster people. We hold strong views on the great British principles of civil and religious liberty and will not tolerate those who persecute, injure or upbraid any of Her Majesty's subjects." He went on: "In the event of a civil war situation being declared in Northern Ireland, the UVF will be to the fore working for physical defence of the loyalist community, especially in those small communities which are in danger of being overrun by enemy forces."

The UVF colonel was at pains to say that the east Antrim

UVF was an entirely upright organisation not involved in running shebeens or in extortion. It had "no connection" with the hauls of stolen cigarettes and alcohol found in shebeens in Islandmagee and Ballymena. The UVF had donated £500 to a youth club in Larne and £200 to another in Carrickfergus.

This bombast did not conceal the fact that the east Antrim UVF was operating in an area from which thousands of innocent Catholics had been intimidated from their homes in the previous two years, and in which only a few tiny Catholic enclaves remained. The clear recollection of people living in the area at the time was that the local UVF was descending quickly into the very type of gangsterism which the "colonel" was at such pains to criticise. The discovery of so much in stolen goods in the UVF club tended to support this view. The UVF in east Antrim was up to its eyes in sectarian violence, extortion, hijacking and the running of illegal drinking clubs.

However, it was certainly growing throughout Northern Ireland and had particular strength in east Antrim. During rioting in Larne, Co Antrim in September 1972, the RUC shot dead a 27-year-old UVF man, Sinclair Johnston. There had been concerted attacks on Catholic homes in the town by the local UDA. On the night of Saturday the 16th, a gun battle broke out between local members of the UVF and the security forces. The RUC said that spent bullet cases were found in Johnston's jacket. Death notices in the local papers described Johnston as a sergeant in the UVF. At his funeral four days later, some 3,000 men, many wearing black leather jackets, black trousers, dark glasses, maroon berets or navy blue forage caps, followed the coffin. The men also wore UVF badges and responded to military commands.

The Rev Ivan Foster, of the Free Presbyterian Church and later a leading figure in the Rev Paisley's Democratic Unionist Party, read a graveside oration. This was the first solid indication that the UVF was a real force. It was a surprise to many of its members that so many turned up. Throughout the second half of 1972 and early 1973 there was undiminished anger in Protestant areas about an increasingly obvious tendency on behalf of the British government to try and negotiate with the IRA. The apparent appeasement of the IRA and the prorogation of Stormont coincided with an intense bout of political rivalry between three contenders for the leadership of unionism. The former Prime Minister, Brian Faulkner, was engaged in a battle for control over the unionist body politic against both his former colleague Bill Craig and the Rev Ian Paisley, who had been steadily building up his Democratic Unionist Party.

The rivalry and attempts to establish new loyalist/unionist power bases extended to efforts to take over control of the paramilitaries, most significantly by supporters of Craig's Vanguard group.

An attempt to impose some form of political control over the UVF in west Belfast in early 1973 failed. The UVF appears from around this time to have decided to remain a dedicatedly independent organisation with its own ideas and ways of doing things. Spence recalls: "They (the unionist political leadership) attempted at times to give them political guidance. It wasn't obviously done, it was done in a surreptitious way. At the same time they used the threat, the potential power the UVF had, in order to try and extract concessions from the British government. You know, 'if you don't talk to us you will have to talk to these armed men.' The UVF did respond to some of the calls being made by the unionist hierarchy and I suppose they knew that they were being used but felt it incumbent upon themselves to respond to these calls."

The "traditional echelons of unionism" feared the UVF, Gusty pointed out. "They feared the UVF for two reasons, number one the UVF had guns and they hadn't. Secondly there was this ideological threat because the UVF were thinking outside the ideological railway lines of traditional unionism." The UVF steadfastly remained outside the main unionist political parties and alliances that were coming into creation in place of the Ulster unionist monolith.

In a series of interviews for Roy Garland's thesis, *The UVF, a Negotiating History,* Spence observed: "The UVF were under no political control. That made them dangerous. It's the same as the Orange Institution in 1795, that was very dangerous to those who held power. The landed gentry took it over because it was a dangerous organisation. It was a working-class organisation which was armed, and the landed gentry didn't want the working-class loyalist to turn their arms against them."

On June 22, 1972, the IRA leadership returned from talks with the British government in London and announced a ceasefire from June 26, apparently on the basis of a misunderstanding. The IRA appeared to have understood that the British were about to accede to their demands to withdraw from Northern Ireland. The entire loyalist community viewed these events with alarm. On June 30 the UDA erected barricades in Belfast and Derry. On July 3 the UDA was involved in another confrontation with the army when the UDA attempted to erect barricades in one of the few remaining religiously mixed areas off Springfield Road. Talks took place between a British army General and Shankill UDA leaders and the situation was defused.

Within two weeks of the IRA-British government talks the UDA staged another confrontation, this time objecting to Catholics moving into formerly Protestant houses in Lenadoon, in west Belfast. Another stand-off with the army ensued and on July 6 a local army commander stopped the Catholics from moving into houses formerly occupied by Protestant families. An estimated 1,400 Catholics assembled on the edge of Lenadoon and a gun battle between the army and IRA marked the collapse of the IRA ceasefire. Almost immediately, the IRA set about wreaking revenge for what they portrayed as British duplicity and pro-loyalism. Gun battles broke out across the city followed by a series of no-warning IRA bomb attacks. By the end of the month, ninety-five people had been killed, fifteen in two IRA car bomb attacks on Belfast and the village of Claudy, outside Derry city. Only eighteen of the deaths in July, 1972 can be attributed to loyalists.

On July 31 the British army flew in massive reinforcements and began the task of removing all barricades and no-go areas and building fortified posts in the areas most affected by violence. By August 1972 there were 21,000 British troops in Northern Ireland.

From this point on, what became known as the "Protestant Backlash" of violence against the Catholic population began. At first the UVF was not heavily involved in sectarian violence, but it was beginning again to move in that direction.

The majority of loyalist sectarian assassinations of this time were the work of the UDA. A UDA gang from the Shankill were using the barricaded roads through Protestant west Belfast as a means to waylay and kill innocent Catholics. Although this was later forgotten, it was the UDA and not the UVF which engaged in the first torture killings, though there was at least one exception. Within hours of the IRA's Bloody Friday wave of bomb carnage and destruction in Belfast on July 21, 1972, members of the UVF unit which hung round a shebeen in a disused garage on the corner of Lawnbrook Street and the Shankill Road abducted a 34-year-old man from the Falls Road, Arthur Matthews. He was overpowered, dragged into a car and brought to the club where he was tied up and subjected to terrible beatings until, at about 4 a.m., he was taken to the rear yard of the club and shot dead. His body was dumped in waste ground at Liffey Street. The man who beat Mathews most severely and eventually shot him was Hugh Leonard "Lennie" Murphy, the man later to earn the soubriquet "the Shankill Butcher".

The same night, Murphy's counterparts in the Shankill UDA abducted Rose McCartney, a young Catholic folk singer, and her fiance Patrick O'Neill, as they drove from a singing engagement Ms McCartney had just finished in Ardoyne to their homes in the Andersonstown area. McCartney and O'Neill were also brought to a social club where several leading UDA figures were gathered. Their bodies were dumped at waste land at the entrance to the new Forthriver housing estate, built in the former demesne of the Fernhill House where the old UVF from the Shankill had paraded. Both had been shot in the head. O'Neill had been badly beaten before being killed.

News about abductions and horrible murders began spreading through the Catholic community. It was fairly well-known within the Catholic community in Belfast that these three victims and other Catholics who had been killed by the loyalists were entirely unconnected with militant republicanism. The murders on the Shankill struck dumb terror into the hearts of Catholics living near loyalist areas of north and west Belfast.

It should be noted that news of these deeds spread almost entirely by word of mouth at this time. The media, like the security forces, were simply overwhelmed by the volume of violence, most of it from the IRA. The newspapers and broadcasting media of the time seemed unaware of what was happening in loyalist drinking dens. A few, mostly young, journalists did try to bring the matter to light. But in most instances these deaths were construed in the local media as "motiveless murders", a term somewhat akin to the type of expression one would expect in state publications in right-wing regimes in South America about the disappearance of suspect peasants. The bodies of other Catholics who had undergone horrific beatings were also turning up in alleyways in the Shankill and Protestant east Belfast.

The IRA was also involved in torture murdering at this time. One mutilated Protestant victim was found in an alleyway in the Catholic Short Strand area of Belfast. But for the most part these actions were the work of the UDA. On August 13, 1972, Thomas Madden, a 48-year-old Catholic man, was set upon by the UDA's butcher gang as he walked home after an evening's drinking. The gang, two of whose members later became leading figures in the UDA, stabbed Madden more than fifty times.

On October 2, 1972, nine members of the UDA in east Belfast took it in turns to beat, stab and otherwise torture James McCartan, a 24-year-old Catholic, at a UDA drinking club. McCartan was semi-crucified. He was stripped, stabbed through the palms of both hands and hoisted by ropes around his ankles. One of the UDA men tried to castrate him. His tormentors repeatedly hauled him up by the ropes to the rafters of their den and dropped him head first onto the concrete floor. Eventually he was also shot in the head and his body dumped in Mersey Street, off the Newtownards Road, in east Belfast.

The IRA violence, and particularly the no-warning bomb attacks in 1972, had tipped the loyalist paramilitaries over the edge into flagrantly sectarian retaliation. None of the UDA's or UVF's random assassination victims of this time had any known connection with the IRA. Most were killed because they lived in or near Protestant areas and were convenient for abduction and murder.

Loyalists are held responsible for sixty-seven assassinations between April 1 1972, and the end of the year. The majority of the other 320 deaths in this period were the work of the IRA, however.

By February 1973, some 15,000 families had fled their

homes, mainly in greater Belfast. It is estimated that 80 per cent were Catholic.

The intimidation increased during the summer of 1972. The worsening sectarian violence of this period is chronicled in the Irish government's submission to the European Commission of Human Rights in its 1976 case against the British government over the "inhuman" treatment of Catholic detainees from August 1971. Page 196 of the submissions records: "Whilst both sides have committed sectarian murders, it is generally accepted that Protestants were responsible for more of them than Catholics. One reason for the outbreak of assassinations by Protestants appears to have been that there was a tendency in loyalist extremist circles to identify any Catholic with the IRA. It appears that the victims of sectarian assassinations were picked largely at random although in some cases they were apparently selected because they had some link with the opposite community. A victim might be stopped whilst he was on foot or in a car, kidnapped and murdered. Sometimes the victims were tortured before they were killed. The body would later be dumped.

"In other cases, mainly in fringe areas on the edge of one particular Catholic or Protestant area, the murder might be carried out by gunmen cruising in cars and shooting down people in the street, either without stopping or stopping only momentarily. Another method particularly common in Protestant or mixed areas was for a gunman to call at a house and shoot the victim as he opened the door.

"This method appears to have been particularly common in cases where the victim was in some way linked with the opposite community, for example, through a mixed marriage. Another method was to kill the victim at work, on the way to, or from work. There were many unsuccessful attempts at assassination in addition to those which succeeded. Most sectarian assassinations appear to have taken place at night."

The Northern Ireland Office statistics for 1972 show that of the 531 people charged with "terrorist-type" offences, three Protestants and ten Catholics were charged with murder; and five Protestants and eleven Catholics charged with attempted murder. In January 1973, sixteen Protestants were charged with murder and no Catholics. In January 1973, 109 people were charged with terrorist type offences of which sixty were Protestant and forty-nine Catholics.

By December 1972 the RUC set up a task force in east Belfast to catch loyalist assassins. From early 1972 onwards, the RUC looked on the UVF as a well-armed and organised body. Whether or not it was succeeding in attacking IRA-related targets is a matter of conjecture but its assassinations did not, yet, have the utterly random characteristics of the UDA's work. Killings attributed to the UVF, through police evidence and other reliable sources, include that of James Teer (21), who was shot dead from a passing car near his home in Ballymurphy by UVF members on May 28, 1972. Another Catholic, Thomas Wardlow (32), was shot dead on the New Lodge Road on May 29.

The UVF was also later found to be responsible for killing John O'Hanlon, a 35-year-old Catholic and father of six, after abducting him in Clifton Street. He was found hooded and shot through the head in the lower Shankill area on July 3. Another Catholic man, Laurence McKenna, was killed in a drive-by shooting on the Falls Road, on July 5.

But there was no immediate response from the UVF to the month of carnage caused mainly by the IRA in July 1972. The next UVF killing was on August 16, when UVF members shot dead William Spence, a Protestant barman, in the Long Bar on the Shankill Road for what are described as "local reasons". Three days later the UVF shot dead another Protestant, James Lindsay (50), in the Glencairn area.

On the morning of August 27, 1972, the bodies of two men were found in an alley way off Agnes Street in the

Shankill area. The two, John Nulty (26) and Patrick Kelly (26), were both Catholics from Antrim who appear to have had the misfortune of coming to Belfast from the countryside to seek work and, not knowing the city well, found lodgings in the Shankill area. When their religion was discovered, they were abducted and shot dead by the UVF in the lower Oldpark Road area.

However, it is impossible to be certain about many of the killings during 1972, when the RUC, still under strength and with a CID structure dating from its foundation, was overwhelmed with a daily rising register of murders, bombings, robberies, assaults as well as the nightly arson and rioting.

The Imperial Hotel on the Cliftonville Road was bombed in September 1972 by the UVF. Doormen spotted the bomb and cleared the premises but three people died in the blast, including the driver of a passing car and a 91-year-old neighbour who died of shock. The hotel was packed with young Catholics attending a disco. About fifty people received injuries.

An out-of-the-ordinary killing of this time was that of Edward Pavis, a petty criminal and supplier of stolen weapons.

Pavis (32) was at his home in Glenvarlock Street in east Belfast on September 28, 1972, when the pillion passenger of a motorcycle called to his front door, asked for Pavis and said to say it was "Lennie". The caller was Lennie Murphy. After engaging Pavis in conversation for several minutes, Murphy produced a gun and shot him dead in front of his family and several neighbours. He then mounted the motorcycle and was driven away. Murphy and the motorcycle rider, Mervyn Connor, were quickly identified and arrested by the RUC. The witnesses who had a clear and close view of Murphy, however, proved to be less than happy about giving evidence.

But the police found that the hapless Connor, who had had no idea he was taking Murphy on a murder mission, when faced with a charge of murder was prepared to turn Queen's evidence if he could escape a life sentence.

Neither Connor nor the authorities had estimated the fact that Murphy's wickedness was matched by his resourcefulness. Both men were being held in Crumlin Road Prison, where Connor was supposedly in a safe isolation wing. Murphy managed to get into his cell. By threatening to strangle Connor he got him to sign a letter retracting his statement implicating Murphy as the gunman at Pavis' door. Once the letter was signed and safely in an envelope, Murphy produced a tube of cyanide which he poured down Connor's throat, killing him. Again, there were no credible eyewitnesses against Murphy who was fast earning a reputation as the UVF's nastiest member.

With Connor's evidence out of the way the case against Murphy collapsed but he was interned under the Special Powers Act and remained in custody in the UVF compound at Long Kesh until 1975. He was described as the compound's most inveterate troublemaker, constantly at odds with the compound officers commanding (OCs).

One day after Murphy shot Pavis, the UVF also shot dead Thomas Paisley, a Protestant milkman, during a robbery at Ballynure, Co Antrim. On September 30, the UVF bombed Conlon's Pub in Smithfield near Belfast city centre, killing one Catholic customer, Patrick McKee. Another man, James Gillen, died two weeks later.

The Portadown UVF killed Patrick Connolly at his home in the town on October 4 with a bomb.

A Catholic woman Olive Campbell (23) was killed when the UVF bombed the Long Bar in Leeson Street in the heart of the lower Falls on October 7. On October 29 the UVF killed 16-year-old Michael Turner, a Catholic youth, as he walked along Cliftonville Avenue. The UVF shot Joseph

McIlroy, a 30-year-old Catholic, in the kitchen of his home in the predominantly Protestant Sandhill Drive area of Belfast.

On November 27, Rory Gormley, the 14-year-old son of a Catholic surgeon, was shot dead when the UVF machine gunned the family car as it passed through the lower Shankill Road, taking Dr Gormley to work in the Mater Hospital and his sons to the adjoining St Malachy's College. The Gormleys were a prominent and greatly liked family among the city's Catholic middle class. Rory's father and brother were seriously injured but recovered.

The Mid-Ulster UVF shot dead Francis McKeown, a 19-year-old Catholic, near his home in Loughgall, Co Armagh, on December 12. Kathleen Dolan (19) was killed in an explosion at her father's public house in Killeter, Co Tyrone on December 14.

In October 1972 the bombing in the Republic started up again. The fertiliser factory at Carrigans, Co Donegal was badly damaged. On the night of November 1, 1972, the Hole in the Wall public house at St Johnston, Co Donegal, and a water plant in Muff, also Donegal, were damaged by bombs. On October 29, 1972, a bomb containing 12 lbs of gelignite was discovered by staff in the gent's toilets in Connolly Station, in Dublin. Army ordnance officers were called and defused it. "It was big enough to kill a lot of people and blast the station if it had gone off in the confined space of the (underground) toilet," an army spokesman said. The bomb had been timed to go off at 10.30 p.m. Later the same night, incendiary bombs exploded in four Dublin hotels: Wynne's in Lower Abbey Street; the Skylon, and the Crofton Airport hotel in Drumcondra, and the Gresham in O'Connell Street. The fires damaged bedrooms but were brought under control by staff and the fire brigades at all four locations. Staff at the hotels reported the rooms where the bombs had exploded had been booked by "Northerners" in the previous twenty-four hours.

On November 26, 1972, a small bomb exploded inside the Film Centre cinema on Burgh Quay, Dublin, injuring forty people, twenty-five of whom required hospital treatment. The explosion occurred just after the Garda had arrested the IRA leader, Sean MacStiofáin, and there were angry protests by republicans culminating in a large rally outside the GPO on O'Connell Street the day after the cinema blast.

It was assumed the blast was the work of the IRA who were now acting in Dublin in much the same way they had been acting for the past year in Belfast. The IRA's "guilt" was compounded when someone rang *The Irish Times* and claimed the bomb to be the work of the IRA.

The serious bloodshed that had been taking place on the streets of Belfast and the provincial towns of Northern Ireland had still not spread south, however. The UVF determined that this should change, bringing the IRA's tactic of city centre car bombings south.

By the end of 1972, the Dublin government, increasingly wary of the violence seeping into their country, was in the process of introducing changes to the state's emergency legislation which would allow detention for questioning without charge for seven days and imprisonment for membership of an illegal organisation on the word of a senior Garda officer.

As the legislation was being debated in the Dáil just before 8 p.m. on Friday, December 1 the army Council of the Provisional IRA was meeting across the Liffey in a north Dublin suburb to plan its response to increased pressure from the southern government.

Both debates were interrupted by an explosion loud enough to be heard over most parts of Dublin. Just over thirty minutes earlier, a telephone caller had told the switchboard of the *Newsletter* newspaper in Belfast: "I will tell you this once. Two bombs have been planted in Dublin and will explode in five minutes. One is planted in Abbey Street, beside Clery's and the other at the Irish Transport and General Workers' building."

The warning had just been received by the Garda in Dublin Castle when the first bomb exploded on Eden Quay, near the ITGWU's Liberty Hall tower block. Fifteen minutes later a second bomb exploded a few hundred yards away in Sackville Place. The second bomb killed two bus conductors, Thomas Duffy and George Bradshaw. Altogether 127 people were injured. The no-warning car bombings of Northern Ireland had, indeed, come south and Bradshaw and Duffy were the first southern civilian bomb fatalities of the Northern conflict (a Garda inspector had been killed by an IRA bomb earlier that year).

The bombs brought a swift end to the Dáil debate on the "anti-IRA" legislation, which had been in danger of defeat by a combination of the Fine Gael Opposition and Fianna Fáil dissidents. Fine Gael abstained in the vote, and the government amendment to the Offences Against the State Act passed quickly into law on a tide of opinion which held the Provisional IRA responsible.

On December 13, 1972, three incendiary devices were found, one in Clery's Department Store on O'Connell Street, and two in the toilets of the Premier Bar in Sackville Place. The devices had apparently been left by the same bomb team which had left the car bombs. The incendiaries did not explode.

Then on December 28, the bombers struck again in the Republic, this time against another civilian target along the Border.

A car bomb exploded without warning in Belturbet, Co Cavan, killing a 15-year-old girl, Geraldine O'Reilly, and a 16-year-old boy, Patrick Stanley. Three people were injured by another car bomb in Clones, Co Monaghan and a public house destroyed at Pettigo, Co Donegal. Cars with Northern registrations were reported leaving the sites of all three bombs, heading northwards.

Residual suspicion that British military undercover units had been responsible for the attacks is based on three main premises: that the December 1st bomb was too closely timed to the Dáil debate to be the work of loyalist bombers who were portrayed in some sectors as amateurish and ham-fisted; that the bomb coincided with the arrest of a British spy, John Wymans, who was arrested in a Dublin hotel with a list of IRA suspects which had been compiled by Gardaí in preparation for a possible internment round-up; and that cars used in the Dublin bombings had English registration plates.

To add to this scenario, at roughly the same time, the Garda Special Branch was seeking Kenneth and Keith Littlejohn, two criminals who also appeared to have been contracted by the British secret services to infiltrate the IRA. The Littlejohns had instead gone on the rampage carrying out armed robberies and enjoying the high life in Dublin. They fled back to England just as they were about to be arrested, but were extradited back to Dublin by the British police in March 1973 and imprisoned.

The three cars used in the Dublin bombing had been hired by a UVF man using a stolen driving licence in Belfast five days before the attack. A fourth car, the one with the English registration, had been stolen from a Derby man visiting Ballymena, Co Antrim. This car, a Ford Zephyr, had been seen in north Dublin shortly before the bombing. The bombers had used commercial explosives which, according to the Irish army, had been assembled professionally. A statement purporting to come from the UVF denied responsibility, saying the UVF was a "military force – a purely military force – whose sole aim is to fight the IRA", and did not "indulge in bombing civilian targets." The UVF now privately admits it was responsible. The bombs were designed to drive the Dublin government to taking stronger action against the IRA and, in loyalist eyes, succeeded.

Another car bomb exploded in Dublin on the afternoon of Saturday, January 20, 1973, again in Sackville Place, just off O'Connell Street. The explosion was designed to cause widespread injury and panic at the busiest shopping time of the week, and killed another bus conductor, Thomas Douglas, a 25-year-old man who had moved to Dublin from Scotland only the previous year. Thirteen people were badly injured. The car used had been stolen from the Shankill Road in Belfast, the same morning.

Other loyalists were attacking targets in the Republic. On the evening of St Patrick's Day, 1973, a Derry UDA member, Lindsay Mooney (19), blew himself up at Cloughfin, Co Donegal, while apparently trying to plant a bomb at a bar in the town. The UDA also shot dead a young couple who accidentally came across one of their units operating inside Donegal.

The question of whether or not these bombs were the work of the UVF or of British agents, even loyalists working with British agents, was to be constantly returned to over the next 25 years. It suits the IRA and its supporters to perpetuate the belief that the British were responsible. The British are their enemy. Republicans, to justify their cause as one of struggle against British rule in Ireland, must also play down the role of the indigenous loyalists and their struggle. To accept that the loyalists have a cause is one step towards accepting the heterodoxy (in Republican eyes) that the loyalist majority in Northern Ireland has a right to remain British in Ireland.

The following story illustrates the point. In March 1974 the Provisional IRA shot dead Senator Billy Fox, one of the few Protestants to serve in the Oireachtas. The Provisional Sinn Féin leader of the time, Ruarí O Brádaigh, attempted to suggest Senator Fox's murder was the work of either British or loyalists, intending to undermine the Republican movement. He was quoted extensively in newspapers as saying: "Once again, as in the case of the Dublin bombings in December 1972, British or pro-British agents have made a strategically timed intervention into the affairs of the twenty-six counties. Their purpose, so obviously, is to pressurise and frighten the Dublin politicians into giving another turn of the screw of coercion to Irish republicans and collaboration with the British forces of occupation in Ireland at this time."

A short while later the gardaí rounded up and charged four Provisional IRA members with Senator Fox's murder. He had been killed by the IRA simply because he was a Protestant.

Over hundreds of years a very great deal of violence in the north of Ireland had been sectarian or ethnic. In the last quarter of the 20th century, nothing had changed.

On February 3, 1973, loyalists were interned for the first time in fifty years after a wave of sectarian assassinations and the disarming of an off-duty UDR man in the Shankill area. During that weekend of rioting, gun battles broke out between Protestant and Catholic areas and thirteen people were shot dead. A loyalist day of action strike was held on February 7. During the day, another seven people were killed, including a fireman who was shot dead by the UDA in Sandy Row.

Loyalist violence continued to rise alongside the continued IRA campaign, and the British government's attempts to find an "equitable form of government" in Northern Ireland increased apace.

During rioting in east Belfast in February 1973, Private Raymond Hall of the Royal Green Jackets Regiment was shot in the back by a UVF sniper at Albertbridge Road. He died a month later from his injuries.

An 18-year-old Catholic, Seamus Gilmore, from Rosscoole Park, was shot dead at the Mount Pleasant Filling Station on the Ballysillan Road by three teenage UVF members on February 4, 1973.

Michael Coleman (30) from Colligan Street, Springfield, and Peter McAleese (38) from Ballymurphy, were shot dead by UVF gunmen who pulled up in a car beside them on the Falls Road on February 18, 1973. Three gunmen were involved.

Stephen Kernan (54), a Catholic taxi driver from Station Road, Whiteabbey, was shot in the chest off Malvern Street when he went to collect his stolen taxi in a hired car on February 28, 1973. His body was found the next day in the hired car.

Patrick Crossan (30) a Catholic bus driver, was shot dead when he stopped to collect two passengers on the Woodvale Road on March 2, 1973. One boarded and shot him dead. Lawrence McMahon (42) was killed by a bomb left at the front door of his house at The Moorings, Circular Road, Jordanstown, by the southeast Antrim UVF on March 15. Robert Millen (23), a Protestant member of the Official IRA, was shot dead while on vigilante duty at McClure Street, in the Ormeau Road on April 14, 1973.

Thomas Ward was shot dead while drinking in a pub at Lavinia Street off Ormeau Road on May 15, 1973. Gerard Barnes (31) was killed by a bomb left at McGlade's Bar, Donegall Street, on May 31.

Alfred Atheson (48) from Ewarts Road and Sadie McComb (48) from Ballymena Street had been out for an evening with a woman friend and had returned to her house for coffee when two masked youths burst in and shot them dead on June 3. It was apparently a case of mistaken identity. Patrick Brack (28), from McQuillan Street off the Falls Road, was shot dead by gunmen in a passing car at Linden Street on July 6. Paul Peter Linauer (24) of Drochtersen, Germany was found shot dead between Jumna Street and Klondyke Street, off the Shankill Road, on July 22.

Leonard Rosborough (38) a Protestant from Hillside Crescent, Templepatrick, Co Antrim, was shot dead when he attempted to tackle armed raiders at his bar, the Horse Shoe, on the Shankill Road, on July 24.

In the middle of this war of sectarian murder in Northern Ireland, UVF spokesmen began issuing incongruously conciliatory political statements. On Monday October 15, 1973, the Ulster Loyalist Front (ULF) was unveiled as the loyalist (for this can be read UVF) political vehicle to "uphold the right of genuine Ulster loyalists to hold and bear weapons in self-defence". The new party said its aims were to work within the law to attain political and social objectives ranging from workers' partnership schemes in factories to the release of all loyalist prisoners, and, particularly, the defeat of the IRA.

The ULF said it already had a member of the Northern Ireland Assembly, in the shape of Mr Hugh Smyth. Its declared aim was "to express the views and opinions of grass-roots loyalists" and to "act as a ginger group". Its policies also included a "return to democracy" and increased use of referendums and workers' partnership schemes. Although in favour of private enterprise, it wanted to curb international monopoly capitalism. The ULF wanted better services for the old, the very young, the sick and disabled. It called for changes in housing allocation and in educational structures.

The UVF announced a 48-day ceasefire in November, 1973 to assist the ULF in working for a political solution to the problems of Northern Ireland. They said they would also bring pressure on the established loyalist parties so that "sound constructive policies" be formulated. At the same time the UVF demanded that the "root causes of subversion and rebellion be stamped out".

Somewhat more in character, the UVF also issued a threat to "flag wavers", those "sectarian" politicians who sought to use the local government elections planned for December as an opportunity to foment further division in Northern Ireland.

The UVF position on the elections was that, as they preceded the Border plebiscite of December 1973, there was the clear probability that the Council elections would become a focus for the upcoming Border question. "We are all sick and tired of the flag-waving type of elections and we want them replaced by elections based on purely social grounds such as housing, schools, more industry and the general welfare of the people of the various districts in which elections are to be held," the UVF stated. The UVF argued that the elections should not take place until the promised Border referendum was held.

The elections were also opposed by the UDA and Craig's Vanguard Party. Meanwhile, from August 1973 the UVF had been escalating its campaign of attacking Catholic-owned pubs and businesses. There was a considerable increase in the level of gun attacks on Catholic areas. Henry Cunningham (17), a Protestant from Carndonagh, Co Donegal, was killed when UVF gunmen opened fire from a bridge over the M2 motorway in south Antrim on the van in which he was travelling in on September 9, 1973. Ernest Drummond (43) was killed in a bomb attack on the Sportsman's Bar, a Catholic-owned pub in York Street on September 15. Charles O'Donnell (60) was killed when a bomb was thrown into his home in Grampian Avenue in east Belfast on September 20. Sean McDonald (50), his brother Ronnie (55) an apprentice, Tony McGrady (16) and secretary, Anne Marie Pettigrew (19) all died in a gun and bomb attack on Ronnie's car repair shop on the Cliftonville Road on September 25, 1973. Sean McDonnell (20) of Carrowannon, Belleeks, Co Armagh was shot dead after being abducted from outside his fiance's house on September 22. Eileen Doherty, a 22-year-old Catholic from Andersonstown, hailed a taxi on Ormeau Road and was joined by two men who said they would share the fare with her on the evening of September 30, 1973. At the Governor's Bridge the men ordered the driver out apparently in order to shoot him. Both the driver and Miss Doherty ran off, pursued by the gunmen in the car who opened fire. Miss Doherty was hit in the head and died.

Francis McCaughey (35) was killed when a bomb exploded on his farm at Glassdrummond, south Tyrone on October 28, 1973.

Also in September 1973, the UDA leader, Tommy Herron, was shot dead in east Belfast after taking a lift in a car with people he apparently knew and felt confident with. His body was found in a lane in the countryside east of the city. His personal handgun was still in its shoulder holster.

There was considerable speculation at the time that he had been shot dead by UVF figures in Belfast but this was never proven. The UDA under Herron's leadership were engaged in unrestrained thuggery and extortion in Protestant areas which was bitterly resented by the law-abiding population. However, three years later a UDA man from east Belfast, Gregory Brown, was shot dead by the UDA as he walked along Cregagh Road. The organisation blamed him for setting up Herron.

Francis McNellis (60), another Catholic, was killed when a bomb exploded at the Avenue Bar, off Royal Avenue, on November 1, 1973. By October 1973 the British army view of the UVF was changing. The UVF was making and planting bigger and bigger bombs, killing more people. A senior British army witness called by the British government during the European Court of Human Rights case of 1975 indicated that before 1973, the army was not greatly concerned with acts of terrorism emanating from the Protestant community. He had regarded the UVF in the early 1970s as a shadow organisation, an object of curiosity and not to be taken seriously. As the Protestant rioting subsided, the British army, now risen to a strength of over 22,000, was able to clamp down on IRA activity in Catholic working-class areas of Belfast.

The IRA switched its attacks to the countryside. Catholic areas were left unguarded and the UVF was able to mount increasingly serious bomb attacks on Catholic pubs and businesses around the city centre.

In October 1973 the UVF bombed six Catholic-owned pubs in Belfast city centre and placed two 500 lb car bombs on the Falls Road, destroying shops and houses. On November 11 Lavery's bar on the Lisburn Road was destroyed by a large bomb. A UVF spokesman was quoted as warning there would be more and worse violence: "We haven't shown the heat yet. It will get worse before next Sunday. We have taken the muzzle off the dog."

The bombings continued up to November 18 when the UVF called a ceasefire to last to New Year to allow the political process to develop. In a rash of last-minute bombings, Charlie Logan, an east Belfast member, blew himself up at a farm house in Desertmartin in Co Derry. Eight east Antrim UVF members were arrested after three bombs were planted at pubs and a filling station in Carrickfergus on the night before the ceasefire. In Belfast a 500 lb UVF bomb destroyed shops and flats in the Catholic Newington area of north Belfast. A warning had been given and there were no injuries. The bombings stopped as the UVF had indicated they would. Until the end of the year there was barely any further UVF action. Before calling its November ceasefire, the UVF was responsible for detonating more than 200 bombs, compared with just under 300 detonated by the IRA.

On December 6, 1973, round table talks opened at Civil Service College at Sunningdale to discuss the future government of Northern Ireland and the establishment of a Council of Ireland. The communiqué issued after fifty hours of talks stated there could be no change in the status of Northern

Ireland unless a majority desired it. There was also to be a power-sharing Executive at Stormont and a Council of Ireland which would involve Irish officials in cross-Border institutions.

The agreement was immediately described as a "sell-out" by horrified loyalists. However, the UVF said it would not end its ceasefire despite its implacable opposition to any moves towards a Council of Ireland.

Reacting to the Sunningdale announcement, the UVF warned that if a political settlement was arrived at with which it did not concur, then it would renew its campaign which would be "of a ferocity ten times that of the original October-November level".

An ominous sign of things to come was the disappearance of twenty tons of ammonium nitrate, the fertiliser used as the main constituent of the UVF's and IRA's home-made explosive (HME), from Belfast docks on December 4, 1973. It had been taken by the UVF. On January 11, 1974, the UVF called on the UDA to stop their sectarian murder campaign, which had been clearly and deliberately stepped-up to undermine the UVF's ceasefire and political ambitions. The UVF statement called on the UDA "to desist from their present murder campaign and to channel their energies and resources into some form of constructive action designed to preserve the glorious heritage of Ulster and to bring about peace and prosperity to our beloved Province."

However, by the end of the month the UVF was also secretly involved in murders. Killings attributed to the UVF during the early period of the ceasefire included Andrew Jordan (41), a Protestant from Dundonald, who was found shot dead in a field at Carrawdore, Co Down, on January 14, 1974; John Wylie (42), a Protestant and Patrick Molloy (40), a Catholic, who were killed in an explosion at a public house in Armagh on February 19, 1974. On general election polling night, February 28, 1974, there were ten bomb explosions in Belfast including one at the Red Star public house in

Donegall Quay in which a 30-year-old Protestant man, Hugh Harvey, was killed. A UVF member was sentenced to life imprisonment for this in February 1978. Two Catholic men, James Mitchell and Joseph Donnelly, were killed when a UVF bomb exploded in Conway's pub in Greencastle on the northern outskirts of Belfast on March 29, 1974.

George Keating (48), a Catholic, was shot dead in a gun attack on the Bunch of Grapes bar at Garmoyle Street on May 11, 1974. Noel McCartan (20) from McClure Street in the Ormeau Road area was shot dead while walking with his sister on March 16, 1974. John Hamilton (46), a Protestant, was shot dead near his home in Spruce Street, off the Ormeau Road on March 24, 1974. James Mitchell (38) and Joseph Donnelly (24) were killed in a bomb attack on Conway's pub in Greencastle on March 29, 1974.

James Hanna (27), from Lisburn, was shot dead on the Shankill Road by a gunman who approached his car on April 1. He was apparently suspected of tipping off the police about a UVF arms dump the previous week. Ellen McDowell (21), from Glengormley, was shot dead as she walked along Tennent Street in the Shankill area on April 6, 1974. James Murphy (40), from Kinawley, Co Fermanagh, was found shot dead near his home on April 21, 1974.

The continued killing did not deter the British government's move towards an overall political solution, to include a Council of Ireland, as set out in the Sunningdale Agreement. The fact that unionist support for the "Irish dimension" of the Agreement had disappeared did not deter the new Labour government's Secretary of State, Merlyn Rees. In April 1974 he removed the proscription from the UVF, making it a legal organisation. The IRA was also pandered to but not removed from the proscription list: Sinn Féin, its political wing, was legalised.

The killings continued. Thomas Morrissey (46), John Gallagher (23), James Doherty (53), Thomas Ferguson (48),

W.J. Kelly (56) – all Catholics from south Belfast – were killed when a UVF bomb exploded at the Rose and Crown Bar on the Ormeau Road on May 2, 1974. The bombing team included a 16-year-old boy who was captured later and sentenced to detention. On April 16th, less than two weeks after Rees's decision to legalise the UVF, Joseph Neill (26) from Union Street, Portadown, was killed when the bomb he was making exploded prematurely at his home on April 16, 1974. He was described in newspaper death notices as a lieutenant in the Armagh UVF.

When the power-sharing assembly at Stormont finally came to vote, on May 14, 1974, on the Sunningdale Agreement – and the acceptance of a Council of Ireland to involve the Irish government in the running of Northern Ireland – the combined weight of the Protestant working-class and the UDA, under the Ulster Workers' Council (UWC), rose against it, calling an indefinite strike. The UWC strike was the high point in the life of the UDA; the two weeks marked the last major successful rebellion in the history of the United Kingdom. UVF members, particularly in east Antrim, played an active role in the action which led to the rundown of electricity power from Northern Ireland's main generating stations in Larne and Carrickfergus.

There were no mass public displays by the newly legalised men in black leather jackets and sunglasses. The UVF's contribution, three days into the strike, was to be the bloodiest single episode in the history of the conflict to date. Just before 5.30 p.m. on Friday, May 17, 1974, as Dublin's offices and shops were emptying and the streets filling with people going home for the weekend, the first two car bombs exploded in Talbot Street and Parnell Street. The Parnell Street explosion killed five people instantly. Six minutes later, the third car bomb exploded in South Leinster Street, south of the Liffey between Trinity College and Leinster House.

The victims included a 15-year-old girl and a baby girl. The dead in the Talbot Street explosion included a French tourist, Simone Chetrit, and a family of four, John and Anne O'Brien and their daughters, Jacqueline, aged 17 months, and Anne-Marie, aged five months. The twenty-eight dead in Dublin included twenty female victims, including two baby girls.

Within thirty minutes of the Dublin bombs, another car bomb exploded in Monaghan town. It was parked outside Graecan's pub in Church Street and killed five people instantly and injured twenty-eight. Again the victims were a cross-section of the humanity that passes along any urban street at 6 p.m. on a Friday evening: a 73-year-old man, two men in their fifties, a 42-year-old woman, a 29-year-old van driver.

The people of Dublin and Monaghan now had experience of the type of carnage visited on the shopping streets of Belfast by the IRA. For days, there was no positive identification of bodies because of the extent of mutilation, with victims referred to simply as "female, aged 17".

The Dublin operation was largely the work of the Belfast UVF. Three cars were hijacked in Belfast on the morning of the attack. The Ford Escort which carried the bomb to Talbot Street was hijacked in the Docks area of Belfast, probably by UVF members from Tiger's Bay or the Shore Road. The Austin 1800 in South Leinster Street was hijacked on Agnes Street off the Shankill Road and the driver taken back to his home in the Torrens Estate where he was held prisoner for the day by armed men. The third Dublin car, an Austin Avenger, was then hijacked in Torrens. It was left in Parnell Street. The car used in Monaghan was stolen from the car park in West Street, Portadown, just after 2 p.m.; the Monaghan bombing was the work of the Armagh and mid-Ulster UVF. The hijackings had gone unnoticed amidst the utter confusion and disarray that had overtaken policing and society in general during the strike in Northern Ireland.

The debate about British military involvement in the Dublin and Monaghan bombings pulls together threads of information about clandestine activity in the Armagh area during the 1970s. A retired British army Major, Fred Holroyd, admitted to recruiting loyalist informants in the Armagh area during his tour of duty there at about this time. Another officer, Captain Robert Nairac – who was abducted and kidnapped by the IRA in south Armagh in May 1977 while attempting to infiltrate the local IRA – was also said to be involved with loyalists. Mystery surrounds Nairac's life and death in south Armagh. His body was secretly disposed of by his IRA killers and has never been recovered.

There is also a list of dead and imprisoned loyalists from Armagh whose names have been thrown into this stew. The fact that UVF members in the Mid-Ulster area also served as members of the Ulster Defence Regiment is a feature of the British army dirty tricks conspiracy theory.

The Garda Special Branch received a list of likely suspects for the bombing from the RUC, but there was never any evidence to link any of the men directly. Some were questioned about the bombings during the course of arrests, but none appeared to have any detailed knowledge of the operation. The fact that UVF members named in files sent to the Garda were not arrested and questioned immediately after the attack is taken by some as evidence that the RUC was involved in a cover-up. The UVF leadership still refuses to reveal any further detail about the bombings. There are understandable concerns that, despite the statute of limitations, police on either side of the Border would still like to prosecute someone for crimes of this magnitude. The UVF simply says the speculation is all wrong, even that which names known active UVF members with bomb-making skills in Armagh who have since died. The UVF leadership does admit that there was British military infiltration of parts of the Mid-Ulster UVF. One leading figure conceded: "There was always the belief they were probably working for British Intelligence. Mid-Ulster leaked. You were never sure who was British Intelligence. It leaked like a sieve." He also suspects that this still goes on to the present. Some UVF members in Belfast claim that some of the more sectarian actions of the Armagh UVF were part of a "dirty tricks" campaign to besmirch the organisation's name.

The UVF, still a legal organisation in Northern Ireland, did not claim the Dublin and Monaghan attacks at the time and recall that as the news of the attack filtered back to Protestant areas of Belfast, local UDA men came on to the streets with plastic buckets to collect money on the pretence that they had carried out the bombings. The UDA did not have the materials or skills to carry out such an attack but it suited them to have people believe it had.

After the collusion allegations resurfaced in a 1994 television programme about the bombings, the Minister for Justice in Dublin, Maire Geoghegan-Quinn, ordered that the files on the attacks be re-examined by the Garda. A senior officer was appointed to carry out the investigation but no announcement was made about the outcome. It is understood the officer found no basis for charges arising out of the programme's allegations.

The attempts in 1994 to establish the case that there was British military intelligence control of the May 1974 bombers led the UVF to finally issue a statement admitting its role. It said: "The UVF avails itself of this opportunity to state clearly and without reservation that the entire operation was, from its conception to its successful conclusion, planned and carried out by our volunteers, aided by no outside bodies." The second paragraph of the statement read: "In contrast to the scenario painted by the programme, it would have been unnecessary and, indeed, undesirable to compromise our volunteers' anonymity by using clandestine security force personnel, British or otherwise, to achieve an objective well within our capabilities. The operation while requiring a fair degree of preparation and not a little courage did not as was suggested by the so-called experts require a great deal of technical expertise. The comments made by some of those interviewed were at best naive, if not deliberately misleading, given the backdrop of what was taking place in Northern Ireland when the UVF was bombing Republican targets at will. Either the researchers decided to take poetic licence to the limit or the truth was being twisted by knaves to make a trap for the fools. The minimum of scrutiny should have revealed that the structure of the bombs placed in Dublin and Monaghan were similar if not identical to those being placed in Northern Ireland on an almost daily basis.

The type of explosives, timing and detonating methods all bore the hallmark of the UVF. It is incredulous (sic) that these points were lost on the Walter Mittys who conjured up this programme. To suggest that the UVF were not, or are not, capable of operating in the manner outlined in the programme is tempting fate to a dangerous degree."

## Five

## A FAILED CEASEFIRE

### RETURN TO SLAUGHTER

In July 1974 the Provisional IRA issued a bulletin to its members warning that a fifth column of one or two Catholic assassins was working with the Ulster Freedom Fighters, a cover name normally used by the UDA in claiming assassinations. The IRA was right about there being a fifth columnist, but wrong about his loyalist associations. He was working with the UVF. His name was Jimmy McKenna. The bulletin from the IRA's publicity wing, the Irish Republican Information Service, claimed the IRA was aware of the identity of a figure who was under the control of "a number of RUC and English Special Branch officers". It also claimed there was a plot to poison IRA members in Crumlin Road Prison.

In his memoirs, published in 1996, the Sinn Féin leader, Gerry Adams, acknowledges that there were some Catholics who worked for loyalists against the IRA.

McKenna's activities stemmed from the early days of the violence in Belfast when the Provisional IRA unit in Ballymurphy in west Belfast was establishing control over the local community. From the outset it pursued well-established methods of creating an environment to enable its growth and eventual domination of its local area. One of the challenges it faced was a small group of professional criminals, some of whom almost certainly had sidelines as police touts. In late autumn of 1970 the Provisional IRA in Ballymurphy announced what it termed a purge of "anti-people" elements. Local criminals, teenage girls suspected of fraternising with British soldiers, minor drug abusers (there has never been any kind of serious problem in Belfast with addictive psychotropic drugs), thieves and anyone suspected of connection with or sympathy towards the Northern state apparatus were forced to leave the area or subjected to a variety of punishments. The press photograph of a young Ballymurphy woman, tarred and feathered and left tied to a lamppost, is one of the starkly cruel images that stands out from this period of the establishment of Provisional IRA control and social values.

As part of this purge, in November 1970 the Ballymurphy IRA had decided to kill two local criminals, Arthur McKenna and Alexander McVicker, for their "anti-people" activities. The two men ran a gambling den in a disused house between Ballymurphy and Beechmount in the upper Falls Road area. McKenna was described by people who frequented the pitch and toss school as a "gentleman gangster". He stood guard outside the gambling school, it is said, sometimes armed with a sub-machinegun. He ensured there were no serious rows and that anyone who won money was safe to leave without being robbed. Likewise, anyone who welshed on debts or incurred their anger faced the prospect of a very severe beating. Gusty Spence knew McKenna from before the Troubles, when they would meet in bars in Belfast city centre, and described him as a "tough monk". If it was to establish control over the street life of west Belfast, the IRA had to eradicate the likes of McKenna and McVicker. Duly, the two were ambushed and shot dead on the Ballymurphy Road on November 16, 1970, apparently as they waited to extort money from a milk roundsman.

The Ballymurphy IRA could not have foreseen the repercussions their "anti-people" purge would have. Arthur

McKenna's brother Jimmy, a former merchant seaman who had emigrated to Australia after the Second World War, returned to Belfast but missed Arthur's funeral by a day. Like his brother Arthur, Jimmy was described as being "built like a bull" and, in his time, a street fighter of considerable repute. He vowed to avenge his brother's killing, setting out to find out who was behind it and to kill them.

This was not something he could easily achieve on his own. Five months after his brother's death, Jimmy McKenna was stopped by a foot patrol of paratroopers in Ballymurphy on April 4, 1971. McKenna was told to stand against a wall with his hands outstretched above his head and was searched. The soldiers found a loaded Webley revolver. McKenna told the soldiers he was a member of a "special investigation branch of the army" and cautioned the soldiers as they removed his gun: "Watch it. It's loaded". He was charged with four offences in relation to the weapon: possession of a firearm with intent to endanger life, the most serious offence; possession under suspicious circumstances; possession in a public place; and, least seriously, possession without a licence. At his trial in June 1971 he told the court he had followed some IRA men to a field behind Corrigan Park Gaelic Athletic Association (GAA) grounds, at Ballymurphy, where he saw them leave something in undergrowth. After they left, he went to the undergrowth and found the gun in a holster and this, he said, was the weapon he had when he was stopped by the paratroopers.

McKenna told the court he had returned from Australia with the intention of finding out who had killed his brother. He had made enquiries in Catholic west Belfast but had made little progress. "Some of the people told me what really happened and I passed on the information to the police. Other people resented my investigations and there were constant threats on my life. Ballymurphy is a very dangerous area at this time". The people of Ballymurphy would like to go to the police, he said, but they "were under the threat of men with the bombs and guns". He had decided to keep the gun for his own protection. He did not, he believed, have it for a criminal purpose.

His contact with the RUC was confirmed by Chief Superintendent Patrick McAndrew, who told the court McKenna had passed on information he had gathered to the police. McAndrew considered McKenna's life was in danger. On Friday, June 4, 1971, McKenna was acquitted of the three serious firearms charges but found guilty of possession of the gun without a licence. He was sentenced to one year imprisonment which he served in protective custody, separated from the paramilitary prisoners.

He then disappeared. Nothing was heard of McKenna again publicly until February 1976, when he was arrested by Australian police after he tried to kidnap his illegitimate daughter from a school in a Sydney suburb. It was reported in the Sydney newspapers that McKenna was sought by the RUC for his involvement in two murders in west Belfast in 1974. One was of John Crawford, a 52-year-old Andersonstown man who was shot dead by gunmen at his upholstery workshop near Milltown Cemetery on the Falls Road on January 9, 1974. The other victim was Vincent Charles Clarke (43) of Ballymurphy who was shot dead near his home on February 4, 1974. The Sydney police were reported as being "puzzled by the apparent lack of interest in McKenna by the Ulster authorities". It also emerged that McKenna had made five return flights to the United Kingdom since his brother's death.

McKenna's name cropped up again during the trial of Raymond Glover, a UVF man from Woodvale in north Belfast, who was sentenced to life imprisonment for having driven Crawford and Clarke's killers. Evidence at Glover's trial in February 1978 suggested that Clarke had spoken to Jimmy McKenna's brother, Arthur, moments before he was shot dead in 1971. Local sources have also said that Crawford was actually one of the gunmen involved in killing McVicker and McKenna. Jimmy McKenna, UVF sources confirm, made contact with their Shankill Road UVF leadership through an intermediary, a man who had supplied guns to the organisation and whom they had reason to trust but will not identify. As the UVF's and McKenna's interests in attacking the IRA dovetailed, they agreed to help him to avenge his brother's death. He moved into the Springmartin Flats and lived under the protection of the local UVF commander. A UVF man from the area recalls: "On one of McKenna's first nights in Springmartin he went into a UVF drinking den for a pint. He was on his own and was quickly recognised by a UVF member as someone from Ballymurphy. UVF members in the bar discussed picking him and interrogating him. McKenna was extremely lucky. The UVF commander came into the shebeen and started talking to him. He explained to his men that McKenna was working for him."

After this, the UVF placed McKenna under the care of the young UVF members from west Belfast who had protected Gusty Spence when he was freed from prison in 1972. One of the Highfield unit recalls: "McKenna wanted to get information on the Provos – those who were involved in the killing of his brother." McKenna, he said, supplied the UVF with the names and addresses of several IRA men in west Belfast and actually took part in their assassinations. McKenna's minders in the Highfield UVF came to regard him as their greatest asset in the fight against the IRA. He was the first source of good quality intelligence about the IRA in Belfast. They still regard his period with them as one of their most successful in their operations against the IRA. "He planned everything. He was an ex-soldier. He was an ould lad to me, probably about forty. I saw him jumping over the bonnet of a car to get this guy, that is how fit he was. He showed us things. He cut socks and put them over your arms (to protect clothing from gun discharge which could be traced and used as forensic evidence in court) then we would throw them away after jobs.

"We would go on recces and we were in disguises. He was something else and if we had been doing that all along we would never have been caught. Remember, I'm talking about the early seventies in Whiterock (the road which runs alongside Ballymurphy). He told us about this guy who had a workshop. Our people were lying in fields for days watching this workshop. We wouldn't move." (This is almost certainly a reference to John Crawford, whose upholstery works was in a clutch of light industrial buildings surrounded by vacant ground, and who appears to have been under surveillance as his movements were known to his killers.) "There was one guy we were doing a recce on, in Whiterock. We were in disguise. This guy had a shotgun and fired it. It went over my shoulder. Jimmy put him down. There was none of them (the assassinations) claimed – admitted as IRA."

McKenna worked with the UVF from the middle of 1973 into 1974, it appears. "It was a short period of time. I'm talking about eight months. He knew the place. We worked in the middle of Ballymurphy. We were sitting in people's gardens with our faces blackened. I could not say where he was getting his information or were they paying him. The UVF knows republicans were not claiming their dead. These people were republicans. Never, at any stage did anybody say to me: 'let's go out and kill a Catholic'." There was some concern over the shooting dead of a young man at a chip shop in the New Lodge area, but McKenna "swore blind that he was a young IRA man". Other loyalists, particularly those with unremittingly sectarian outlooks, distrusted McKenna's presence on the Shankill. "McKenna used to drink in the Loyalist Club and Chuck . . . did not like this and he used to make snide remarks. I told him to fuck off. Jimmy grabbed his arm and pulled the arm out of the socket and pulled his gun on him. Then he stuck his arm back into the socket. He was in the navy, some special unit."

Eventually, even the UVF felt things had got "too hot" for McKenna. He was taken to Newtownards Airport, a small aerodrome in Co Down, where the UVF had chartered a light aircraft to fly him out of Northern Ireland. They did not see him again.

McKenna is believed to have lived as a semi-vagrant in Australia until his death from a heart attack in 1986. His parting remarks to his young UVF minder were: "You are safe. Don't worry, I was working for the Special Branch. Good luck."

It is not clear if there were other victims of the UVF unit working with McKenna. One possible victim was Patrick Bracken (28) from McQuillan Street in the Falls area, who was shot dead as he walked along Linden Street on July 6, 1973.

Despite the horrors of the period, much of which emanated from the UVF, the organisation had also begun to engage in political dialogue with a spectrum of political organisations and with the other republican paramilitary organisations. It was formulating its own political ideas and a strategy for peace.

After the organisation was made legal by Merlyn Rees in early 1974, Ken Gibson, the east Belfast UVF figure who had been released from prison the previous year, emerged as the voice of the UVF, then as leader of the newly named political wing, the Volunteer Political Party (VPP).

The VPP was formally established in June, 1974 with Gibson appointed as chairman. Gibson stated from the outset that his party represented the men of violence on the Protestant side who, he believed, had a voice that must be heard. He proposed a forum for all-party talks, an idea which found favour with a British government seeking to fill the latest political hiatus that had followed the ending of the

Executive. "The sooner the political consultative body is set up, the sooner we can talk to people and, I mean, talk to people," Gibson said. But he added: "Let me say this: if, in fact, the democratic efforts which are being put into the situation in Northern Ireland at the present time fail, then there's going to be nothing left in Northern Ireland but for the Ulster Volunteer Force to go ahead and fight for Ulster." Despite what was to come the UVF had made apparently sincere efforts to stop the fighting during this period. In February 1974 it issued a statement appealing to all sides to "pause, to stretch out the hand of forbearance and conciliation, to forgive and forget and to join in making for the Province, which they love, a new era of peace, contentment and goodwill."

The UVF had a new outlook on life, he said. "They see Ulster not simply through the eyes of sectarian bigots and gunmen but through the eyes of enlightened Ulster men, Ulster men who now see that life in Ulster can only be enjoyed to the full by the creation of a new society based upon the unity and sovereignty of the ordinary rank-and-file Ulster people, Protestant and Roman Catholic alike. Just how this new Ulster can be achieved must be the subject of much discussion and hard bargaining between the people of Ulster themselves, not just the upper middle class who have exploited the religious fears of both sections of the community for fifty years in order to achieve political power and material wealth, but the ordinary rank-and-file people who have suffered so much and have so much to offer in a peaceful and prosperous land. First and foremost, the people of Ulster must realise that sooner or later they are going to have to live together."

Coming from the organisation which had sunk Captain O'Neill's government on the grounds of its readiness to accommodate the views of Catholics a few years earlier, this was very radical stuff. It was certainly not to the taste of

144

many in the loyalist community who adhered to more traditional, sectarian and anti-socialist views. After calling its ceasefire in November 1973, the UVF held a series of talks with representatives of the main political parties in Northern Ireland. Its view, later expressed publicly, was that, aside from the radical former Stormont MP Desmond Boal, and the electorally insignificant Northern Ireland Labour Party (NILP), none of the others had any sound constructive policy to put forward. Boal had by this stage formulated a federal Ireland plan, which the UVF disagreed with, despite finding much of his other political thinking to their taste.

These contacts extended to secret meetings with the Provisional and Official IRA. The February 1974 UVF peace proposals were given a guarded welcome the next day by the Provisional IRA leadership. Daithi O Conaill, the IRA leader, said republicans would give careful consideration to the UVF proposal for setting up a council of Ulster to advance the cause of reconciliation. Maire Drumm, the Belfast Sinn Féin leader, was even more welcoming. There was no reason, she said, why the Catholics and Protestants of the North should not work together to solve their age-old problems. She said the IRA's political party, Sinn Féin, supported a policy of federal Ireland in which Ulster would be one of four self-governing provincial areas, in which "the Protestant community would still be in the majority and would have all their rights safeguarded by a central federal government." On January 29, 1974, the UVF called on the UDA to stop sectarian assassinations and called on the IRA to stop killing members of the Ulster Defence Regiment. Two days later the Provisional IRA issued a statement saying it had instructed all its units to stop shooting UDR members.

Despite the fact that the UVF and Provisional republicans were still clearly reading from very different hymn books, a meeting was arranged with O Conaill. The Shankill UVF leadership had come to admire and trust a young freelance reporter working in Belfast, Kevin Myers, who was given an extraordinary degree of access to the UVF's affairs. Jim Hanna, a leading local UVF man, so trusted Myers that he gave him photographs of himself with two British army intelligence officers taken in his own home. One of the pictures showed Hanna holding one of the officer's rifles.

In February 1974 Myers agreed to act as intermediary between the UVF and IRA and a meeting was arranged. Billy Mitchell, the leading UVF figure and editor of the UVF magazine *Combat*, Jim Hanna and Myers drove across the Border to a hotel in Co Cavan where they met O Conaill and the Belfast IRA leader, who introduced himself using the pseudonym Sean Murray, although all present were fully aware of his real identity.

Two weeks before this, Myers had also brokered a meeting between the UVF and the Official IRA. This took place in the bar of the Europa Hotel, in central Belfast. The venue was chosen, Myers recollects, because the hotel was a relatively gun-free environment. The hotel had been bombed a dozen times by the IRA and was, by this stage, surrounded by a large security fence. Everyone entering the grounds was thoroughly searched. However, both delegations took the precaution of having armed units waiting outside the hotel. In February 1974 the Official Sinn Féin President, Tomás MacGiolla, said his party had held peace talks with representatives from the VPP. Newspaper stories accompanying this suggested the loyalists had stayed in a house in Balbriggan, north of Dublin, over a weekend. The UVF denied this. Nothing was written about the other meetings and little is still known about what was discussed.

By this stage, someone should have realised that a meeting needed to be brokered with the other loyalist paramilitary organisation, the UDA. The UDA leadership sensed the UVF was taking some kind of leap forward and was clearly unhappy. The UDA issued a statement saying its position was that the Provisional IRA "covertly aided by the Roman Catholic hierarchy" was Ulster's main enemy and that it would "continue to carry out the function for which it was created: the defence of the Protestant people and the preservation of the Protestant faith". It stepped up its attacks on Catholic business and civilian targets and also carried out a number of bombings for the first time, attacking two Catholic-owned pubs in Belfast.

The VPP set its sights, impossibly high as it turned out, on contesting the next Westminster general election in the Belfast West constituency, which included the Shankill Road but which was a seat with an inbuilt nationalist majority. The Protestant side of the Belfast West constituency was traditionally represented by Johnny McQuade, who by 1974 had aligned himself with the Rev Paisley while running as a United Ulster Unionist Council (UUUC) candidate. By August 1974 there was considerable speculation surrounding the VPP's intentions. It was suggested at one stage that the UPP would come within the UUUC umbrella to stand in the general election.

Some elements within the UVF expected that McQuade could be encouraged to stand aside and allow Gibson to run as the agreed unionist candidate in the West Belfast constituency at the October general election. The UVF magazine *Combat* predicted that "given a free run", Gibson, the ex-internee, could win the west Belfast seat back from the SDLP MP Gerry Fitt, who had beaten McQuade by 2,000 in the previous election. The VPP election literature included a pamphlet attacking the disgraceful social conditions on the Shankill and pointing the finger at the patrician political figures who continued to dominate unionist politics: "In the past our representatives have paid very little attention to Ulster's economy. In the old days, the unionists would vote slavishly with the Tories, whatever they did, and the Tories did very little for the outlying regions of the UK like Ulster.

As long as a unionist shouted 'No surrender', he could vote against the introduction of a regional employment policy which brought considerable benefit to Ulster's economy. Those days are now over. If Ulster men want to be more than second-class citizens of the UK they must send MPs who will behave like representatives of a first-class region rather than at present, when we have eleven indecisive representatives vainly pleading a special case for an area with which fewer and fewer Britons have sympathy for anymore. Ulster MPs must join with others from Scotland, Wales, northeastern England and southwestern England to resist the cutting of government expenditure on social services and social security and rises in unemployment. Unity is strength."

Seeking parity of representation with the rest of the United Kingdom, the VPP added: "We will support any evolution that will work for the good of all the people of Ulster, not just for the fur coat brigade as the old Stormont governments did, and not for a United Ireland as the SDLP did in the Executive." The VPP was totally opposed to any form of united Ireland "because it would mean breaking the link with Britain which directly benefits all working people, Protestant and Catholic and because Southern politics are dominated by Fianna Fáil and Fine Gael parties, both of which are subservient to the political control of the Roman Catholic Church. We believe that in a united Ireland, not only would Protestants find that social and education policy was controlled by the RC church but that the economic policy would be based upon the interests of business and agriculture at the expense of the industrial Ulster man." It firmly rejected the notion of a unilateral declaration of independence for Northern Ireland which was being mooted by some figures within the UDA. "UDI means anarchy and anarchy means civil war, the outcome of which would be too horrible to contemplate." The October 1974 election campaign was full of the usual negative campaigning, with insults and smears coming from all sides, much of it directed against the upstarts in the VPP. The United Ulster Unionist Council Assembly member from north Belfast, Frank Millar, claimed there was Marxist infiltration of the UVF. Billy McGrath, the embittered TARA leader, chipped in and accused the UVF of fraternising with the enemy. The UVF issued a sharply-worded reply referring to McGrath's homosexuality. The UVF had met the IRA only "through the sights of SLRs (self-loading rifles) . . . Such meetings were, however, reserved for the men of Ulster and naturally enough, TARA was not invited."

There were strong suspicions, at this time, that the media was also being fed stories about left-wing, even Marxist, leanings in the UVF by the British army's press office in Lisburn, which was earning the nickname, the "Lisburn Lie Machine" because of the amount of misinformation emanating from it. As part its duties, the press office did have a propaganda function which was referred to as a "psycops (psychological operations) plan" to undermine the terrorist organisations, including the UVF. Many journalists working in Belfast at this time had experience of the eccentric and occasionally dangerous misinformation from Lisburn. However, in the welter and mystery of the early 1970s some journalists did allow themselves to be taken in, and now laugh about it; and some of the stories they were fed were relatively harmless. Several papers, for instance, carried a story that the static electricity in women's nylon knickers was causing bombs to detonate prematurely. This was dreamed up in Lisburn, apparently as a ploy to make IRA bombers nervous.

The attempts to subvert the loyalist paramilitaries involved a particular line about a supposedly radical left-wing group within the loyalist paramilitary world. This involved a non-existent group called the Ulster Citizen's Army (UCA) which described itself in anonymous letters to newspapers as the revolutionary army of the working classes. It also used the socialist symbol of the Starry Plough on its press releases during 1974. However, the UVF leadership, which might be expected to know about such things, and other reliable loyalist sources say it was all dreamed up by someone at the army headquarters in Lisburn. Certainly, it seems suspicious that the life span of this non-existent, supposedly left-wing loyalist group coincided with the UVF's attempts to move into politics on a broadly socialist agenda.

Finally, in reply to continued "red under the bed" slurs, the UVF issued a statement on October 10, 1974, saying it and the VPP held no "left-wing or communistic views" and were opposed to "all shades of communism, socialism and liberalism". It added: "We have repeatedly attacked such communist doctrines as the redistribution of wealth, nationalisation of British industry, economic co-operation with communist dictatorships and the drastic cuts in defence spending. No loyalist organisation has done more to oppose the inroads of communism and liberalism than the UVF." It offered a £500 reward to anyone who couild substantiate charges that it was dominated by communists. No one took up the offer.

Gibson failed to gain support as the agreed loyalist candidate in Belfast West, but ran in the October 1974 general election against Johnny McQuade for the Protestant share of the vote. He gained only 2,690 votes compared with Johnny McQuade's respectable 16,265 votes. After Gibson's poor showing, the decision was finally made to drop out of politics. "The low poll for the VPP candidate indicates that the general public does not support the political involvement of the UVF. It would therefore be fruitless to promote the Volunteer Party as a party political machine," the UVF announced after the election. Ominously, it indicated that at a recent meeting of volunteers there had only been a narrow majority in favour of maintaining what was left of the UVF ceasefire. Recalling the foray into politics and the VPP, a senior UVF figure later felt it was a "haphazard attempt to organise politically, a bad move. The UVF was a coalition of sorts – fascists, socialists, liberals, etc, all under one umbrella. There was a Pol Pot approach to politics. If you wore a beard or glasses and read books you were suspect among some members of the organisation. There was a lot of confusion in the early days about politics, the conditions just weren't right.

"We could have easily infiltrated the DUP or UUP. For example, I recall going to a unionist branch meeting in Stranmillis. The meeting was packed with old dears who hadn't a clue. We could have run it without a problem." Gusty Spence later observed: "The beauty of the Volunteer Political Party was that they thought that they were the first ones that had the ideas. Whenever one embraces enlightenment, whenever one suddenly has the scales from the eyes removed, you think this is the secret of the world. You think you're the only one with this particular secret and you are inclined to be euphoric. You are inclined to be impractical, unpractical and unrealistic."

Speaking twenty years later, Gusty Spence observed: "1974 was a golden opportunity to end the destruction. Feelers were sent out to republicans but to no avail." He had been doing his bit in prison, negotiating with his counterpart in the IRA wings about ways of making a truce. Finally, he felt the mistake on the UVF's behalf was that it rushed the fence in attempting to contest the Westminster election without having established an electoral base. "I was against contesting elections. We weren't ready. And the choice of west Belfast as a place to stand in was disastrous."

Another senior west Belfast UVF figure at the time recalls how the UVF finally pulled back from politics in 1974. "Ken Gibson was trying to put people in key positions. I was in charge of the YCVs (Young Citizen Volunteers, the group which had surrounded Spence during his period of liberty). He (Gibson) wanted to overthrow me."

This figure firmly blamed Gibson's supporters for assassinating Jim Hanna, the Shankill UVF man who had taken part in the talks with the Provisional IRA leadership. Hanna was shot dead as he sat in a car with a girlfriend outside the Rumford Street drinking club, just off the Shankill Road on the evening of April 1, 1974. Hanna had played a prominent role in the Springmartin and other gun battles and was much admired within the junior ranks of the UVF in Belfast. At the time, the reasons for his assassination were unclear, nor was it at all clear who was responsible. No group admitted responsibility. Then rumours emerged that Hanna had been uncovered as an informer. He was known to have consorted with the British army intelligence officers, whom Myers later named in a magazine article. The army had found a UVF arms dump in the area where he was shot just two days earlier.

Hanna was certainly living in a murky world. However, it gradually emerged that his own organisation had killed him. It was noted at his inquest some months later that he was a member of the UVF and that he might have "offended this organisation in some way". The view later on was that Hanna was a victim of other people's political ambitions within the UVF at the time. The YCV leader recalled how the tables were turned on Gibson and his supporters after the election failure. "The whole politics of it was that people were trying to take over and they started saying they were the political wing. They put people in positions and they ended up at larger meetings. The company commanders called a meeting and they put security on the doors and we surrounded everybody and no one was allowed to carry (guns). There was the Special Services (another young unit which had taken part in the Springmartin gun battle) and the YCV. We pulled guns out. We took the UVF over and changed the brigade. We were not opposed to the politics but we were against the direction the military operations were going – that no one could carry out an operation unless someone had sanctioned it and had looked at it and said it was viable and it wouldn't lose men or weapons. Then these political people were going to come and say you need to bomb Dublin or shoot a taig here or a taig there. We were always suspect of all of them, who they were working for. The military people took over."

The return to militarism in the UVF was also a reaction to the fact that the IRA had massively stepped-up its violence and Northern Ireland again appeared to be on a political knife edge. Ironically, the same process that had gone on in the UVF a year earlier had now begun in the Provisional IRA. At the end of a period of intense violence in the autumn and early winter of 1974 – during which the IRA carried out the Birmingham pub bombing in which twenty-one people were killed, as well as other ferocious attacks in Britain and Northern Ireland – the Provisional IRA had also reached the point where it decided to call a ceasefire.

Negotiations with British officials soon led to graduated concessions to the IRA in Northern Ireland. IRA members would not be arrested on sight, unless they were in the commission of a crime. Incident centres were set up and paid for by the British in republican areas where the IRA could report to officials in the Northern Ireland Office if they thought there was any infringement of guidelines set down for the security forces. Then in early 1975 Rees moved quickly to fill the political vacuum with an elected Constitutional Convention at which all parties could discuss the internal government of Northern Ireland. As with the UVF, the Provisional IRA had its hawkish element, well-equipped with explosives and firearms, who wished to continue the "struggle". They began the same process of undermining their organisation's own ceasefire. Part of this process involved the deliberate provocation of loyalists through blatantly sectarian attacks on Protestant targets. By the time the Provisional IRA was moving towards its ceasefire, however, the UVF was beginning to move back towards the gun. By the autumn of 1974 UVF members were using the Ulster Protestant Action (UPA) and Protestant Action Force (PAF) cover names to deflect attention from the fact that it had restarted its campaign of assassinations. The PAF pseudonym was first used in an admission for the murder of Albert Lutton, who was shot dead in Newtownabbey, on October 10, 1974, and then used to claim a further nineteen of the 110 UVF killings in the following year.

Another contributory factor to the need to reassert itself militarily was the increasing belligerence of the UDA. Tensions that had been building for years between the UDA and UVF had broken out almost immediately after the UWC strike. Fighting between local UDA and UVF units began within a year or so of the UDA's creation, but this was usually restricted to brawls. During 1973 one Shankill Road UDA man had been before the courts on a charge of attempting to murder men in a UVF club after a local row got out of hand. In August 1974 a drinking club used by the UVF in Monkstown in south Antrim was destroyed in an arson attack for which the local UVF blamed the UDA. The most serious conflict between the two organisations broke out in east Belfast in July 1974. The UDA massively outnumbered the UVF in the east of the city. Systematic harassing of UVF men in pubs developed into attacks on UVF men's homes. A grenade was thrown at Ken Gibson's home. The UVF retaliated, bombing a pub, the Bunch of Grapes, which was used by the UDA. The UDA retaliated with more gun attacks on UVF members' homes. The feud spread to prison during the summer. In Long Kesh, UVF and UDA prisoners who had been sharing the same compound segregated themselves on the evening of Saturday, July 25, 1974, amid vicious fighting in which forty-five prisoners and eleven soldiers were injured. The UDA announced it would no longer sit on the co-ordinating committee of the UWC with the UVF, which it accused of bombing loyalist property and endangering loyalist lives. Ken Gibson retorted by saying the UVF stood for the people of Ulster and "takes no part in gangster activities".

One east Belfast UVF figure said he carried a weapon for personal protection at all times during the feuding. The UDA attempted to kill him twice. On the first occasion, a meeting between the two sides had been arranged for a bar in east Belfast. "After the meeting I went out and they had let down my tyres. I went back and put my gun to Billy . . .'s (he named a senior UDA figure in east Belfast) belly under the table. The tyres were blown up when I went out." The second occasion was to a drinking club in Lord Street. The bar man, who was in the UDA, greeted him as "wee Gusty", then he left the premises pretending to go to the toilet. "He went downstairs. I ran back out and when he came back I had the gun trained on him from the entry. I did not shoot. There was eighty of us and 8,000 of them." The UDA in east Belfast was, in fact, fortunate not to have lost large numbers of its members in the feud. After a series of attacks on UVF members' homes in November 1974, an attempt was made to blow up the UDA headquarters at Roberta House on the Newtownards Road. However, a British army patrol stopped the stolen car containing the UVF bomb shortly before it was delivered. After talks in the autumn of 1974, the feuding died down, but flared again the following Spring. Two UDA members, John Fulton (20) and Stephen Goatley (19), were shot dead in a UVF gun attack on the Alexandra Bar on York Road in north Belfast on March 15, 1975. A row had broken out between UVF and UDA men in another loyalist drinking club in the same area. The UVF said Goatley and Fulton had shot dead a UVF member, Joe Shaw, in May 1974, during the UWC strike.

During March 1975 there were nine incidents of gun attacks arising from the UVF-UDA feud. Two men were dead and seven wounded. Three pubs were shot up when the feud flared in east Belfast on the weekend of March 30–31, 1975. One pub in the Willowfield area was hit by thirty bullets but no one was injured.

The following week the UDA figure Sammy Smyth was shot at in his home in southeast Belfast by two young UVF members. Six shots hit the house but he escaped injury. The same night shots narrowly missed a child sleeping in a UVF member's home in the Tiger's Bay area of north Belfast. The UVF in east Belfast threw a pipe bomb into a UDA man's house in east Belfast but the inhabitants escaped injury.

The Shankill UVF then struck at the UDA leadership. Hugh McVeigh, a leading member of the UDA's inner council and its representative in talks with the UUUC, was kidnapped while driving a van belonging to the furniture store he worked for on the Shankill Road on April 7, 1975. His assistant, David Douglas (18), a junior UDA member, was also taken. Three days later the leaderships of the two organisations met, largely in response to a call by McVeigh's wife, Ellen, for the UDA leaders to hold talks with their UVF counterparts and end the feuding. The UDA principally wanted to know what the UVF had done with McVeigh and Douglas. At the outset, the UDA was not entirely certain that the UVF had abducted and killed their men. At one point the UDA threatened to kidnap twenty Catholics and kill them if McVeigh and Douglas' whereabouts were not revealed.

McVeigh was an important, experienced member of the UDA who might have emerged as one of its leading figures. He had led a delegation of UDA members to Holland to take part in peace talks organised by the European Council of Churches a month before his disappearance.

Despite a massive amount of publicity, nothing was heard or seen of McVeigh and Douglas until the end of August 1975. The discovery followed from the plight of a minor north Belfast UVF figure who had moved to east Antrim and drifted into involvement with the local UVF, but had come under suspicion of the local leadership. He was called to a meeting in a drinking club which had been taken over and was being run by the UVF and there made to wait in a back room while the other UVF men discussed their suspicions. Fearing for his life, he jumped from a window and ran to the town's RUC station. Within a few days he had given police a hugely detailed list of the local UVF members and their activities. He also brought the RUC to an unmarked grave on a hillside on Islandmagee overlooking the North Channel, where the skeletons of Hugh McVeigh and David Douglas were recovered.

Actually, the UDA had not needed to wait for the recovery of the bodies to know who to blame. On May 6, 1975 more fighting broke out and a serious attempt was made by the east Belfast UDA to kidnap the UVF spokesman, Ken Gibson, outside a public house. He broke free although his arm was broken in the struggle. UVF men in the pub came to Gibson's assistant, one armed with a handgun. A UDA man was shot in the stomach and another UDA man stabbed. On the morning of July 13, 1975 two UVF men ambushed and shot dead a UDA member, Denis Berry, as he left a UDA club in south Belfast.

However, after this the two sides largely agreed to avoid feuding. The internecine loyalist feuding did not interrupt the flow of predominantly sectarian killings in Northern Ireland by members of the UVF. Michael Browne, a 16-year-old Catholic schoolboy of Abbot's Walk, Bangor, Co Down, was found shot dead on playing fields near his home on July 12, 1974. He was shot by local UVF members who had identified his religion, probably by his school uniform.

Thomas Braniff (25) was killed in a bomb explosion at the Sunflower Bar, Corporation Street, on July 16.

Michael McCourt (26) of Pomeroy, Co Tyrone, died in an explosion at the factory where he worked in the town on September 16, 1974. Patrick McGreevy (15) was shot dead by gunmen in a passing car on Clifton Street, on September 19. Kieran McIlroy (18) a Catholic from Andersonstown was shot dead by gunmen who ambushed him as he left a training centre on the Limestone Road on September 25, 1974. Ralph Laverty (54) another Catholic from Andersonstown, was shot dead at the Sunblest bakery where he worked in east Belfast, on September 30, 1974. James Willis (30), a Protestant, was shot dead near his work on the Lisburn Road, Belfast on October 4, 1974, possibly as a result of mistaken identity. Albert Lutton (68) a Catholic was shot dead while visiting friends in Ballyduff, Newtownabbey, on October 10, 1974. James Hasty (40), a Catholic, was shot dead near his home in the New Lodge area on the morning of October 11, 1974. Ciaran Murphy, a 17-year-old Catholic from Ardoyne, was abducted, beaten and shot dead and his body dumped off the Hightown Road, Ligoniel on October 13, 1974. Kevin Regan (26), a Catholic from The Roddens, Larne, was shot dead in a public house in Larne on November 17 and died three days later.

There were still forays across the Border. On the weekend of March 9, 1975 the Greencastle, Co Donegal trawler fleet was attacked and fire-bombed by the UVF. Both the Red Hand Commando and UDA claim responsibility, although the UVF says now it was their operation. A statement purporting to come from the Londonderry UDA made the unlikely claim that the fleet had been used to ferry arms ashore for the IRA after a rendezvous with a Russian submarine. Fourteen fishing boats were damaged.

By the spring of 1975 the UVF had decided that it should publicly admit it was back at war, whatever the consequences.

On March 17, 1975, the UVF held a press conference in the Shankill area and admitted carrying out six killings and two pub bombings in the previous month. It admitted responsibility for killing Michael Adamson, a Catholic student, at his home in the Cliftonville area which the UVF spokesman referred to a "bed of Irish Republican Socialist Party members" (the IRSP and its military wing, the Irish National Liberation Army, had just been set up by ex-members of the Official IRA who wished to continue fighting in Northern Ireland but did not want to join the Provisional IRA). The UVF spokesman said its Provost Section had executed the two young UDA men, Fulton and Goatley. The UVF had also killed John Francis Green, an IRA man who had escaped from the Maze Prison and had been living in Co Monaghan. He was found shot dead in a farmhouse just across the Border in Monaghan on January 10, 1975. The UVF also admitted killing Patrick Bracken (28), of McQuillan Street, Belfast, who was shot dead on the Falls Road, in July 1973; James Sullivan (30) of Lesley Street, Ligoniel, who was shot dead on February 8, 1975.

On March 14, 1975, the UVF shot dead a 19-year-old Catholic youth, Robert Skillen, as he stood at a street corner on the Falls Road. The UVF man took the occasion to swipe at both the UDA and Official IRA, describing the Official IRA, with its avowedly socialist agenda, as the most dangerous group in the country. He refuted claims that the UVF was mixed up with the Official IRA and said the UDA had a history of gangsterism and thuggery. The largest newspaper in Northern Ireland, the *Belfast Telegraph*, raised the point that a legal organisation was holding a press conference to announce that it was engaged in murder. "The government has had its face slapped by an organisation which it legalised last year and which it regularly receives in deputations to Stormont Castle," the paper's editorial ran. "Mr Rees must make it clear that he cannot deal with the UVF at least until it can enforce a ceasefire. The simple reaction would be to ban the UVF but the simplest solution is not always the most effective." The UVF continued remorselessly on its path, not always as successfully as it would have wished. Six Belfast members were killed by premature explosions. In one incident in April 1975, members of a UVF unit kicked open the door of the Jubilee Bar in the Markets area, pointing a rifle at drinkers and shouting: "take that you bastards". The rifle failed to fire. The fuse on a bomb which was carried into the bar fizzled out and, to compound their difficulties, as the squad was running from the bar a British soldier spotted them, opened fire and shot dead Robert Wadsworth, a young UVF man from north Belfast.

On March 13, 1975 a UVF man was badly injured when the bomb he was planting at Conway's Bar in Greencastle, Co Antrim (which the UVF had attacked a year previously) exploded prematurely. Another UVF member ran from the building with his clothes on fire, and he and the third member of the gang were arrested. A 38-year-old Catholic woman, Marie Doyle, died in the explosion. George Brown, the UVF bomber, died from his injuries a month later. Two UVF men, James McGregor and Thomas Chapman, both aged 28, were killed when a bomb exploded in their car at Great Patrick Street on June 12, 1975, while on their way to bomb a Catholic-owned pub in the Docks area.

The attrition rate among UVF men was beginning to climb alarmingly. In the first six months of 1975, as well as the six UVF men killed when the bombs they were handling exploded, some forty-five members were arrested in the act of either bomb or gun attacks. A series of attacks on Catholic workmen's huts ensued. One Catholic building worker, Gerald De'ath, was killed at Rushe Park, Glengormley on May 22, 1975, when a booby-trap bomb in a thermos flask exploded. Two Catholic workmen who were playing cards with Protestant workmates at Mount Vernon in north Belfast

160

were shot dead on May 23, 1975. Two youths, Kevin Kane and Michael Coyle, were killed in a bomb explosion at McLoughlin's Bar in the New Lodge area on April 5, where they had been watching the Grand National on television.

Immediately after this attack, the IRA drove to the Shankill Road and placed a bomb in the Mountainview Tavern, killing five people. A week later the UVF retaliated again, with a bomb at the Strand Bar in the Short Strand which killed six customers. On March 17, a UVF booby-trap bomb killed a seven-months' pregnant Catholic woman and two men at a house outside Dungannon, Co Tyrone. The UVF, using the Protestant Action Force cover name, shot dead three Catholic, members of the darts club in Bleary, outside Portadown, on April 27.

Altogether in April 1975 the UVF killed twenty people, seven people in May and six more in June. That month the SDLP Convention member, Paddy Devlin, held a press conference to lay the blame for recent assassinations at the door of the UVF. Devlin, a tough trade unionist, also accused the emerging republican organisation, the INLA, of carrying out sectarian assassinations of Protestants. When the UVF issued a statement attacking Devlin, he advised them to avail of the services of a taxidermist (get stuffed).

Then in the early hours of July 31, 1975 the UVF carried out one of the more horrible attacks in the history of the conflict. Ireland's best known popular music band, the Miami Showband, was driving home to Dublin after playing at a dancehall in Banbridge, Co Down. At about 2.30 a.m. the band's van was stopped at what appeared to be a routine UDR checkpoint on the main Dublin road between Banbridge and Newry. The checkpoint was a fake. The uniformed soldiers were all members of the UVF. The Land Rover parked at the side of the carriageway was stolen from a farmer. The band was ordered from the van and made to stand along the grass verge while their identification was checked. Two of the uniformed men had opened the back of the van and were apparently carrying out a routine vehicle search when an explosion occurred where they were standing at the rear of the van. The two "soldiers", Harris Boyle, from Portadown and Wesley Somerville, from Dungannon were killed instantly.

The fake UDR checkpoint was part of an elaborate plot by the UVF to kill the members of the band, who were nearly all southern Catholics who had been näive enough to think they could safely travel through Protestant areas of Northern Ireland at night. The UVF's intention was to plant a bomb in the back of the band's van and let it drive on southwards so the bomb would explode south of the Border. The convoluted reasoning was that when the bomb exploded it would be assumed the band had been carrying explosives for the IRA. The plan went awry as Boyle and Somerville mishandled the bomb and it exploded in their faces. A few seconds after the explosion, one of the other UVF men who had been training his sub-machinegun on the band members opened fire, killing Tony Geraghty, Brian McCoy and Fran O'Toole. A fourth member of the band, Stephen Travers, was seriously injured and another escaped injury when the force of the blast knocked him into a ditch and he was overlooked by the remaining UVF men.

In an attempt to disguise the real train of events, the UVF issued a statement later saying its members had mounted a patrol and were questioning the "suspicious" occupants of the Miami minibus and a second vehicle, a car, when a bomb exploded in the minibus. It added: "At the precise moment of the explosion, the patrol came under intense automatic fire from the occupants of the other vehicle. The patrol sergeant immediately ordered fire to be returned." The UVF statement also claimed it had recovered two Armalite rifles, a weapon associated in Ireland with the Provisional IRA.

The Miami massacre had a profound effect. The Miami was

the most popular live pop music band in Ireland and Fran O'Toole one of the best-known faces in the music business. Opprobrium rained down on the UVF. There was a controversy over whether or not Somerville and Boyle should receive a funeral service in a Protestant church. Eventually, Somerville and Boyle were buried with full UVF honours with about 3,000 men attending the funerals, during which volleys of shots were fired over the coffins. Prayer services were held at each funeral by the Free Presbyterian Minister, the Rev Willy McCrea.

The bogus checkpoint ploy was used again by the UVF in south Armagh on the night of August 24, 1975. The UVF men stopped two Catholic men, John Farmer from Dungannon and Colm McCartney from south Derry, who were returning from the All-Ireland Gaelic football semi-finals in Dublin. The RUC confirmed that one of its cars had actually passed through the same UVF checkpoint less than an hour earlier but that its men had taken the checkpoint to be a genuine military operation. The UVF patrol took the two men to a nearby quiet lane and shot them both in the head and back. Their bodies were found the next morning.

The IRA was equally determined to keep the sectarian conflict alive. Ardoyne IRA members carried out a bomb and gun attack on the Bayardo Bar on the lower Shankill Road, killing four people and injuring forty on August 13, 1975. A leading member of the Ardoyne IRA was arrested immediately after the bombing while still in the car from which the gunmen had sprayed the front of the bar with gunfire, forcing people to run back into the bar for cover only to be caught in the bomb blast. After the Bayardo, the UVF demanded that the British government immediately pull out of the ceasefire deal with the Provisional IRA which, it pointed out, was clearly not adhering to any kind of a military cessation. The UVF gave Rees one week to pull out of the bargain with the Provisionals or it pledged to "consider full-scale war to rid the Province of Popish terrorists". Two weeks later another IRA unit machine-gunned the Tullyvallen Orange hall at Newtownhamilton, in south Armagh, killing four Protestant men, one of whom was eighty years old. On the same day the UVF shot dead a 36-year-old SDLP member, Denis Mullan, at his home in Moy, Co Tyrone.

The UVF's plan to force an end to what they saw as British capitulation to the IRA involved the use of a term which harked back to the original UVF's moment of sacrificial glory at the Somme: the Big Push on June 29, 1916. The later UVF leadership set the date for their Big Push as October 2, 1975. One of the first UVF units in action on that morning was from the Shankill Road. The group of four young men was led by Lennie Murphy, the man who had tortured and killed an innocent Catholic at a Shankill drinking club in 1972, then killed another loyalist and poisoned another prisoner while in Crumlin Road jail. He was among the loyalist prisoners who had been released from detention in early 1974. Murphy led his unit to Casey's Wholesale Wine and Spirits, a Catholic-owned bonded warehouse in Millfield, between the centre of Belfast and the Shankill Road. Murphy had apparently been ordered only to rob the warehouse. He ordered the proprietor's wife, Mrs Marie McGrattan, a 47-year-old mother, and her younger sister, Mrs Frances Donnelly, to kneel on the floor of the office, and shot each in the head. Two young warehouse men, Gerard Grogan and Thomas Osborne, were similarly dealt with.

The new UVF also suffered casualties in its Big Push. Four UVF men – Samuel Swanson, Andrew Freeman, both from Coleraine; Mark Dodd, the 17-year-old son of a policeman, from Ballymoney, Co Antrim, and Aubrey Reed, from Belfast – were killed instantly when the bomb they were carrying in the boot of their car exploded outside Coleraine. A Catholic photographer, Thomas Murphy, was killed when his studio on the Antrim Road was demolished by a UVF bomb at lunchtime. Mrs Irene Nicholson, a 37-year-old Protestant, was killed when a UVF bomb planted outside a Catholic-owned bar in Killyleagh, Co Down exploded. Later in the evening a Catholic man was killed when another bomb was thrown into McKenna's bar, at Aldergrove, Co Antrim.

The IRA in the Markets area added to the general tone of the evening by kidnapping a Protestant man, John Stephenson from Carrickfergus, as he walked from work in east Belfast, beating him and then shooting him dead.

Eleven people were killed on October 2, 1975. On October 3, a UVF delegation attended a pre-arranged meeting with senior Northern Ireland Office officials at Laneside house, in Co Down. The NIO wanted to determine whether the UVF was prepared to pull back from its war footing. The UVF delegation, accompanied by the Independent Unionist Convention member, Hugh Smyth, demanded that the Provisional IRA's incident centres be closed and British contacts with the Provisionals ended. They also sought the ending of the policy of allowing Provisionals to carry arms and to virtually police the Catholic working class areas of Belfast which they now controlled. On October 4, 1975, the Secretary of State, Merlyn Rees signed the order proscribing the UVF and ending its eighteen months of legal existence. He said it had become clear the UVF was wedded to violence. Under Section 9 of the Northern Ireland (Emergency Provisions) Act 1973, the UVF was again named as a proscribed organisation from October 4, 1975, with conviction for membership an offence punishable by imprisonment. (At the time of writing, twenty-two years later, this is still the case). In a statement the next morning, the UVF said it was not worried and that some commanders had welcomed it as it would help tighten security.

The British government security policy of conciliation to

the paramilitaries was now turning back towards retrenchment.

An exasperated Rees also announced that special category status, under which people convicted of terrorist offences were allowed to wear their own clothes, would no longer apply for people convicted of offences committed after January 1, 1976. As a carrot to accept the new regime he also announced that remission for those who accepted the new imprisonment terms would be 50 per cent of the jail term.

On October 5, 1975, the state moved against the UVF. During the early hours of the morning the largest police and army operation mounted against loyalists took place across north and west Belfast and southeast Antrim. By that time it was estimated the UVF had around 1,500 members with a hard core of about 400 to 500 active gunmen and bombers. Dozens were arrested, including almost thirty on the basis of statements made to detectives by the UVF man who had given himself up to the police in Carrickfergus and led police to the graves of McVeigh and Douglas, the two UDA men who had been kidnapped in April. Several top UVF members were caught in the raids, including the editor of *Combat*, Billy Mitchell. The police raided dozens of UVF offices and clubs, seizing documents, equipment, arms and stolen goods.

One of the areas of most concern to the government and security forces at this time had been the sectarian war which was paralysing large parts of the mid-Ulster area. The area of countryside between Dungannon, Portadown and Armagh, centred on Loughgall, Co Armagh – where the Orange Order had been born almost two centuries earlier amid sectarian conflict – earned the distinction of being named the Murder Triangle. The name sprang from a booklet prepared by two local priests, Father Denis Faul and Father Raymond Murray, about the murders in what they termed the "Triangle of Death". Some horrific murders were perpetrated by both sides in this area. On August 5, 1973, the local UVF unit shot dead a married couple, Francis and Bernadette Mullen, at their home at Broughadowey, outside Dungannon. The gunmen also fired at the couple's two-year-old son hitting him in the leg.

On October 23, 1975, the Armagh UVF broke into the home of Peter and James McKearney, a Catholic couple in their 60s, outside the village of Moy and shot both of them dead. It is believed they were mistaken for the family of a local woman who had been named by British police in connection with an investigation into IRA attacks in Britain. On December 19, 1975, three men, two local Catholics and the third a young English tourist, were killed in a UVF bomb and gun attack on Donnelly's Bar in Silverbridge, Co Armagh.

This wave of UVF killing was a simple reaction to the IRA's campaign of violence and particularly its assassinations of (mainly) Protestant members of the local security forces in areas where Protestants were in the minority. In areas where Protestants were in the majority, the local Catholic community could expect the same, and worse. Gusty Spence said that it had been a policy of the UVF at this time to kill Catholics. "It was seen that Ulster had entered a dangerous phase. Violence had worked for the IRA who were engaged in talks with government agents as part of the political process. The UVF took a conscious decision to give the British government a message that if republican violence could get them to the conference table, the use of indiscriminate violence with a terrible rationale, a 'terrible beauty,' the UVF could commit more violence than the IRA. Volunteer violence was not totally indiscriminate, it was directed at male Catholics."

The victims didn't always have to be Catholics. Being married to a Catholic was sufficient for a member of the Protestant community to find himself or herself on the death list. On October 17, 1975, the UVF stabbed and shot to death John Greer, a 35-year-old Protestant married to a Catholic in north Belfast.

There was still residual interest in attacking targets in the Republic. Despite the talk about some kind of relationship with the Official IRA, in May 1975 the UVF tried to bomb a train carrying 300 Official republican supporters to the annual Wolfe Tone commemoration at Sallins, Co Meath. The UVF bombers were disturbed by a local man, Christopher Phelan, who happened on the unit as they planted their bomb. The UVF men stabbed him to death before escaping. The bomb was defused after Mr Phelan's body was discovered the next morning. On December 1, 1975, two explosions at Dublin Airport killed an Aer Rianta employee, John Hayes (38), a married man with three children and injured eight others. This was claimed by the UDA, who also said it had carried out a bomb attack in Co Donegal sometime previously. Three weeks later two men were killed when a bomb exploded at Kay's Bar in Dundalk. This was claimed in the name of the Red Hand Commandos. The two were John Hayes (38), who was passing the bar when the bomb exploded, and Jack Rooney (61) a customer. On July 5, 1976, four bombs were planted in luxury hotels in Dublin, Rosslare, Limerick, Killarney and Galway. Warnings were given from "Captain Black of the Ulster Freedom Fighters" and the hotels all cleared. The only casualty was a 10-year-old boy injured by a 10 lb bomb in the gents' lavatory at the Royal George Hotel in Limerick. The other explosions were at the Gresham Hotel, Dublin, the Great Southern in Rosslare and Torc Great Southern, Killarney. The bombs caused some disruption and severe, if temporary, damage to the tourist industry, the Republic's second largest source of foreign currency after farm produce.

An explosion at a meat plant in Clones, Co Monaghan, on the night of July 4, 1977 was not the work of the UVF, it insists. The explosion damaged the factory belonging to one of the Republic's major meat processors, Hugh Tunney. Local garda sources have confirmed that loyalists were not suspected. The bomb, it appears, was the work of local IRA members.

At least 110 of the 212 victims of the conflict in 1975 are believed to have been killed by the UVF. The rest were the work of the IRA, UDA and the emerging second republican paramilitary organisation, the INLA, which was randomly killing Protestants.

The sectarian warfare in Armagh reached new levels of awfulness in January 1976. On New Year's Day, an IRA bomb killed a Protestant woman, Sylvia McCullough, in Gilford, Co Armagh. Three days later the UVF shot dead five men: three Catholic brothers, Anthony (17), Brian (23) and John Reavey (25); their 61-year-old neighbour, Mr Joseph Dowd, and his 19-year-old son, Declan, at the Reaveys' home in Whitecross, Co Armagh. The following day, a gang of about twenty IRA men stopped a minibus carrying ten Protestant workmen from a mill in south Armagh, ordered the workmen to line up at the roadside and shot them all dead. The incident became known as the Whitecross massacre. By the end of January 1976 forty-two people had died as a result of sectarian attacks across Northern Ireland.

The violence in Mid-Ulster continued later in the year when a UVF bomb killed four people at the Catholic-owned Hillcrest Bar in Dungannon on St Patrick's night, 1976. The dead included a 13-year-old boy who was walking past the bar when the car bomb exploded. On May 15 a UVF bomb killed another three customers in yet another Catholic-owned bar, Clancy's, at Charlemont, Co Armagh.

The Armagh pub carnage went on into the summer. Two people were killed in the Catholic-owned Step Inn, Keady, Co Armagh on August 16, 1976. The mainstream UVF was still capable of identifying, targeting and shooting Provisional IRA members. A senior IRA figure, Gerard Masterson, was shot dead while sleeping in his home at Alworthy Avenue off the Antrim Road on May 27, 1976. However, one of the UVF men who had broken into Masterson's bedroom, Brian Garvin accidentally shot himself. Garvin was taken to a house in Sandy Row where he was treated by a doctor who had been struck off the medical register, Harvey Jackson. Jackson, a raging alcoholic, managed to sever one of Garvin's arteries, causing his rapid death from what should have been a minor wound.

There were similarly random assassinations by the IRA and by the end of the year, eighty-one Catholics and forty Protestants had died at the hands of the "travelling gunmen". In March 1977 two important UVF bomb-makers, Joe Long and James Cordner, blew themselves up while handling explosives. Also, throughout 1976 and 1977, the UVF men rounded up by the police during the previous year were brought before the Northern Ireland judiciary, who meted out exemplary punishments. The men were vilified in the local media for having dragged the good name of their Province into the mire.

Two men arrested by the RUC for the Miami killings, Thomas Crozier and James McDowell, were brought before Lord Justice Jones in Belfast City Commission. In an extraordinarily charged atmosphere in the courtroom, it actually appeared at one stage as though the judge was contemplating the idea of sentencing the two to be hanged. Instead he pointed out that the Law precluded him from handing down what he thought was the appropriate sentence in this case. Calling Crozier and McDowell to their feet he sentenced them to life imprisonment and told them they would serve thirty-five years before they could be considered for parole. Five years later, another member of the gang, James Somerville, whose brother, Wesley, blew himself up while planting the bomb in the minibus, was also convicted and also told he should do thirty-five years before being considered for release. The "ruthless" UVF leaders captured in the October 4, 1975, police raids were also hit with stunningly severe sentences. George Anthony, the east Antrim battalion commander, was given a life sentence with the recommendation that he serve thirty years. Billy Mitchell, whom Lord Justice MacDermott felt was the UVF leader, was given life with the recommendation that he served 25 years. George Sloan and Norman Cook were given the same sentence as Mitchell. In all, eight of the twenty-six accused were given life sentences, mostly with the recommendation that they serve minimum periods of between twenty and thirty years.

During 1977 the RUC was able to state that almost every single member of the UVF in Co Antrim was brought before the court. In June 1977, twelve members of the north Antrim UVF were sentenced, one for life, for a series of crimes in the Coleraine area. In October 1977 an RUC officer was able to say that the UVF in east Antrim was by that stage "practically non-existent". Ten members from Ballyclare appeared in one case in July 1977 and were given sentences of up to fourteen years for possession of firearms and other offences. Twelve members of the Ballymena UVF received similar sentences at a single trial in November 1977. A further eleven east Antrim men appeared on UVF-related charges in September 1980.

Those defendants who were said in court to have served with the security forces, usually the UDR, received no mercy. The intelligence gathered by the RUC during the intensive seven-day interrogations to which most of the UVF prisoners were subjected led them to solve a high proportion of killings carried out by the UVF, and to uncover arms caches and supply routes for weapons. Several Scottish UVF men who had sent weapons were rounded up and imprisoned in Glasgow. The Belfast and Mid-Ulster UVF were also severely depleted. One man, George Farrell from Fermanagh, was even extradited to the Republic from Northern Ireland and charged before the Special Criminal Court in Dublin with causing the explosion at Pettigo, Co Donegal on September 28, 1973. The explosion was the work of the UVF. Farrell, a former member of the UDR, was sentenced to fifteen years' imprisonment in Dublin on November 3, 1976 but the sentence was quashed on appeal the following July. He served a total of eighteen months in the Republic for other offences. The UVF was on the run.

Six

# CUTTING THROATS
## LENNIE MURPHY AND THE SHANKILL UVF

Enthusiasm for inflicting excruciating pain on their enemies, making them suffer before killing them, is a common feature of ethnic or religious conflicts. The loyalists of Northern Ireland are guilty of this, as are republicans. The loyalists had an expression: "terrorising the terrorists". If the avowed aim was to terrorise the Catholic population which supported the (IRA) terrorists, in some people's eyes the more horrible the violence, the more terror you inflicted.

In the early days of the Troubles there were some disturbing signposts to horrors ahead, particularly in areas of Belfast where Catholic enclaves abutted on to loyalist heartlands like the Shankill or Newtownards Road. A series of incidents in which gangs of Protestant youths chased and caught Catholic boys or girls and carved initials on their skin began in the early 1970s. It was an uncommon and disturbing enough phenomenon to be reported on extensively in the local newspapers of the time. The level of public interest might have caused some of the victims to have inflicted injuries on themselves to attract attention, but they could not all have been faking. The carving attacks inevitably concerned the UVF, if only in name. On April 28, 1971, a Catholic schoolboy had the letters UVF carved on the back of his hand with broken glass by a gang of boys in the Ardoyne area of north Belfast. A Catholic factory worker in

173

Newry, Co Down claimed he had been stripped and beaten by other workers who then carved the letters UVF on his stomach. Two Catholic boys claimed the same had happened to them in May 1971 in the Duncairn Gardens area, and a 12-year-old Catholic boy from Ardoyne claimed the same had happened to him later the same month. His family refused to go to the RUC with a complaint.

In August 1971 two Catholic boys claimed they were attacked by Protestant youths on the Crumlin Road and one of the Catholic boys was pinned by the group and the letters UVF carved on to his arm with a nail. In September 1971 two Catholic schoolboys said they were attacked on their way home from school on the Antrim Road in Belfast and had the letters UVF carved on to both their arms. On April 9, 1972, a Catholic schoolgirl from the New Lodge area reported that members of a gang had used chloroform to render her semi-conscious, forced her to sing "The Sash" and then used a knife to carve UVF on her forearm. Three Catholic girls reported being attacked by a gang of Protestant girls in the Millfield area, being beaten and having UVF carved on their arms on August 20, 1973.

And so it went on. Any doubt that this kind of attack was real was dispelled on the evening of November 16, 1973. Two men forced their way into the home of the SDLP figure, Austin Currie, outside Dungannon, Co Tyrone in an apparent attempt to assassinate him. He was away but his wife Anita, along with their children, were in the house. After the men had searched the house and failed to find her husband, they set upon Anita, kicking and punching her. One tore her nightdress. She passed out and when she woke up she found the letters UVF scratched on her chest.

Savage beatings were meted out by all sides in the conflict, but there is a subterranean level beneath all the other horrible violence of the conflict that involves the UVF. One of its members, Lennie Murphy, with his associates from the

Shankill, were at the heart of this darkness. Murphy had been involved in the beating and torture of Catholics from the same time the UDA was "rompering taigs" and their own errant members.

The "rompering" term was a deliberately callous one. It derived from the name of a children's playschool programme on local television. Murphy and the other UVF men who drank in the shebeen in Lawnbrook Street off the Shankill Road had their first taste of the torture murders that were being carried out by the UDA in their clubs in west and east Belfast when they murdered Arthur Mathews on the evening of Bloody Friday, July 21, 1972. However, Murphy was prevented from further killing when he was imprisoned two months later after his arrest for the murder of Samuel Pavis, in east Belfast. Although acquitted, he remained in prison under a detention (internment) order until 1975.

Murphy's release in 1975 coincided with the fixation, in some loyalist minds, that the Victorian slums and lower middle-class suburbs of north Belfast were being annexed by republicans intent on driving Protestants from the north of the city. There had been a gradual increase in the Catholic population in this area, but this was only because the expansion of the Catholic population within Belfast was limited within certain well-defined territory. Much of north Belfast was not definable as either Protestant and Catholic, so this made the area a natural place for Catholics, who simply would not be safe living in the Shankill, east Belfast or Shore Road areas. The population displacement of the early 1970s had created tremendous housing pressure on north Belfast. More than 30,000 Catholics had been displaced in predominantly Protestant areas of north Belfast and southeast Antrim. They had to find homes somewhere. The UVF was now blaming these families for attempting to move into areas which lower middle-class Protestants had already begun leaving through upward migration anyway.

175

The autumn 1975 edition of the UVF magazine *Combat* stated: "The following areas have been marked down by the enemy for take-over: Cliftonville Road and Antrim Road. Soon, the whole of the Antrim Road from the Carlisle Circus to Fortwilliam will be dominated. Stem the tide of Popery's penetration policies. The policy of the Papist Church is to buy as much property as it can in so-called residential areas and let it out at fixed rents to Papists. The idea is to replace the Protestant population with Papists and Republicans." The territorial imperative in Belfast, a source of violence in the city since it was an early 18th century maritime town, had never changed and was still a cause of friction. The conflict over the streets of north Belfast in the mid-1970s was, however, to provide a quality of violence that not even Belfast's misshapen history could have prepared it for. Just as Armagh/Tyrone had its Murder Triangle, north Belfast achieved the similar sad status of having the stretch of road from Clifton Street, northwards along the Antrim Road to the Cliftonville and Oldpark Roads, renamed, in popular parlance of the time, Murder Mile.

The notoriety of the sectarian violence in this area predated the arrival of the Shankill UVF unit led by Lennie Murphy. As the only book dedicated to the modern UVF is Martin Dillon's horrifying and accurate account of the activities of the Shankill UVF unit which became known as the Shankill Butchers, attention has tended to focus on the UVF as the only group which engaged in torture murder.

This is by no means the case. Murphy and his associates were only among the worst of the people who did this. The east and west Belfast UDA carried out some savage murders involving the use of knives and hatchets in the early 1970s. The IRA also kidnapped and stabbed victims to death in the 1970s, although in smaller numbers. It should also be remembered that working-class Belfast life is not unfamiliar with violence. It is common for people to be beaten or stabbed, even sometimes to death, on Friday or Saturday nights. There has never been any significant period in the city's history when Protestant and Catholic youths were not seeking each other out for attack.

Among the first Catholics to meet a truly gruesome death in this area in the 1970s was Thomas Madden, a middle-aged bachelor who was found stabbed to death on the Oldpark Road in August, 1972. He had suffered 150 stab wounds, caused by a sharp knife, probably nine inches long. However, none of the wounds was sufficient to kill. Madden had been tortured by someone who had the mental capacity to inflict 150 shallow wounds on a bound and naked middle-aged man, not in particularly good health, over a period of four to five hours. Madden finally died from strangulation. It was speculated at his inquest that he might have been kept upright with a rope tied around his neck to a garage roof when the knife wounds were inflicted. A woman resident of a house in Hillview Street, near where Madden's body was found, reported hearing a man screaming: "kill me, kill me" at around 4.30 a.m. Madden appears to have been the victim of the Shankill UDA.

These savage killings were not exclusive to Belfast, it should be said. At around the same time as Madden's murder, the charred and battered body of a 19-year-old Catholic youth, Eamon McMahon, was found floating in the River Bann in Portadown, Co Armagh. A rope was tied around McMahon's neck. It was reported at the time that McMahon was beaten to death and an attempt made to hang him in a UDA club in the town. In an attempt to hide their work, his killers wrapped his body in a mattress and set fire to it. They finally dumped the smouldering remains in the Bann.

Five other Catholics were stabbed to death in 1972, including two Fermanagh farmers, Michael Naan and Andrew Murray, who were killed by members of a Scottish

Regiment of the British army who went berserk after having been posted to an isolated barracks near the Border.

Given the rate of killing in Northern Ireland during the early 1970s, relatively little attention was paid to these torture killings. One incident which did attract more than cursory attention in the media was the slaying of the well-known Catholic political figure, Senator Paddy Wilson of the SDLP, and his friend, Irene Andrews, an opera singer, in June 1973. They were abducted by a UDA gang as they left a public house in central Belfast, taken to a disused quarry on the Cave Hill on the outskirts of the city, and each repeatedly stabbed. Wilson's body was found to have thirty-two stab wounds. Miss Andrews had nineteen wounds.

Torture murders were by no means the exclusive territory of loyalists. Another terrible case of torture and stabbing occurred in the Catholic Markets area on November 25, 1973. Francis Joseph Benson (27) a Catholic from the New Lodge area, was found with multiple stab wounds in a derelict house in Stewart Street. He had been killed by local IRA members.

Then in May 1974 Alfred Stilges, a middle-aged Catholic man from the Markets, was found beaten to death in an empty house in the loyalist Ballygomartin area of west Belfast. Gerry McWilliams (24), a Catholic who had returned to Belfast from London and was living on the Lisburn Road, was attacked by a UDA gang after he left the Club Bar on the night of September 9, 1974. The UDA gang stabbed McWilliams in the body, cut his throat and dropped a heavy concrete post repeatedly onto his prostrate body.

After this, there was a period relatively free of this kind of brutality. Then, in November 1975, it started again. Lennie Murphy was released from prison and within a few weeks, the badly mutilated body of Francis Crossan, a 34-year-old Catholic man, was discovered on November 11 in an entry leading off Tennent Street in the lower Shankill. Bodies were regularly found in back entries in Belfast, usually shot dead or dead from severe beatings, but this was abnormal. An apparent attempt had been made to decapitate the victim.

Crossan's murder harked back to the worst of the nightmarish "romper room" killings of the east and west Belfast UDA and of the killing of Arthur Matthews in the Lawnbrook shebeen on the evening of Bloody Friday. Crossan had been abducted by Lennie Murphy and his associate Billy Moore at Upper Library Street as he made his way home to west Belfast from a night's drinking in the Catholic Ardoyne area. The geography of Belfast makes it possible to work out someone's religion simply by the routes they negotiate after the public transport system has closed down at night. Murphy and Moore beat Crossan unconscious in their car and then took him to an alley way in the lower Shankill where Murphy attempted to cut Crossan's head off with a butcher's carving knife. He almost succeeded. He cut deep incisions in the neck until the victim's head was only attached to the torso by the spinal cord.

Thomas Joseph Quinn, a 55-year-old homeless man who had been staying at the Carrick Hill hostel for men beside Unity Flats, was next to be abducted, on the night of February 7, 1976. His body was found the next morning in the demesne of Fernhill House at Forthriver. It was reported at the time that Quinn, an entirely innocent man, was killed in retaliation for the IRA's murder of two policemen on foot patrol in the Cliftonville area the previous day.

The manner of his death, however, was considerably different. He had been abducted by Murphy and other members of his gang and beaten unconscious. On arrival at Forthriver, Murphy cut Mr Quinn's throat and then ordered his accomplices to drag the body further into the river valley's undergrowth. Here, Murphy set about Mr Quinn again, cutting his throat back to the spine.

Two days later Murphy's unit opened fire on two delivery

men in their van when it stopped at a newsagent on the Shankill Road. The men, Raymond Carlisle (27) and Archibald Hanna (51), were both Protestants but were shot dead because Murphy was fixed on the idea that they were Catholics. On February 22, 1976, Francis Rice, a 23-year-old man from the New Lodge Road, was abducted and had his throat cut. His body was left in an alleyway off Mayo Street in the Shankill. Again, Murphy cut through the victim's throat to the spine.

There were other people using similar, if not quite so horrible, methods at this time. Four days after Rice was killed, an off-duty Protestant UDR man, Joseph McCullough, was stabbed to death by republicans near his home in Tullyvallen, Co Armagh, only a few miles from the Tullyvallen Orange Hall where the IRA had shot dead four Protestants a few months previously.

The loyalist butchery of this time was also not all the work of the Shankill UVF men. On St Patrick's night, 1976, the UDA abducted a 40-year-old Falls Road man, James Donnelly, took him to east Belfast and stabbed him to death. There were more than twenty stab wounds on his body. A Catholic woman, Margaret Gamble, was found stabbed to death on the Antrim Road, on April 4. No one was ever convicted of this murder, but it is felt she was killed by a loyalist gang looking for Catholics on the Antrim Road. She was walking home from the Lansdowne Hotel when she was stopped and stabbed to death at the top of Glandore Avenue. There is an abiding belief that Murphy carried out this killing on his own, though he never admitted it.

Another homeless man, Herbert Spring, who had been staying at the Morning Star Hostel run by the Catholic church on the Falls Road, was abducted and beaten to death by unknown loyalists on June 4, 1976. Spring was a Protestant. The mere fact that he was staying in the Catholic hostel was sufficient to warrant his murder.

Another Catholic, Edmund McNeill (22), strayed into the Protestant part of Ardoyne while drunk on the night of June 20, 1976. He was found dead from stab wounds the next morning. Another man was stabbed in the same area thirty minutes later, but recovered. The RUC said at McNeill's inquest that his injuries were so severe it appeared a maniac had carried out the killing.

Daniel Mackin, a 20-year-old Catholic, was attacked as he turned the corner off the Cliftonville Road towards his home in Orient Gardens on the night of June 25, 1976. He was returning home from a drinking club in Ardoyne and could have been identified as a Catholic because of the direction he was coming in and the fact that Orient Gardens was predominantly Catholic. His mother heard the commotion and went out to find a dying man with head and face wounds so severe that his own mother literally did not recognise him. She alerted the police about the barely alive man at the top of her street. The same officers later had to inform her that the victim was her son. Again, no one was prosecuted for this murder.

On July 10, 1976, a Protestant man, Thomas McKenzie from Solway Street in east Belfast, was abducted near his home, taken to the Falls Road and stabbed to death by republicans. The next definite Shankill butcher victim was Cornelius Neeson, who was abducted in the Cliftonville area taken to the Shankill and killed by repeated, heavy blows with a hatchet to the head. He was killed by an obese drunkard in Murphy's gang, called Sam McAllister, who later admitted he had decided on the night in question – May 23, 1977 – to kill a Catholic, possibly out of boredom.

By this stage, however, Murphy was in prison and his associates were carrying on his work for him. Murphy was arrested after attempting to shoot two young Catholic women in a car on the Cliftonville Road, on March 3, 1976. He was not caught at the scene but arrested later as he attempted to retrieve the gun he had used from a hedge. He was sentenced to twelve years' imprisonment. With the 50 per cent remission rule, he served only six years.

Catholics continued to be seized in and around the interfaces between the Shankill and Falls at night, despite the clear warnings about the danger of movement in these areas during darkness. On September 2, 1976 the body of Patrick Cunningham, a 29-year-old Catholic from Co Down, was found in Conway Street between the lower Shankill and Falls. He had been tied up with wire, beaten terribly and shot through the head. The next known victim of the Shankill Butchers, without Murphy, was Stephen McCann, a Catholic youth who was abducted by the gang while walking home from the city centre with his girlfriend on October 30, 1976. The couple were stopped by the gang at Millfield, just off the lower Shankill. The girl was let go and McCann bundled into one of the UVF's black hackney cabs. It is possible he was quickly stunned with a blow to the head from a hatchet in the vehicle. He was taken away to the wooded river valley below Fernhill House. There he was shot and had his throat cut.

Word circulated in Belfast after this that McCann and some of the other victims had been decapitated. The story was nearly true. After shooting the young man in the head, Billy Moore, Murphy's lieutenant, had copied his leader and severed McCann's throat back to the spine.

They struck again on December 20, 1976, when McAllister beat Thomas Easton – an innocent Protestant man half his size – to death outside a drinking club in Ballygomartin. Having knocked Easton unconscious, McAllister proceeded to smash his skull with a heavy concrete block. He dragged Easton's body to the car park of St Andrew's Church in Forthriver, where it was discovered the next morning.

Cornelius McCrory (17), a Catholic from Beechmount

182

Grove, was found in a field at Glencairn, in the upper Shankill on November 4. John Patch (35) another Catholic from the Cliftonville area, was beaten and shot to death near Alliance Road in north Belfast on November 13, 1976. These murders were the work of others.

The Shankill UVF unit killed five customers when they machine-gunned the Chlorane Bar in the Smithfield area of Belfast city centre on June 5, 1976. Three weeks later the IRA, using the cover name Republican Action Force, shot dead three customers in the Protestant-owned Walker's Bar at Templepatrick, Co Antrim. A week later, the UVF shot dead six customers in a Catholic-owned pub, the Ramble Inn, outside Antrim. Five of the victims were Protestant. A member of Murphy's unit, Robert "Brasher" Bates, was widely held to be responsible for beating to death a UDA man, James Moorehead, in the lower Shankill on January 30, 1977. Three days later Bates and the others captured another Catholic, Joseph Morrissey (52), as he made his way home from an evening's socialising in the city centre along the Murder Mile to his home in north Belfast. The procedure was similar to that used with other victims. Morrissey was struck several times on the head with a hatchet to stun him and then stabbed repeatedly. Finally, on the sloping, wooded grounds at Forthriver, Billy Moore cut Morrissey's throat. Another member of the gang, Artie McClay, then set about decapitating Morrissey with a hatchet.

The unit's next victim was Francis Cassidy, a 43-year-old Catholic, a quiet bachelor who lived alone in a respectable lower-middle class suburb area in north Belfast. Again, he was abducted as he walked along the Murder Mile (Antrim Road), and found with two bullet wounds to the head in a field in the Highfield estate on March 30, 1977. He also had his throat cut. In statement evidence later, the butchers confirmed that Cassidy's was the quickest death. The abduction, beating, torture, shooting and near decapitation with a butcher's knife took place in under ninety minutes. The others' torture lasted longer.

It would appear this bloodthirsty crew were finally losing their appetite for this activity. The Butchers' last intended victim was Gerard McLaverty, a 20-year-old Catholic from north Belfast, who was captured by the gang on May 11, 1977, not surprisingly as he made his way along the Cliftonville Road late at night. McLaverty survived and was able to recount what befell him. In his statement to police, he told of being overpowered and pushed into a Ford Cortina car by men who claimed to be RUC. They took him to a building, a disused doctor's surgery, on the lower Shankill, where he was made to sit on a chair in a room, containing only a sideboard and two electric heaters. He said: "The fat man (McAllister) and the driver (Billy Moore) went behind the counter and came back with sticks. The stick that the fat man had had a nail driven through the end of it. They both started beating me around the head with the sticks. I put my hands up to protect my eyes. I was afraid of the nail in the fat man's stick piercing my eyes. The fat man said: 'Get your fucking hands down or we'll give you more'." McLaverty said he started to scream with fear and pain and the two stopped and began to make tea with a kettle and cups they produced from the sideboard. McLaverty said McAllister actually asked him if he wanted any tea. When they had finished their tea, they set about McLaverty again. He was knocked to the floor then kicked in the face. Moore then removed McLaverty's bootlace and began strangling him with it while McAllister slashed at McLaverty's body. McAllister cut two very deep gashes into McLaverty's wrists to sever the artery. Confident he had achieved this, and believing their victim to be well and truly dead, they dumped him in the alleyway beside the disused surgery in Emerson Street that they had turned into a charnel house.

McLaverty was found a few hours later barely alive.

However, after six days of treatment in the intensive care unit of the Royal Victoria Hospital, he was well enough to talk to police and give a good description of his torturers. Ten days later McLaverty was driven along the Shankill Road by police from Tennent Street RUC Station. The UVF and UDA had ordered all its men onto the streets as part of the week-long loyalist protest which brought paramilitaries on to the streets in large numbers. There, in broad daylight on the Shankill Road, within a few yards of where he and other innocent Catholics had been butchered, McLaverty pointed to two of the worst corner boys in history, Billy Moore and Sam McAllister.

They were arrested and, at their homes, police recovered the butcher's knives they had used on their victims. The other principal figure, Robert Bates, and six other members of the gang were also arrested quickly and all made statements implicating each other in the series of murders.

The UVF still has difficulties coming to terms with what Murphy and his associates did. Many simply did not suspect the UVF was responsible, as such killings were previously the exclusive work of the UDA and it was presumed they were still at it. Then, as one senior UVF member confessed: "There were people who would still think Murphy was a great guy. It could be said that the enemy dictates your behaviour. But there was something sinister and ridiculous about using shovels and knives to mutilate people. They probably enjoyed it. They were shit bags." This man remembers being in a car driven by Murphy in the lower Shankill when Murphy spotted an injured pigeon on the road. The passenger at first thought Murphy might be interested in saving the bird. Murphy, he said, captured the bird and pulled its head off.

Prison did nothing to cure Murphy of his maniacal desire to kill people. As a postscript to this period, Murphy was released from prison on July 16, 1982, and on his arrival in the Shankill was immediately taken to the Rumford Street loyalist club for drinks by his associates. During the evening a homeless, mentally ill man, Norman Maxwell, wandered into the club. Murphy and another man pulled Mr Maxwell to the back of the club where they beat him until he was unable to rise from the ground. Murphy then drove a car over the prostrate man, several times. He loaded the corpse into the boot of the car and drove to playing fields in north Belfast where he dumped the body. Six weeks later, Murphy killed again. This time it was a former associate, a Shankill Road UVF member, Brian Smyth, who had built up a small car business. Murphy bought an ostentatiously large car – a canary yellow Rover – from Smyth, but failed to pay. Smyth began asking for his money and Murphy shot him dead on August 9, 1982. Two months later, Murphy struck again. On October 22, the IRA in Armagh kidnapped and killed a UDR member, Tommy Cochrane, but did not disclose the whereabouts of his body. The following evening, Murphy drove into the Falls area and abducted a middle-aged Catholic man, Joseph Donegan. Taken to a disused house in the Shankill, Mr Cochrane received the full force of Murphy's sadism. Murphy used pliers to pull out Mr Donegan's teeth and then had one of his associates beat him to death with a shovel. Murphy lasted another month, and then on November 16, 1982, he was shot dead by IRA gunmen outside his girlfriend's house, in the Forthriver housing estate. He had been set up by loyalists whose territory he was trying to muscle in on.

Only the manner of the Shankill unit's butchery makes it stand out during a period of slaughter restrained only by the fact that Britain had established a security force contingent in Northern Ireland numbering almost 38,000. The revolting symmetry of retaliatory sectarian assassinations was evidenced in north Belfast at the end of 1976. On November 30 Elizabeth Lyon, a 36-year-old Protestant woman, was shot by the IRA at her home in Ballysillan. Nine days later, local loyalists drove to Mountainview Gardens, half a mile from Ballysillan, and shot dead a Catholic teenager, Geraldine McKeown, in her home. Other UVF killings of this time were as callous. Two Catholics working as delivery men for the main unionist newspaper, the *Belfast Telegraph*, were abducted, driven to the upper Shankill and shot dead in the back of their own van on October 30, 1976. On Easter Sunday, April 10, 1977, a UVF land mine, concealed in a barrel disguised as a road bollard, exploded in Beechmount Parade off the Falls Road as the annual demonstration by the political wing of the Official IRA was assembling to begin its annual march to its commemorative plot in Milltown Cemetery. The bomb killed Kevin McMenamin, a 10-year-old boy from Ballymurphy. The explosion and death had the benefit, from the UVF's point of view, of precipitating a sharp but bloody outbreak of fighting between the Provisional and Official IRA after the Officials blamed the Provisionals for the bombing. Ten days later a similar opportunity arose when Provisional republicans were assembling for the funeral of Trevor McKibbin, an IRA man shot dead in an exchange with British soldiers. A car bomb exploded as the funeral was about to start in Ardoyne, killing two young men, Sean Campbell (19) and Sean McBride (18). The next day the IRA machine-gunned a group of Protestant men walking along Snugville Street off the Shankill Road, killing one man, Brian Smith, aged 24. Two days later the UVF sprayed the Legahorey Inn in Craigavon with gunfire, killing a 72-year-old Catholic customer, Patrick Devlin. During the loyalist stoppage in May 1977, when McLaverty identified the Butchers, the UVF bombed a filling station on the Crumlin Road in Belfast because the owners had refused to close their business. The explosion killed an off-duty member of the Ulster Defence Regiment, Corporal John Geddis (26).

From 1975 to 1977 the UVF plumbed new depths of violent activity in Northern Ireland. The organisation had held innocent Catholics responsible for the IRA's assault on its community. While the IRA has made a small industry out of venerating its dead, no epitaph exists for the Stephen McCanns, Francis Cassidys and Joseph Donegans who suffered for the IRA's sins. By the end of the 1970s the UVF was rendered almost inactive, largely as a result of the RUC's reorganised headquarters and regional crime squads. From some seventy murders in 1976, deaths at the hands of the UVF fell to twelve in 1977, to seven in 1978 and to six in 1979, levels at which they would remain for most of the next decade. Figures supplied to the House of Commons on July 14, 1975, showed there were 256 UVF prisoners. This figure doubled by 1979. Throughout 1976 and 1977, prisoners flowed into the UVF compounds in the Maze, arriving sometimes in batches of up to a dozen. At one point as much as a quarter of the organisation was behind bars, many serving very long sentences.

In 1977 there were three compounds for serving UVF prisoners and one for prisoners on remand for UVF crimes, all packed. As a result of the pressure and anger in the loyalist wings, antipathy developed between the loyalist prisoners and the prison staff. Several attacks were made by the UVF on prison officers' homes. On March 11, 1977, a prison officer's wife was shot in the neck and almost killed at her home in Glengormley, a suburb north of Belfast. Another officer was shot dead in 1980. Largely out of frustration, the UVF prisoners in Compound 18 at the Maze Prison managed to dig a 36-foot long tunnel using only cooking utensils before being caught in December, 1978. In February 1979 it was reported that UVF prisoners in the Maze were following the example of the Provisional IRA prisoners and refusing to wear prison uniform. The disruption in the loyalist wings continued through until 1980.

Gusty Spence announcing the loyalist ceasefire at Fernhill House on 13 October 1994

Samuel "Bo" McClelland (left) laying a wreath at the Belfast City Hall in November 1978

UVF murals, painted during the loyalist ceasefire, spell out the terror group's message to republicans.

UVF men training along the North Antrim coast.

UVF prisoners, one wearing a prison officer's cap and another brandishing a replica rifle, stand defiant during a protest at the Maze prison outside Belfast

The scene outside Boyle's pub in Cappagh, Co Tyrone,
after the UVF shot dead three IRA men in March 1990.

Armed UVF men stage a show of strength in the Shankill area in 1993 during the height of the loyalist terror campaign.

Billy Hutchinson, a former UVF prisoner and Progressive Unionist Party spokesman, marching on the Shankill to demand the release of loyalist inmates.

A reassuring message for Shankill loyalists twenty-four hours after the IRA ceasefire in August 1994.

Gusty Spence's period of freedom in 1972 had cost him dearly. In 1974 he was refused leave to attend his mother's funeral. In March 1977 he was refused leave again for his brother William's funeral. And in October 1980 there were calls for Spence's release after the death of his brother, Robert. Robert, who was serving a 14-year sentence for bombing a pub on the Falls Road, collapsed while exercising and died. Gusty Spence announced his resignation from the UVF in 1977 while still in prison, but continued to encourage political debate among the other UVF inmates. He was finally released after serving eighteen years in prison in December 1984. Times had changed. He had met the Catholic Cardinal, Tomás O Fiaich, while he was serving as a chaplain to the Maze and, on his release, Spence sent the head of the Catholic Church in Ireland a Christmas card. On the outside, Spence slowly rebuilt his life in the tight-knit community of the lower Shankill Road and eventually gravitated into community activism.

Meanwhile, the cost of making payments to the families of hundreds of other prisoners, as well as the amounts of money needed to run a military campaign, placed considerable strain on the UVF. By 1975 large numbers of men were engaged almost full-time in carrying out robberies and selling stolen goods. Robbers ran a high risk of arrest and this only added to the burden on the organisation.

At one stage the UVF was organising outdoor markets to sell its stolen goods in a desperate attempt to support its operations and the families of its felon population.

UVF activity continued but with far less frequency than before. A Co Antrim priest, Father Sean Murphy, was kidnapped after Constable William Turbott's body was taken from a car during an IRA ambush on June 17, 1978, in which his colleague Constable Hugh McConnell was shot dead. It is not clear why the IRA took Turbott, who was either dead or near death when the gunmen removed his body. The location of his body in a derelict farm nearby was revealed by the IRA on July 9. Murphy was kidnapped by the remnants of the Armagh UVF, led by the aberrant RUC Special Branch officer, William McCaughey. McCaughey eventually freed his hostage as a result of a personal plea by the Rev Ian Paisley.

On February 12, 1978, Mary Smyth (70) died in a fire which broke out in her house in Oldpark Avenue in north Belfast after a UVF bomb exploded at her front door. On April 14, 1978, a UVF unit shot dead Robert McCullough as he slept in his bed beside his wife in their home at Rathcoole. The gang used a silencer and Mr McCullough's wife woke to find her husband lying dead beside her from a gunshot wound to the head. Two men received life sentences for this murder in September, 1979. In August 1979 the RUC recaptured most of the remaining army-issue rifles which had been stolen by the Armagh UVF in the early 1970s. Twenty-nine rifles and 10,000 rounds of ammunition were found at a house in Tandragee, Co Armagh. The police also recovered £200,000 stolen from the local post office the previous month.

On October 7, 1979, Mark McGrann (24), a Catholic from the New Lodge Road, was shot dead by a lone gunman on a bicycle as he walked across the Albert Bridge from the Short Strand. The gunman rode off towards east Belfast. An unsuccessful attempt was made to wipe out the leadership of Sinn Féin in 1979 when the UVF planted a bomb concealed in a fire extinguisher in the Mansion House in Dublin just before the party's annual conference. The 10 lbs of gelignite failed to explode. On June 20, 1979, two gunmen called at the home of Francis Sullivan (36) in Bombay Street near the Falls-Shankill peace line and shot him dead. John Harvey (43) was shot dead at point blank range while at dinner with his family by two men who burst into his home in the New Lodge Road on August 28, 1979.

The UVF shot dead Sara Larmour (44) at her home in

Rodney Parade in west Belfast on October 3, 1979, possibly after mistaking her home for that of a local IRA man.

In 1980 the UVF assault on republicanism gave way to a burst of activity from a reorganised UDA under the military leadership of John McMichael. McMichael targeted and had his men assassinate a list of republican figures who were seen to be leading the political campaign surrounding the IRA "H" Blocks prison campaign. The dead included Miriam Daly, the IRSP figure; Ronnie Bunting, the INLA leader in Belfast; and John Turnley, a republican from a Protestant background who was shot near his home in Co Antrim.

Another of their intended victims, Bernadette McAliskey, narrowly survived when she and her husband were shot by McMichael's team at their home on the southern shores of Lough Neagh. The couple were saved when a British army undercover unit which was watching the house called a helicopter ambulance which had the McAliskeys in hospital within forty minutes. The UDA team, including the organisation's future political mentor, Ray Smallwoods, was arrested by the same army unit.

The UDA was also attacking targets in the Republic but with little success. In 1977 Freddie Parkinson, a UDA man from west Belfast, was arrested when an incendiary bomb he was trying to plant in Clery's Department Store on O'Connell Street in Dublin exploded in his pocket. He was sentenced to twelve years' imprisonment but released in 1982 after having spent almost his entire period of detention in the protective custody wing of Mountjoy Prison. Two other UDA men, Albert Taylor and Thomas Mullan, from Newtownabbey, also served sentences in Mountjoy after they were caught on a foolhardy mission to assassinate Francis McGirl, the Co Leitrim IRA man who was acquitted of murdering Lord Mountbatten in 1979. The UDA still continued with regular attempts at planting firebombs in Dublin and Donegal. A few shops were badly damaged. In November 1981, the UDA did succeed in shooting up the Sinn Féin headquarters in Parnell Square, Dublin, injuring two republicans.

On February 23, 1981, an east Belfast UVF man, Robert "Squeak" Seymour, cycled his way into UVF folklore when he rode across the city late at night to a house on Rodney Parade where James "Skipper" Burns, one of the most senior IRA figures in the city, was living with his girlfriend (Burns had beaten his wife to death six months earlier). Seymour broke into the house, hiding downstairs until the couple came home and went to bed. When they were asleep he made his way up the stairs, shot Burns dead as he lay in bed, using a silencer, and left the house without waking Burns' girlfriend. Snow was beginning to fall and, concerned that his tyre tracks would be followed, Seymour carried his bicycle on his back down the Donegall Road and across the M1 Motorway until he was safely back in the loyalist Village area. After this, his associates say, Seymour became a bit of a legend. He was a quiet single man who later opened a video shop in east Belfast. Seven years after he shot Burns the IRA eventually caught up with Seymour and shot him dead in his shop.

At the time of Seymour's ride to fame, the UVF was undergoing another change. The long-term prisoners who attended Gusty Spence's political education classes began, in Spence's words, to ask: "What is in it for us? We don't want to go back to the same old things again. We want something new, not only for the Prods, we want something new for everyone whereby everyone would have had some form of input into society, where they could be listened to."

A signal that members of the UVF in prison were changing came in a statement from the former east Antrim leader sent to a local paper in October 1978. The statement called on young men in the UVF to quit and leave the job of taking on the IRA to the police. The UVF, he said had been amateurs.

He added: "I make no apologies for being a member of the

UVF because I was in it for what I believe in. But it has gone wrong and before any more young fellows waste their lives in a jail, I'm saying: stop it. I don't want to see them end up as H-Block prisoners offered remission for cleaning IRA H-Block cells." He advised loyalists to pursue the political path. "Get rid of the watered-down politicians and get staunch men instead who will represent your cause and not men who will jump off and visit the other side."

In June 1979, amid increasing IRA attacks on part-time security force members among the Border Protestant community, the Rev Ian Paisley again set about raising political pressure for a major response to the republican threat. Again there were threats, as in the old days, that if the government would not respond then loyalists would take matters into their own hands. The UVF issued a statement pointing out that the "H-Blocks at the Maze jail are full of loyalists who took it upon themselves to retaliate."

During the visit of Pope John Paul II to Ireland in September 1979, the UVF again offered to call a ceasefire if the IRA would lay down its arms. It called on the IRA to respond to the obvious desire for peace in Ireland and call a ceasefire. The UVF would "immediately reciprocate by standing down all active military personnel. The UVF feels that the climate is right for a new political initiative such as a devolved administration and would hope that the British government would respond to a cessation of violence by endeavouring to arrive at some political settlement." This time the IRA did not even reply to the overture.

On the military side, in 1979 the UVF and UDA decided, like the IRA, to reorganise and to do so in a way which would make it not as easy as it had been for the police to round up entire units of the organisation. Using the experience they had gained, the UVF leadership began coaching members in anti-interrogation techniques, instructing their members in the type of questioning they would meet. They also devised a cell system where smaller units were engaged in specific roles and operations. The theory was that members of one cell would not be privy to what another cell was doing and so would be unable to tell the police.

Very slowly, UVF attacks began to pick up. There was a series of attempted assassinations in later 1979 and 1980 in Belfast, although altogether only ten people were killed by the UVF in these two years. In February 1980 the UVF in south Belfast accidentally shot dead an innocent Catholic man, William McAteer, while trying to kill a local republican.

The internal UVF security reform, combined with a British government decision to restrict the use of rough interrogation in Castlereagh, once again began to push the pendulum back in favour of the terrorist organisations. But for the UVF, the frenetic and bloodthirsty activity of the mid-1970s was becoming a bad memory. A decision was taken not to return to civilian bombing, and aside from one or two instances in the early 1980s, the UVF refrained from using the bomb again. The IRA was also reeling from the effects of the RUC arrests and it was clear the threat to the Union was receding. In Westminster, the new British prime minister, Margaret Thatcher, made it abundantly clear that while she was in office there would be no retreat in the war against the IRA. The UVF could afford, for a while, to take a back seat.

## Seven

# FRIENDS ACROSS THE SEA

In the spring of 1978 the Lebanese capital Beirut was in chaos. The city swarmed with armed militias on both sides of the Green line separating Moslem west from Christian east. Thousands were dying in gun battles, shell barrages and hand-to-hand fighting during the civil war. Into this sectarian maelstrom stepped two Belfast loyalists on a mission to buy guns for the UVF.

Through contacts via criminals in the European underworld, the two UVF envoys travelled into the heart of Lebanese Christian power. The two UVF men met representatives of the Gemayel family, the leading Maronite clan which had just began to forge the links with Israel which culminated in the disastrous invasion of 1982. There was a certain irony to the link-up. Here after all were Belfast Protestant loyalists, reared on a politico-relgious diet of anti-Catholicism, sitting down to discuss an arms deal with a paramilitary force whose members soldered pictures of the Virgin Mary onto their rifle butts. The Christian Phalangists whom the UVF men met were members of the Maronite faith, a Lebanese sect which, although strongly independent from the Vatican, still had strong Catholic undertones in its iconography and ritual. All this meant nothing to the UVF men in Beirut. They were only interested in securing arms and cared little as to whom they came from.

Their mission to Beirut proved fruitless. When they were about to travel to the Gemayel family home they were informed of a death in the family. The UVF men decided to get out of Beirut quickly even if it meant returning to Northern Ireland. They were aware of the dangers of hanging around the Lebanese capital waiting for the Gemayels to contact them again. It would not, however, be the first time the UVF and other loyalists colluded with Lebanese arms dealers.

The aborted Lebanese mission in 1978 points to a central logistical problem for the modern Ulster Volunteer Force. Their "friends across the sea" were and are generally financial, as opposed to ideological, allies. From time to time the UVF did come across supporters and sympathisers abroad who out of conviction rather than gain sent guns to Northern Ireland for the loyalist cause. But on the whole the UVF had to seek their weapons from whoever was willing to sell them on the international arms market. There was no Colonel Gaddaffi type figure sending guns and explosives to the UVF because he supported their goals. The UVF was and still is at the mercy of arms dealers who for a few dollars more are always willing to betray their clients.

The original UVF had fewer problems acquiring the weapons to fight a war. Carson's army was a pan-class alliance with support and succour from inside the Unionist and British establishment. The organisation's greatest logistical achievement had been the importation of 35,000 guns and 2,000,000 rounds of ammunition on the *Clyde Valley* in April 1914. This operation was backed by a cabal of Ulster business leaders as well as British army officers such as the adventurer Major Frederick Crawford, who actually guided the *Clyde Valley* into Larne.

There was one striking comparison between the guns brought to Larne in 1914 and those smuggled into Northern Ireland during the present Troubles. The *Clyde Valley* arms were bought from the German Kaiser's army. Indeed the stub of the cheque paid to the German middlemen who negotiated the deal with the UVF is still in the hands of the Cunningham family, who owned Fernhill House where many of the guns were stored. The German connection was deeply ironic given that within two years thousands of UVF men would die in French battlefields at the hands of the Kaiser's soldiers firing the same type of weapons smuggled into Ulster on the *Clyde Valley*.

Many of these old UVF guns were constantly resurrected from arms dumps across the Province during later crises. There were so many weapons around in 1936 that the Stormont regime decided to send 6,000 Mauser and Steyer rifles to Haile Selassie's troops resisting Italian invaders in Abbysinia. The remaining guns from the 1914 shipment were hidden in houses, farms and Orange Halls. Gusty Spence makes the point that none of the original UVF arsenal was ever decommissioned even though it had been brought into Northern Ireland by the Ulster Unionist Party in 1914, the same party which today insists on terror groups disarming.

Some of the guns are still turning up in the 1990s. In the middle of the loyalist terror campaign in 1992 the RUC announced news of a major arms find in North Belfast. It later transpired that the 200 or so guns were old rusting German Mausers which had been discovered by locals in the Tiger's Bay area after derelict houses had collapsed. It seemed the guns had been holed up and left there for more than eighty years.

Up until the early 1960s loyalism had little need for a UVF, since the original organisation had been amalgamated into the Stormont state militia at the creation of Northern Ireland. It was not until unionism started to fragment under the liberal policies of Terence O'Neill that the UVF began to emerge again. This time however it found itself pitted against the very forces it pledged loyalty to. The legal state forces, the RUC and "B" Specials, now had the weaponry and the manpower to defend the union. The modern UVF was left with very little.

Then and now most unionists supported the legal state forces and the most talented within their community joined the police, "B" Specials or army. The UVF's illegality made it extremely difficult for the descendants of the middle and upper classes who once supported Carson's army to give help to Gusty Spence's militia. The type of people who once supplied the money and the technical know-how to the UVF now joined the security forces. The UVF had to do with second best.

The flight of the middle and upper-class unionists from the UVF has only increased the sense of isolation felt by working-class loyalists. The modern UVF knows full well it is on its own at home and has even fewer true friends across the sea.

Their most reliable ideological allies are in Scotland, given the strong historical, religious and cultural ties between there and Ulster.

From the beginning of the modern Troubles the Scottish connection has proved valuable, at least in terms of boosting the morale of Ulster loyalists. Support from their Scottish brethren at least makes the Ulster loyalist feel he or she is not alone in the world. But UVF leaders in Belfast are sceptical that their brethren across the Irish sea can do much else for them. One member of the UVF Brigade Staff confessed that he personally kept his distance between himself and most Scottish loyalists. "I've always kept them at arm's length. There might be the odd one or two who have been invaluable to us. But there have been far too many more who have caused us nothing but trouble. There have been plenty of Scottish loyalists caught by the security forces. I've always believed the police in Scotland were always on top of them."

His scepticism about the usefulness of the Scottish connection is borne out by the history of the Troubles. Scores of Scottish UVF men have been tried and convicted for sending arms to Northern Ireland. In the early days of the conflict, the Scottish connection was used to send a steady stream of gelignite stolen from mines to Ulster. This was carried out by UVF supporters in mining villages in Lanarkshire when there was still a Scottish mining industry to talk about. In the 1970s the gelignite was smuggled over via ports such as Stranraer and Cairnryan. In 1973, for instance, twenty sticks of gelignite were found in a cistern of a toilet at Stranraer railway station, possibly to be picked up by someone boarding the ferry to Larne. The same year the Strathclyde police, acting on a tip-off, raided a house in Drongan in Ayrshire where they found fifty sticks of gelignite. Most of the explosives came over in small quantities, usually in something as innocuous as a lunch box or briefcase.

Some observers have gone much further and imagined that the modern UVF emulated Carson's army by shipping huge quantities of weapons in boats across the Irish sea. They look at fishing ports on the Co Down coast such as Portavogie or Kilkeel as possible pick-up points for the guns from Scotland. According to long-standing UVF members these routes have rarely been used. The organisation has preferred to use individuals, cars or lorry containers to smuggle gelignite and guns via the western Scottish ports.

The UVF has done much better in Scotland raising money, especially in collections and raffles at loyalist functions along the central belt. The Loyalist Prisoners Welfare Association has collected hundreds of thousands of pounds through the last 25 years which has lifted the financial burden on the war chest at home. One of the UVF's biggest fund-raising events are concerts by the loyalist folk band, Platoon. The Belfast band plays to huge audiences in loyalist social clubs across central Scotland. They are known as the loyalist version of the Wolfe Tones and even do a competent rendition of "The Fields of Athenry". Platoon tapes are also a popular buy with young loyalists at events such as Orange marches or Rangers matches.

Recently some enterprising loyalist stallholders have made money from the sale of UVF badges, flags and even tea towels. One of the most popular T-shirts at the moment is a take-off of the cult film, *Reservoir Dogs*. In the Scottish loyalist version, the black-suited killers in the sunglasses also wear Orange sashes and are known as "The Reservoir Prods".

Up until very recently UVF supporters also collected money for loyalist prisoners outside Rangers and Hearts football matches. Loyalist supporters have even gone into the enemy's territory to collect money for UVF prisoners' aid. In one infamous episode several years ago, young men belonging to the Edinburgh Loyalist Coalition travelled to Celtic Park in Glasgow's east end. Posing as republicans, they carried collection tins onto "The Jungle" – the terracing where the hard core Glasgow Celtic fans used to stand before the stadium was made all-seater two years ago. The Edinburgh loyalists told the Celtic fans they were collecting for IRA prisoners and spent the afternoon filing their tins with money from Scottish republicans. The Coalition's venture into the lion's den won't happen again. It is a sign of changing times, as much as in football as politics, that Celtic's millionaire owner Fergus McCann has banned any political collections or paper sales in the ground. This also goes for Glasgow Rangers.

The ability to raise funds in Scotland is severely hampered by the attitude of that country's Orange Order. Since 1989 the Order's leadership has banned any collections for loyalist prisoners at Lodge dances or functions. That same year the Grand Orange Lodge of Scotland expelled one hundred and sixty members from the organisation after they collected money for loyalist prisoners at a social night in Edinburgh. The expulsions produced a split in the Orange Order, with the dissidents forming the Independent Orange Order. This has been a much smaller, less significant body than the mainstream Orange movement in Scotland. Scotland's

Orange establishment has also, unlike their counterparts in Northern Ireland, banned loyalist bands which have a strong association with the UVF or UDA. In the North the "blood and thunder" bands are seen as good recruiting agents for loyalist terror groups. In Scotland they are seen by most militant Protestants as an embarrassing aberration.

The exclusion of loyalist paramilitary supporters from the mainstream Orange movement has retarded the UVF and UDA's growth in Scotland. It is worth adding that while most Scottish Orangemen are deeply attached to the union and see Irish nationalism and Catholicism as twin heads of the same beast, they are still by and large law-abiding citizens. The Grand Lodge in Scotland has gone so far as to outlaw acts of support for the UDA and UVF as fundamentally anti-unionist as well as illegal. Loyalist aid groups therefore operate at the fringes of Scottish society where financial and technical resources are at a minimum. Unlike the United States, where the Provisional IRA has some wealthy backers, the vast majority of loyalist supporters in Scotland are usually working class, poorly educated and politically unsophisticated.

Despite these handicaps the UVF has been marginally more successful than the larger UDA in Scotland. The UDA's record in Scotland has been, with a few exceptions, a series of debacles. Statistically far more Scottish UDA men have gone to jail for paramilitary offences, compared to the UVF. The latter organisation was always smaller and tighter in Scotland whereas the UDA at one time boasted of having thousands of members. In very broad terms the UDA is stronger in western Scotland along the Ayrshire coast as well as in areas like Paisley. The UVF strongholds have been based around the Bridgeton area in Glasgow's east end and towns along the eastern central belt.

The UDA were also more vocal. In 1976 the UDA's leader

in Scotland, Roddy MacDonald, said in a BBC television interview that he would be happy to supply arms and send them to Ulster. MacDonald boasted that the UDA had 6,000 members in Scotland. He also predicted that thousands of Scottish loyalists were preparing to travel to Northern Ireland and fight in the defence of their Ulster comrades. MacDonald's outburst cost him his membership of the Orange Order. It was also used as evidence in MacDonald's trial in 1978, when he was charged along with five others for soliciting people to hand over rifles and pistols for use in acts of terrorism in Britain and Northern Ireland.

Within less than a year of the MacDonald trial, the Scottish police had arrested forty people they believed were connected to the UDA, eight from Northern Ireland staying in Scotland and the remaining thirty-one native-born Scots. The UDA in Scotland had been badly mauled by the arrests and never really recovered from the blow.

The UVF also took a hammering from the Strathclyde police. In June 1979 nine of their members were given jail sentences of between twelve to eighteen years in Glasgow's High Court. The nine defendants faced sentences totalling up to 500 years. Four of the men were found guilty of bombing two Catholic owned bars in Glasgow in 1979. The Old Bairns and Clelland pubs were targeted, the UVF said, in retaliation for the IRA bombing campaign in England which was claiming scores of lives. On the same night as the Glasgow explosions the UVF also attacked an Irish pub in Kilburn, North London and bars in Belfast and Dublin. The Glasgow bombings were the only offensive operations ever undertaken by loyalist terror groups in Scotland.

The 1979 trial shone a light into UVF terrorist activity in Scotland during the first decade of the Troubles. It focussed on the role of Scottish supporters who supplied explosives to their colleagues in Ulster. During the court case a miner, Thomas Powell, confessed that he stole thirty sticks of gelignite from the Montonhall pit in East Lothian after being approached by one of the accused, Colin Campbell. Powell told the court he stole the explosive sticks one and two at a time and then buried them in his back garden. Over the next few months, the miner continued, he received phone calls from Campbell. Eventually a meeting was arranged at a social club in the area. Powell then started to hand over the gelignite sticks on different occasions at the club. All of the gelignite was then transported to a house in Cambuslang in Glasgow shortly before the pub bombings.

Ten people were injured in the Clelland pub attacks but the device left at the Old Barnes bar was so ineffective that after it exploded the customers continued drinking in a haze of dust. Less than 48 hours after the bombings the UVF men involved were all picked up by the police in dawn raids.

The subsequent court case painted a picture of life inside the Scottish UVF which seemed to be a mixture of bizarre ritual and farce. Members swore an oath of loyalty on the bible to the Queen. Some of the former UVF who gave evidence against the nine accused claimed they had joined a loyalist welfare organisation. They insisted the UVF in Scotland was simply there to provide money and succour for embattled loyalists in Ulster. The court also heard that disagreements over the role of the Scottish UVF resulted in a split. James Laing, one of the prosecution witnesses, admitted he had been a driver for the Bridgeton UVF. He said that in the early days of the Scottish UVF he believed it was simply a "charitable organisation". Once the group started to look out for weapons and explosives, the Bridgeton UVF divided. Laing said that those opposed to the UVF embarking on terrorist actions in Scotland simply kept their views to themselves and did nothing.

The 1979 trial also threw up a puzzle for the security forces monitoring the UVF in Scotland. Three years earlier the Scottish UVF had been taken over by William Campbell.

Under his leadership the UVF was re-activatated and urged to collect "war materials". The mystery however was why the Glasgow UVF men, to whom secrecy was meant to be paramount, would suddenly decide to go public and bomb pubs in their own city. Senior UVF figures were also worried about the exposure of their support group across the Irish sea. The Ulster UVF wanted the Scottish connection to be kept as quiet and clandestine as possible while the money, guns and explosives continued to come over to the real theatre of conflict.

Ironically, the Provisional IRA adopts the same policy regarding Scotland. It does have cells operating throughout the Scottish central belt. However, they are in place for purely logistical back-up for the IRA's England department. Some of the Provisional's most prominent volunteers, including Patrick Magee, the Brighton bomber, have used Glasgow as a base to enter England. Magee kept the explosives used in the bomb which nearly wiped out the British Cabinet at a house in Glasgow, before they were transported down to Brighton. While the IRA has used Scotland to store explosives and hide activists, there has been an unwritten understanding that their units do not carry out bombings or shootings there. The potential for stoking up the latent fires of sectarianism in cities such as Glasgow and Edinburgh is far too great a risk. The Catholic population is small and potentially vulnerable to a backlash if such a campaign was set off. Most importantly, the Provos do not wish to jeopardise vital bases in Scotland which would receive even more attention from the police and the public if bombs were going off in Scottish towns and cities.

The IRA's relative inactivity in Scotland means the UVF does not have to deal with the same threat it faces back in Northern Ireland. The loyalists too want to keep their heads down and get on with the business of supporting the war back at home.

The business of backing the boys in Ulster suffered another major setback two years after the 1979 trial. Nine further suspects were arrested in Glasgow for their part in a UVF gun-running operation. They were found guilty of using Glasgow as a conduit for arms being shipped from Canada to Northern Ireland. The operation centred on the importation of weapons via the Royal Mail from Canada to Scotland and onwards to the Province. Once again, however, the Scottish police seemed on top of the situation. Working with customs officers, they handed over hidden taperecorders to Royal Mail employees who delivered packages containing the Canadian guns and ammunition to Glasgow addresses. As soon as the postmen delivered the parcels the police swooped. The parcels, which purported to contain car spares, were ripped open in Glasgow's Wellington Street Post Office in April 1981. The first packages contained a sub-machine gun, ammunition and a silencer. Another parcel they found later contained two revolvers while a third one the police intercepted included a hand gun and a small quantity of ammunition. Whoever was sending the packages had been doing their homework. The parcels were all covered inside with lead sheeting to beat detection by X-ray machines.

Among those arrested was one of the UVF's most senior members from Northern Ireland, Norman Sayers, from the Glencairn estate in Belfast. The Glasgow trial ran in conjunction with that of an English man, George Hill, who was also charged with aiding the UVF. Hill, a commissionaire for Marks and Spencer, was arrested after handing over sixty-three pounds of the weed killer, sodium chlorate, to a Scottish loyalist contact at London's Euston station. Sodium chlorate when combined with sugar and diesel oil makes up the key ingredients for explosive mix. The substance is naturally banned in Northern Ireland but can be easily obtained in Britain.

The English court was told that Hill was meant to pass on

the heavy packets of weed killer to a UVF member and then they would be shipped from Glasgow to Belfast.

Back in Glasgow the judge, Lord Ross, noted that in the 1979 trial he had warned that "severe sentences would be imposed on those who chose to wage war on society by obtaining arms and explosives to be sent to Ulster." He added that his warning at the original UVF trial appeared to have been ignored. He then handed down sentences running from four to eleven years. Lord Ross's warning should have been heeded by the UVF for another reason. It was crystal clear that the majority of their gunrunning operations on the mainland were severely compromised. The lessons of 1979 and 1981 were harsh ones which the UVF leadership back in Belfast took on board.

Since those two trials UVF activity in Scotland has slackened off considerably. The organisation prefers to keep an extremely low profile, primarily raising money and from time to time providing the odd piece of logistical support. In general the UVF in Northern Ireland prefers to keep its Scottish operation on a tight rein. Both loyalist terror groups confess the Scottish connection is of limited value.

Sitting in Ibrox stadium on a Saturday afternoon listening to the chants of "U-U-UVF" and "The Sash my father wore" might give one the impression that there is a potential army of young Scottish loyalists ready and able to fight for No Surrender. The reality is somewhat different. Sectarianism and loyalism in Scotland are minority sports. With a few exceptions it is forty-five minutes each way on alternating Saturday afternoons. Dougie Currie, a long standing Scottish UDA supporter from Renfrew, best sums up the disappointment committed loyalists feel towards their arm-chair soccer-singing counterparts: "When Gerry Adams came over to Glasgow to speak in Govan town hall in the Autumn of 1995 we organised a protest. The week before there were 40,000 people singing Derry's Walls and the Sash at Ibrox.

Yet even though Govan town hall is close to Ibrox only 400 loyalists turned up to stop Adams and his cronies speaking. That says a lot about the armchair loyalists."

The cynicism of the dedicated minority of Scottish loyalists towards the less than committed but vocal majority is shared by many in the UVF in Belfast. UVF leaders regard hardline Scottish loyalists as an embarrassing irritant to be tolerated for a few days over the Twelfth of July. They point to the fact that some Scottish loyalists, particularly those based around the extreme pro-UVF *Red Hand* magazine in Edinburgh, have supported anti-ceasefire rejectionists like Billy Wright in Portadown. As one Belfast UVF member put it: "There are plenty of good Scottish loyalists over there but there are also many more who are much more extreme than loyalist people in Ulster. The Scottish loyalists, some of them, are a bit like the Irish Americans. More Irish than the Irish themselves, more Ulster than the Ulster people themselves."

The extremism of some Scottish loyalists is matched by their political confusion. Unlike loyalists in Northern Ireland, they have no real natural party any longer to gravitate towards. There is no longer a Protestant Action Party with any serious support. Most Scottish loyalists are working-class and find it uncomfortable supporting an increasingly unpopular Conservative and Unionist Party. Supporters of the UVF and UDA also find it difficult to give their full allegiance to the Labour Party. This is for two reasons. The first relates to Labour's long-term objective of a united Ireland by consent. The second is that Labour has the overwhelming backing of Scotland's Catholics who in certain parts of the country dominate the party.

The most recent illustration of Scottish loyalist confusion occurred after the death of Labour leader John Smith in 1995. At the by-election for his Monkland's East seat, the campaign was dominated by allegations that a "Catholic mafia" ran the local council to the detriment of mainly

Protestant areas of the constituency. Smith's successor to the seat, Helen Liddel, dismissed the allegations as "tittle tattle". However loyalists from the pro-UVF Edinburgh coalition latched on to the Monkland's campaign. They ran what they called an "anti-mafia campaign". Helen Liddel's closest challenger was the Scottish nationalist candidate, so the pro-UVF group supported the SNP urging loyalists in mining villages in the constituency to vote for the nationalist. These were some of the same villages which helped supply mining explosives in the early 1970s. The absurdity could not have been greater. Here were loyalists who swore allegiance to the British Crown, some of whom were even prepared to finance and arm the UVF in Ulster, voting for a nationalist candidate at home. In other words their anti-Catholicism superseded their unionism. The ridiculousness of their stance was not lost on their comrades on the other side of the Irish sea.

The 1981 Glasgow UVF trial illuminated an infinitely more useful connection for the organisation on the other side of the world. The court case had thrown light on a link between the UVF and loyalist supporters in Canada. At the time of the '81 trial, Scottish newspapers reported that the Canadian connection had been smashed. This was far from the truth, for between 1979 and 1986 the UVF was able to smuggle up to 100 machine-guns, as many rifles, grenade launchers, magnum revolvers and hundreds of thousands of rounds of ammunition from Canada. The shipments were a considerable shot in the arm for the organisation.

As far back as the early 1970s some Canadian loyalists were prepared to ship arms to Northern Ireland. In April 1974 two men, Ronald Whiteside and George Hall, both from Toronto, were arrested and charged with sending guns to the UDA. The shipment included nine M1 Carbines, thirteen Sten guns, sixty-six sten gun ammunition clips and 2,000 rounds of ammunition. The arms seizure was a result of a parallel operation in Southampton in which the English police found a small amount of guns and explosives at the port which were also destined for the UDA.

Toronto is to Ulster loyalists what Boston or New York is to Irish-Americans. The Canadian city has a number of Orange lodges and Ulster cultural societies set up by expatriates. There is even an Orange Lodge of Canadian Mohawks, whose traditional feathered headdresses and war paint light up the Twelfth parade in Belfast, normally a dull black and Orange blur of bowler hats and sashes. Most Ulster Canadians restrict their loyalism to these kind of harmless cultural activities. There is, however, a hardcore minority who feel they should go one step further and help arm the boys back in Ulster in exactly the same way as Noraid did for the Provisional IRA at the start of the Northern Troubles.

Until the late 1970s the supply of guns from Canada to the UVF was an insignificant trickle. Eventually the UVF came across one Canadian who was every terrorist group's dream – a true believer. William Charles Taylor from the Toronto suburb of Etobekoq was different. A gun freak, he was also a member of one of North America's countless private militias and most importantly of all, a fanatical anti-communist. Taylor was never so happy as when attending gun fairs across Canada and the United States. At the end of the seventies Taylor became friendly with several expatriates from Ulster who had relatives in the loyalist community back at home.

They included Albert Watt, who had emigrated from the Province to Canada at the start of the Troubles. Through their long conversations Taylor became fascinated with the loyalist cause. He started to imagine that the Provisional IRA was a Soviet-backed front and that only the UVF was a bulwark against the red menace in Ulster. (Yet at the same time Irish-Americans also believed the PIRA was an anti-communist force. In one infamous editorial in 1975 of

Noraid's *Irish People* newspaper, a writer referred to the Provos as the "wedge against communism".)

Taylor's attitude deeply impressed the loyalist hardcore living in Toronto. He seemed a cut above the average committed loyalist abroad. He had an exceptionally high IQ and was known to be a dab hand at converting guns from semi to fully automatic. Moreover, he was well-read and had a good working knowledge of the Northern Ireland political situation.

It was not until 1980 that any solid connections were made between Taylor and the UVF. His estranged wife Gayle later confessed to the Royal Canadian Mounted Police that the genesis of his relationship with the UVF began during an adventure south to the USA. Taylor was joined on the trip by another unusual character, Howard Anthony Wright. Taylor met him through the gun club fraternity in the Toronto area. Both had a mutually unhealthy interest in firearms and they shared a loathing of communism. Wright, a former officer in the Canadian Reserve Army, also had a working knowledge of firearms. He had been born in Manchester of Catholic parents but eventually became very sympathetic to loyalism through his admiration of British soldiers being killed by the "communistic" IRA in Ulster.

The two buccaneers travelled to Ohio in March 1980 along with Gayle Taylor. There they attended a gun show where Bill Taylor bought some weapons. Afterwards the trio concealed the weapons in a petrol tank of the pick-up truck they travelled from Canada in. Gayle Taylor recalled that en route back north her husband mentioned to Wright that the guns would be "shipped to Ireland."

Through the expatriate, Taylor got in contact with several Belfast UVF men who travelled to Canada, including John Bingham. Money was handed over by Bingham to Taylor, who then concealed the first consignment of guns inside hollowed out tractor engines. It was Taylor's idea to cover the guns with lead sheeting to prevent detection by X-ray.

Meanwhile, back in Belfast, the UVF got their hands on an import licence and used a Belfast shipping company to import the tractor engines to the province. This was the preferred method for the Canadian connection over the next few years. During this period Taylor and his colleagues managed to smuggle hundreds of rifles and sub-machine guns as well as thousands of rounds of ammunition. Among the arsenal were Ingrams, known in the arms trade as the "Rolls Royce of machine-guns". The UVF was particularly delighted to get their hands on the Ingrams. It was only slightly bigger than a hand-gun, looked like the Israeli Uzi-machine gun and like the Uzi could fire hundreds of rounds per minute. Taylor's shipments also included Mac 10 sub-machine guns which he personally tested at his truck repair shop.

Taylor and Wright were so determined that the UVF should get the best equipment that they also converted scores of semi-automatics to full automatics. Under American law it was extremely difficult to buy fully automatic weapons at the kind of gun fairs the two men were attending.

Another weapon the Canadians sent over was the Colt Commando rifle, a slimmed down version of the Armalite, once the preferred weapon of the Provisional IRA. The UVF's Canadian arms suppliers even managed to get their hands on grenade launchers for the Colt Commando, which, oddly, the terror group has yet to use in the Northern conflict. One of the most popular weapons supplied by Taylor and Co. was the Magnum revolver. A senior UVF man who knew Taylor said the Magnums, which the UVF never had access to before, became a favoured weapon for those involved in close quarter assassinations over the next ten years.

The fact that most of the weapons had been bought in the United States was an additional advantage for the UVF. In the early days of the Canadian connection the RUC appeared blind to the origin of the guns. Detectives admit that they were initially puzzled as to how the UVF had got its hands on guns from the USA given that they had next to no base there.

The UVF, however, asked Taylor to avoid sending explosives given the obvious dangers of shipping such unstable material across the Atlantic. The UVF commander who knew Taylor recalled: "Taylor was something else. He was a god-send. He could do anything with his hands. The beauty of it all was that he was a true believer. He didn't want money. I think he enjoyed the thrill of it all. Most arms dealers you work with are untrustworthy. They are always willing to sell you out to the highest bidder. Taylor was different. After we established trust with him we knew we had a great asset."

The UVF were so pleased with Taylor and Wright's contribution to the cause that they were invited over to Northern Ireland in October 1986. While in the Province both men were taken to Belfast City Hall to discuss the receipt of a new arms shipment they were planning to send over.

The meeting took place in an ante-room in the City Hall shortly after the two Canadians had a conversation with the then Lord Mayor, Sammy Wilson of the Democratic Unionist Party. At the time Taylor, Wright and Wright's girlfriend were staying with the Lord Mayor's chauffeur, Alan McIvor.

Sammy Wilson recalled speaking with the two Canadian arms smugglers, although he denies he knew what they were up to. "I remember Alan McIvor asking me to meet a number of people. I can't really remember much detail about them but I agreed to meet them." Wilson remembered that McIvor's wife, who has relatives in Canada, was herself later implicated in the court case which signalled the end of the Toronto connection.

The shipments of arms came at a crucial time for the UVF, given the upsurge in paramilitary violence after the Anglo-Irish Agreement. John Bingham played a pivotal role in renewed UVF activity in Belfast. He also had a key position in helping to pack some of the weapons Taylor had hidden in tractor engines which were sent on to Northern Ireland. A few weeks after a trip to Canada Bingham was murdered at his home by the Provisional IRA. The UVF then obtained information that one of those suspected of his murder had gone to live in Canada. Discussions were held with Taylor about the possibility of tracking him down and killing him on Canadian soil. The revenge plot, however, came to nothing as the Canadian link was about to be broken.

On Christmas Day 1986 the Royal Canadian Mounted Police raided Taylor's home. They had been acting on a tip-off. Inside the house they found a shipment of arms including five Ingram sub-machine guns, six Armalite rifles, a number of handguns and at least 10,000 rounds of ammunition. As well the guns they uncovered weapons manuals and a briefcase containing parts for a Mach 10 sub-machine gun under Taylor's bed. As the Mounties ripped Taylor's house apart they came across a chemical mace gun, tear gas canisters, bullet-proof vests and a book about Protestants being killed in Ulster. They also found a set of negatives and raw film. When these were processed the Mounties saw pictures of Taylor and Wright, along with a number of others dressed in paramilitary uniforms, carrying machine-guns under the flag of the UVF.

The arms-smuggling network had been betrayed from within. The tip came from one of Taylor's girlfriends who in subsequent court hearings was referred to only as Linda. Taylor was caught in a spurned lover's pincer movement, for besides Linda his ex-wife Gayle also started to talk. As the Mounties probed further they exposed a web of intrigue which stretched across the Atlantic from the quiet suburbs of Toronto out to Liverpool in England and ultimately to Belfast. The UVF had used Liverpool as their mid-way point for shipping arms from Canada to Northern Ireland once the Glasgow route had been compromised. In a security operation the combined forces of the Mounties, the RUC and the Lancashire police force discovered that a Liverpool businessman, Trevor Cubbon, was also implicated in the conspiracy. Cubbon, a director of a road haulage firm, was arrested and charged with importing the shipments of arms and ammunition. He admitted that he had been asked to take delivery of a consignment of weapons being transported to Belfast from Canada.

In Belfast the RUC picked up Albert Watt three weeks after the initial raid on Taylor's home. Watt, a native of Belfast, had emigrated to Ontario where he remained committed to the loyalist cause. After he was arrested he confessed that his truck was to be used to transport the guns that Taylor was assembling at his Toronto home prior to the Mounties' raid on Christmas Day.

Things were rapidly falling apart, with several of the conspirators on both sides of the Atlantic starting to talk. Wright signed a statement which revealed his extensive contacts with loyalists in Belfast. He described the trip to Northern Ireland in October 1986.

His detailed revelations showed that he was not the usual type of loyalist abroad. "The Anglo-Irish Agreement. That was my prime motivation for going to Ireland. I had studied Northern Ireland, and in particular in university, and written a paper on it," he said in conversations with the Canadian police.

Then he told his interrogators that he met two men allegedly in the UVF leadership. One of the UVF men had just been released after the collapse of the Supergrass system. Wright described his trip to Belfast and the meeting with Sammy Wilson.

"Prior to meeting them I had been introduced to the Lord Mayor of Belfast, spoke with him for perhaps ten or fifteen minutes on various aspects of the economy and developing the tourist industry, believe it or not, in Belfast." When pressed by the Mounties about his trip to Belfast, Wright finally cut to the chase and revealed his real intention.

"We had dinner in the company of Alison Spibey and Bill Taylor on another occasion while we were in Belfast." Wright was then asked if during that discussion the subject of guns being provided from Canada to the UVF was raised. His reply was categoric. "I got the impression that that was a definite possibility," Wright told the Mounties.

The conspirators were not tried until September 1988, with "Linda" and Gayle Taylor testifying against the accused. A month later Bill Taylor was sentenced to three and a half years in prison for his part in the gun-running plot. Wright meanwhile was also found guilty and received five years. He did manage to beat another rap for illegally exporting guns and ammunition in late 1986, because the weaponry never actually left Canada.

When Taylor was freed he was then extradited to England in 1992 to serve another year for his part in the Liverpool side of the arms network. Watt and Cubbon had by this time already served their four-year prison sentences. On his release a year later Taylor returned to Canada and merged back into the gun freak fraternity. As far as the UVF was concerned his days of smuggling arms to Northern Ireland were over. Taylor had lived for and thrived on guns. It was no great surprise that he met his end at the end of a gun. In 1995 he was shot dead in a bar-room brawl in Toronto. One of Taylor's friends, James Hill, was charged with the murder. The UVF on learning of his death paid this tribute to Taylor in the April 1995 edition of *Combat*:

"We have lost a friend who had no hesitation doing what he saw was his duty and for this Ulster will remain forever in his debt. Breathes there a man with soul so dead, who never to himself hath said. This is my own, my native land."

Taylor was driven by a fanatical hatred of communism. Other anti-communists around the world have also seen the

Northern Ireland conflict as a simple struggle between the Soviet-backed IRA and the right-wing freedom loving loyalists. The true picture of course is much more complex.

The connections between loyalists and fascists in Britain and further afield have been exaggerated by sections of the British left. Far-left apologists for the Provisional IRA have been only too quick to equate Loyalism with neo-nazism. They forget that many UVF members and their families have long-standing links with the British army, and some UVF men's fathers fought and died against Hitler in the Second World War. Ulster loyalists are also keen to point out the clear collusion between the old IRA under Sean Russell and the Nazi dictatorship during World War Two.

When neo-fascist groups did establish links with loyalists, it was always at the former's iniative and produced nothing but embarrassment for the UVF. In the early years the modern UVF was a politically confused creature. The bulk of its members would have been at home in the British Labour Party had they grown up on the other side of the Irish Sea. A smaller number were working-class Tories who were tied into a conservative network of Orange halls, Masonic orders and Evangelical sects. An even smaller number flirted with the political extremes of right and left. As one founding UVF member who joined up in the late 1960s put it: "The UVF was a broad alliance. There were communists, fascists, liberals, Tories, democratic socialists. All kinds of people. They were only united on two things – defending their communities and ultimately the union."

This political confusion was reflected in the pages of *Combat*. In the early 1970s, the UVF faced constant charges of being tainted with communism and socialism. These allegations came from three quarters. Firstly there was the extreme fundamentalist unionists, especially those who emerged from the wreckage of TARA. These claims were compounded by the rival UDA, who also alleged the UVF was moving too far to the left. The UDA pointed in particular to the growing relationship and mutual respect between UVF prisoners and the Marxist Official IRA inside Long Kesh. Finally the loyalist reds-under-the beds scare was fanned further by sections of British intelligence working out of British Army headquarters in Lisburn.

There was little or no truth to these accusations. Nevertheless they allowed right-wing elements inside the UVF to propagate their views in *Combat*. The climate of paranoia opened the door to fascists within the UVF. It was clear that by mid-1974 those in control of *Combat* had extreme rightist inclinations. The April 1974 edition of *Combat* welcomed the establishment of National Front branches in Belfast. It read:

"*Combat* wishes every success to the National Front in Northern Ireland and trust it can grow from strength and be of assistance to Ulster." Bizarrely the same edition of the magazine praising the racist NF ran a lead article criticising religious bigotry under the title "Sectarianism, who stands to gain?"

The following month, still stung by the communist slur, the UVF magazine ran a piece lifted straight from the NF magazine *Spearhead*. The feature detailed the "evils of communism" in the Soviet bloc.

On the basis of the light strain of fascist sympathies within the UVF, the far left in Britain and Ireland have jumped to the conclusion that the loyalist terror group was connected into the network of Euronazi groups on the continent. This was based on a simple reductionism. If the IRA was anti-imperialist then loyalists must be right-wing and reactionary. The truth is that the relationship between the UVF and fascist terror groups was always one-way, the latter invariably approaching the former.

UVF leaders stress that British fascist organisations are regarded with distrust and hostility. The European neo-nazi groups were also fanatical but with one vital difference –

they at least had access to arms and more importantly explosives.

Just before Christmas in 1980 representatives of the fascist Flemish Military Order (VMO) came to Belfast and asked to speak with the UVF. The Belgian neo-nazis had taken an interest in Northern Ireland since the start of the Troubles. At one time the VMO supported the IRA and invited Sinn Féin members to their annual political rally. The VMO was vehemently anti-British as well as deeply anti-semitic. Around the end of the 1970s this crackpot fascist organisation changed its policy on Ireland. It switched to backing the loyalist cause against an imagined communist IRA.

The VMO envoys offered the UVF guns and explosives. The fascist terror group had a frightening arsenal of weapons stored up illegally in Belgium to defend the Flemish people in the event of some racialist doomsday. According to UVF members who agreed to meet the VMO, the Belgian nazis took a keen interest in the loyalist's ability to manufacture their own guns. Since 1969 the expertise gleaned in the North's heavy engineering industries has been used to make thousand of home-made rifles and sub-machine guns. Indeed several large arms factories have been discovered by the RUC, including one which was operating under the cloak of a light engineering works and actually received a government grant.

Despite their reservations the UVF agreed to see what the VMO had on offer. Three men, including the supergrass Joe Bennet and the late Jackie Irvine, travelled to Antwerp to have further discussions with the Belgian group. In his testimony during the Supergrass trials Bennet described the Antwerp meeting. "This Nazi character asked us if we would be interested in bombing targets on the British mainland – Jewish targets – in exchange for guns and explosives. Jackie Irvine said it was not the policy to bomb that type of target and he would have to take it back to his brigade staff."

This lunatic request, for the UVF to attack Jewish people in

218

Britain, effectively killed off any link-up between them and the VMO. When the three UVF representatives left Belgium they had promised the VMO that they would come back with £50,000 for guns and explosives. The money was never paid. The UVF's brigade staff said the VMO's request for an anti-Jewish bombing campaign was totally unacceptable.

"We knew these guys, the VMO, were real loopers when our lads who went out told us about the place they met them in. It was at the back of a bar where there was a picture of Adolf Hitler flanked by two black candles. The suggestion that we attack Jews was the last straw."

The VMO's wish was particularly incongruous given the strong strain of support within loyalism for the state of Israel. Many UVF members and their supporters associate the plight of Ulster Protestants surrounded by nationalists on the island of Ireland to that of the Israelis swamped in a sea of Arabs in the Middle East. The admiration for Israel's exploits in the 1970s battle against terrorism was so great that the UVF even approached members of the Jewish community in Belfast to ask they could get loyalists some assistance from Israel including arms. Wisely the Jews rejected the UVF overtures, preferring to remain absolutely neutral in the Irish conflict.

But the fact that the UVF was at one time willing to petition Israel for support while later on trying to get guns from European fascists once again shows that the search for weapons abroad is an ideologically-free one. A founding member of the UVF said that his organisation cared little whom they bought weapons from as long the operation was free from penetration by the security services.

There has been some "on the ground" cross-over between fascists in Northern Ireland and the UVF and UDA. In the early 1980s, with the revival of the Skinhead sub-culture in the UK, many young Belfast Protestants joined the NF and the British National Party. Some of those later associated with the UDA's Second Battalion were originally nazi skinheads who took part in NF rallies in Belfast. In April 1983 three young Shankill Road men who referred to themselves as "NF SKINZ" were jailed for killing a young Catholic man, Patrick Barkley, at a derelict flat in the area.

During the early 1980s the NF had around 200 members, most of whom were teenage skinheads. By the end of the decade the organisation faded away. The NF and other fascist groups won little support in loyalist communities. In 1987 for instance the local NF leader David Kerr (a close associate of Ulster Unionist councillor and fundamentalist Nelson McCausland) gained just twenty-seven votes in a by-election in Newtonabbey. The demise of the NF was hastened by the growing hostility of the UVF towards neo-nazi gangs. In 1989 the UDA had ordered the NF to shut down its offices in Templemore Avenue in east Belfast. Five years later the UVF threatened another neo-nazi group, Combat 18, which was also attempting to organise in the east of the city. Combat 18, a collection of nazi Hitler-loving crackpots, had also tried to organise at Queen's University. But the organisation was not exactly true to its own militaristic name and offered no combat at all against the UVF threat.

By the mid-1980s the UVF and its allied party the Progressive Unionists, were already moving away from the extreme right. In July 1986 *Combat* reported a meeting between representatives of the African National Congress and the PUP in Belfast. Much to the chagrin of the neo-nazis the PUP declared that they now supported Black majority rule and an end to the racist apartheid regime.

The PUP's public opposition to the old South African regime appeared at variance with the attitudes of other loyalists to Pretoria. In 1985 the UDA leadership sent army agent Brian Nelson to South Africa. While there, Nelson met up with Ulster-born Richard Wright who showed him a full warehouse of weaponry. Nelson returned to Northern Ireland and informed the UDA what the South Africans wanted. At

220

the time the Pretoria dictatorship was engaged in a desperate war with Angolan and Cuban troops. South African soldiers were pitted against the well-armed Cubans who were supported by modern Soviet MiG 23 jets. On the ground the South African army lacked a reliable air defence missile system to combat the MiGs. In one infamous incident in 1987, eleven South African troops were killed when their armoured vehicles were caught in the open and attacked by Cuban pilots flying MiGs. After that debacle the South African state-owned arms industry, Armscor, decided to seek out and steal an effective western-built missile defence system. Armscor's eyes turned to Shorts, the Belfast aerospace company which had just won a British army contract for "Starstreak" – a supersonic missile system guided by the most up-to-date electronics on the international arms market.

Richard Wright went back to Northern Ireland and met one of the UDA's top officers at the time in his east Belfast home. Wright offered to supply guns but stressed that he was only willing to accept a deal worth a quarter of a million pounds or more. In addition Wright told the UDA that South Africa wanted missile technology from Shorts. If loyalists could steal missile parts or the blueprints for such weapons, this would be regarded as acceptable currency for weapons from South Africa.

Over the next two years there were several bungled attempts to steal missile parts from Shorts. By this stage the two main loyalist terror groups had joined forces to secure a huge arms shipment from abroad. They were also offered some assistance from Ulster Resistance, a mainly rural-based militia, formed originally by loyalist politicians including Ian Paisley and Peter Robinson to combat the Anglo-Irish Agreement. (Paisley later insisted he had no idea that other members of the UR were engaged in illegal activity and had linked with the UVF and UDA.)

The desire to import huge arms shipments into Northern

Ireland reflected deeper political concerns among loyalism's leadership in the mid to late 1980s. One of the prime movers behind the deal with South Africa was John McMichael. The UDA leader was convinced that the only way to save Northern Ireland from creeping Dublin rule was for loyalists to stage a coup d'etat. McMichael therefore set up the Ulster Defence Force, the auxiliary wing of the UDA. He envisaged that the UDF would become a mass army, enabling the loyalists to seize power to put down any nationalist rebellion. Naturally such a mass army would require weapons. McMichael became so enthusiastic about the idea that he even planned to appoint the DUP's deputy leader, Peter Robinson, and the late Upper Bann Ulster Unionist MP, Harold McCusker, as leaders of the new UDI-style government. (Needless to say Robinson and McCusker were flummoxed when told of McMichael's plans for their futures!)

The UVF's reasons for seeking new arsenals abroad at this time were somewhat less grandiose. Their leadership simply wanted to create enough violence to destabilise the North and make the Anglo-Irish Agreement unworkable. They were less than enthusiastic about the idea of a coup.

Unable to steal missile parts, the three loyalist groups decided to raise the money which Wright said they needed to buy guns. In June 1987 the UVF staged a daring bank robbery in Portadown which netted more than £300,000. The loyalists then sent representatives back to Richard Wright who in turn put them in touch with an international arms dealer, Douglas Bernhart. Bernhart, an American citizen who had worked for Armscor, had long-standing connections with other arms traffickers across Europe and the Middle East.

Bernhart then passed the loyalists down the chain towards a Lebanese Christian arms dealer, Joe Fawzi. The UVF, UDA and UR (Ulster Resistance) were promised 200 Czech-made AK47 rifles, Browning pistols, a small cache of RPG-7 rockets and warheads and Soviet-made hand grenades. The weapons had actually been captured from one of the IRA's old Third World heroes, the PLO. They had fallen into Lebanese Christian hands after the PLO were ejected from south Lebanon by the Israelis during the 1982 invasion. The deal was signed with Fawzi at a meeting in Cyprus. He then shipped the weapons to Northern Ireland in crates marked as containing ceramic tiles. The vessel taking the deadly cargo came out of the southern port of Naquoora which ironically is right beside the headquarters of the United Nations peacekeeping force in Lebanon. Since the Irish Army had sent a battalion to the UN mission, including a detachment of troops to the headquarters, it is likely that the guns for the UVF sailed past Irish soldiers living at the UN camp beside the port. No doubt that brought a few smiles to the faces of loyalists involved in the deal.

The consignment arrived in Belfast docks in December 1987 and in the following weeks the weapons were split three ways. Some of those on the UVF side of the deal were getting increasingly nervous about security. "Everybody seemed to know about it. The whole thing was so transparent that I started to worry if it had been infiltrated from the beginning," one UVF man said.

His suspicions were justified. On January 8, 1988, Davy Payne, a long-standing UDA veteran with a violent sectarian record, was stopped in a car on the Mahon Road outside Portadown. The police found sixty-one rifles, more than 120 rifle magazines, more than 11,000 rounds of ammunition and 150 hand grenades concealed inside the car. A court was later told that there were enough weapons in Payne's possession to supply a small army. Within hours of his arrest removal vans arrived at the home of another UDA man in west Belfast. He and his family were spirited out of the country. The message was clear – he had betrayed Payne. There was, however, a list of other candidates who could have compromised the Lebanon shipment. They included the late Tommy "Tucker"

Lyttle who was still the UDA's west Belfast battalion when the guns came in. Lyttle acted as an agent for RUC Special Branch and had managed to provide information which effectively hampered the UDA terror campaign.

The RUC and British army both knew that the Lebanon shipment had come into Northern Ireland. Both loyalist and security sources admit that the weapons were allowed to reach the Province. The UVF themselves believe the object of the undercover RUC operation was to catch the conspirators inside the Province. One of those central to the conspiracy concluded that the UVF and Ulster Resistance managed to slip through the net, although a significant portion of the guns and ammunition were captured in north Belfast a year later.

Nevertheless the new weapons were used to increase loyalist violence over the next five years. Many of the guns which killed nationalists and Sinn Féin/IRA members came from the Lebanese shipment. Moreover, a third of the weaponry has never been used. The arms taken by Ulster Resistance remain secreted in arms dumps in North Armagh although the UVF's mid-Ulster brigade can have access to this arsenal.

Ulster Resistance also maintained contacts with arms dealers working for the South African regime. On April 11, 1989, three UR members, Noel Little, a former UDR man, Samuel Quinn, a sergeant in the Territorial Army and Jim King were arrested in Paris by French intelligence agents. The trio had been attempting to set up another arms deal with a South African diplomat, Daniel Storm, in a Parisian hotel when the French pounced. Parts of a Blowpipe ground to air missile together with an electronic guidance system were seized. Missile parts and blue prints for the Blowpipe had been stolen from a TA base in Newtonards in Co Down the previous week.

The French with the aid of MI5 had been tracking Quinn, Little and King for several weeks. The arrests smashed the connection between Armscor and UR. Douglas Bernhart later confessed that Armscor saw Shorts in Belfast as a prime target for South Africa in its clandestine search to gain missile technology for the Angolan war. The Paris debacle caused further embarrassment for the DUP leader Ian Paisley. One of the Paris three, Noel Little, was commandant and chief marshal for Ulster Resistance when it was founded in 1986. Dr Paisley and his deputy Peter Robinson were also prominent at UR's foundation. The DUP leader actually led the first march of about 1,000 supporters in Co Down. At the head of the march was Noel Little.

The UVF insists to this day that unlike UR, their organisation established no formal links with the South African regime. After the interception of the UDA tranche of the 1987 shipment and the Paris arrests, the UVF decided to distance itself from any dealing with apartheid's agents.

The UDA took a different view. The largest loyalist terror group continued to try and court Pretoria in a further bid to get arms from the racist state. South African agents offered the UDA information on dissidents they alleged were working as links between the ANC and IRA. A dirty tricks operation by South African spies in their London embassy resulted in a murder bid on an academic who had been living in Belfast since 1976. South African-born lecturer Adrian Guelke was shot in his bed by UDA gunmen who broke into his home in the city's university area on September 5, 1991.

Guelke survived the shooting because one of the guns used in the attack jammed. He later claimed that he had been set up by BOSS, the South African secret service. The UDA had got the wrong man. The real target was another South African working in Belfast who did help the IRA arrange an arms shipment. Guelke was ironically an opponent of political violence in Northern Ireland. He was simply the victim of the UDA's incompetence and BOSS's sinister intent.

The South African connection to the UVF has been grossly exaggerated. In 1992 the visit of the UVF's mid-Ulster commander, known as the Jackal, sparked a wave of media hysteria. There were reports that the Jackal was linking up with racist extremists to establish another arms shipment. The reason in fact for his trip was more prosaic. He had made two previous journeys to South Africa in 1983 and 1984 to visit relatives who had emigrated there. By this time anyway the UVF was turning its attention to new arms bazaars.

After the Berlin Wall fell and communist regimes collapsed across eastern Europe, anarchy reigned throughout the former Soviet bloc's armed forces. The UVF had established relations with English arms dealers. They had linked up with the English criminals since the mid-1980s, when a member of the UVF in Mid-Ulster helped Dublin criminals "fence-off" stolen paintings, including a number of Dutch masters. This odd relationship involving southern criminals, the mid-UVF man and English criminal gangs, involved in every kind of shady deal from art theft to gunrunning, was one of the UVF's key routes to weapons in the 1990s.

According to one of the RUC's most senior officers, the central figure for UVF operations abroad is a businessman from east Belfast. He runs a tight team of activists. The openings to arms dealers are made by the mid-Ulster UVF which has a relationship with the English criminals. Once the introductions are made the east Belfast team take over. The connections into Eastern Europe were made around 1991 when several UVF men travelled to Poland. They were shown around a factory which contained massive amounts of weapons including guns, ammunition, grenade launchers and large stocks of plastic explosives.

The UVF was impressed by what their men saw and agreed to pay out a quarter of a million pounds for a shipment. The arsenal included two tonnes of plastic explosive, thousands of detonators, hundreds of AK47 rifles and phosphorous grenades.

The weapons, however, were never destined to reach Northern Ireland. British intelligence along with their Polish counterparts had known of the transaction and tracked the shipment from Gdansk to Teesport in England. On November 24, 1993, at the height of the loyalist terror campaign, the shipment was intercepted. The Teeside Police put on display the weapons which according to one report would have "tipped the military balance" towards the UVF.

There were reports in the Irish media the next day that the whole Teesport find had been an MI5 propaganda ploy and that the British wanted to use the arms shipment to "scare off" Dublin from supporting the Hume-Adams initiative. The proposition was that the sight of a vast loyalist arsenal including explosives and detonators would be enough to throw the Irish government off course.

It is clear MI5 knew about the Polish arms deal, but the real reason for its interception at Teesport relates to what happened to the Lebanese arms shipment in 1987, when the RUC had taken a chance and allowed the guns to come into the Province. Their aim had been to arrest the key players involved with the guns in the North. It was no accident, for instance, that the RUC even provided broadcasting organisations with video footage of the AK47s found in Davy Payne's car. However, the RUC operation was far from a success. The UVF and UR guns got through. This time they were taking no chances with the Polish shipment which was much larger than the previous one. It should also be remembered that the UVF had sought out arms from Poland two years before the Teesport shipment, well before the Hume-Adams process was publicly underway.

Meanwhile, the UDA was also busy in Eastern Europe, searching across the former Soviet bloc for arms to buy. Senior RUC officers believe the UDA may have been more successful. Wire taps from conversations by members of the UDA's Inner Council suggested that the terror group had managed to import a shipment on the same scale as Teesport at the end of 1993. UDA leaders were heard to boast that their weapons and explosives had got through despite the

UVF's failure. This was a matter of ongoing concern for the RUC through 1994. Indeed the UDA shipment was one of the main items on the agenda at the ill-fated meeting of top intelligence chiefs in Scotland in June 1994. The RUC, MI5 and Military intelligence officers were planning to talk about the UDA response if the British government accepted an IRA ceasefire. The discussions, of course, were never held as all 26 anti-terrorist experts were killed in the Chinook helicopter crash off the Mull of Kintyre.

The leadership of the UVF was not surprised that their Polish weapons route was compromised. They were again at the mercy of arms dealers who had clearly gone to a higher bidder and betrayed their customers.

None of this has stopped the UVF searching for arms and explosives abroad. Recently the organisation toyed with the idea of approaching the Chinese for weapons. It was suggested that UVF members contact the Chinese community in Northern Ireland to ask them to act as conduits in a deal between the loyalists and China's burgeoning arms industries. The idea of the UVF getting guns from Communist China may seem unlikely, but in the murky world of international arms deals ideology is meaningless. The dictatorship in Beijing has sold guns to countries and terrorist groups ideologically opposed to China's brand of Marxism-Leninism. China, for instance, has helped beef up the armed forces of the Islamic Republic of Iran over the last few years despite Teheran's fierce anti-communism.

While nothing has ever come from the proposed Chinese connection, it does again show the lengths organisations such as the UVF are prepared to go to arm themselves. German imperialists, Canadian anti-communists, Belgian neo-nazis, Lebanese Maronites and even Chinese communists have all at one time been or may have been potential allies for the UVF in their search for arms and "friends" across the sea.

## Eight

# JUST ANOTHER SELL-OUT

In their heart of hearts loyalists have always suspected that Britain has an exit strategy. They fear the mandarins at the Foreign Office are devising a long-term scheme to withdraw from Northern Ireland. The process starts with economic pull-out and slowly but surely, through giving Dublin a greater influence, the political link is severed. The long-held belief in a plot to disengage was bolstered on November 15, 1985, when Britain and the Republic signed the Anglo-Irish Agreement. Less than two years before, Margaret Thatcher had rejected the recommendations of the pan-nationalist Forum report with the infamous "Out, Out, Out," dismissal. Now she was in the centre of British power in the North, Hillsborough Castle, signing the accord with the then Taoiseach, Garret FitzGerald.

In unionist eyes Thatcher had committed the ultimate turn-about by giving the Republic a say in the governance of a province she once said was as British as her own Finchley constituency. Another link in the chain connecting the North to the United Kingdom had been broken. In addition Britain was now declaring itself neutral, whereas the Republic's government continued to sponsor Northern nationalism.

It is an axiom of Irish history that in times when the union was perceived to be under threat loyalist violence would increase. In the years following the Anglo-Irish Agreement, the index of murder and intimidation from both the UVF and UDA soared back up to levels not seen since the early to mid-1970s.

In the years just before the Agreement UVF violence had been severely curtailed. In the 1970s the organisation was killing scores of people, sometimes at least one a week, every year. By the early 1980s their murder rate was down to about four to five victims per annum. This was mainly due to the RUC's use of the Supergrass system.

It was not an entirely new weapon for the police to deploy against terrorist organisations. The testimony of informers helped to convict more than twenty UVF activists in East Antrim in 1976. The crucial difference, however, was that the supergrass system allowed paramilitaries to be held solely on the uncorroborated evidence of informers, who betrayed their former comrades for immunity from prosecution or a sharp reduction in their sentences.

The first Supergrass was the Ardoyne IRA man, Christopher Black, who went on to implicate thirty-eight men he alleged were active Provos. Once Black began to bargain the signal was sent to other terrorists who also offered to help the police by selling out their colleagues. The first to turn Supergrass on the loyalist side was Clifford McKeown, a UVF man who agreed to give evidence against twenty-five men, mainly from the mid-Ulster area. They included a young loyalist from Portadown called Billy Wright. They were all held on serious charges including murder.

McKeown changed his mind in mid-July 1982 and refused to give any more evidence. The trial continued and eighteen of the men were eventually convicted, mainly on minor offences. More importantly, McKeown's original decision to co-operate sparked a chain reaction among loyalist remand prisoners who started to offer themselves up as Supergrasses. Two of the key "grasses" in the UVF camp were Joe Bennett and William "Budgie" Allen. Bennett's testimony started in

December 1982 and it painted a fascinating picture of life inside the terror group. He had been arrested in May of that year following a botched armed raid on Killinchy post office in Co Down. An elderly post-mistress, Maureen McCann, was stabbed to death during the robbery. Bennett, who later confessed that he joined the UVF at an Orange Hall in west Belfast in 1972, struck up a deal with the police once he was arrested. He would testify against his former comrades in return for immunity from prosecution, money and re-settlement out of Northern Ireland.

Bennett implicated eighteen suspected UVF men who were charged with a total of seventy offences. The suspects included senior UVF commanders, including the organisation's so-called Brigadier General. They were accused of a vast range of crimes including murder and the importation of arms from Europe and Canada, as well as several bombing attacks against republicans. The majority of those accused by Bennett were held for up to two years on remand inside the Crumlin Road prison, living in cramped Victorian conditions on the same landings as their republican enemies, also incarcerated due to their Supergrasses.

Yet by the end of September 1984 Northern Ireland's judiciary were under severe pressure to abandon the Supergrass system. Lord Justice Lowry admitted in court that it was probable that the accused were important members of the UVF. However, he also ruled that Bennett was not a reliable witness. Most of those accused by Bennett were freed but a small proportion remained in custody. They had the misfortune of being with other UVF supergrasses including William "Budgie" Allen, John Gibson and Joseph Crockard.

Allen implicated forty-seven people on charges totalling up to 226 offences. His testimony also collapsed in 1984 when the judge concluded that he was "totally unreliable". Twenty of the defendants were initially found not guilty.

Later that week another sixteen were freed. The Supergrass system never produced the ultimate result the security forces sought, the smashing of terrorist organisations. All of the loyalist informers' testimony had been judged unsafe. There were nevertheless some important by-products of the system.

It clearly damaged the UVF for several years. One of the immediate results was that the arrest of up to one hundred men put incredible strain on the UVF and its support organisations. Their war chest had been severely drained of funds while the Loyalist Prisoners' Welfare Organisation had to find the funds to support men on remand. In addition the UVF's command structure was disrupted, although according to senior members of the organisation they were able to set in place an emergency leadership within hours of the Supergrass arrests. Time and resources had to be devoted to the long court cases. The security forces had successfully diverted the attention of all the major terrorist organisations away from the day-to-day business of killing and maiming. That didn't stop, but it severely reduced, their ability to cause mayhem.

In the medium term the Supergrass system inadvertently created a huge public intelligence bank of names, addresses and other snippets of information about paramilitary organisations. The UVF in particular, a group normally known for its secrecy, now had a face. For instance John Bingham, who was accused of several serious crimes, publicly denounced the Supergrass system on television outside Crumlin Road courthouse on the day he was released. Two years later Bingham was assassinated by the IRA. Another man identified during the Supergrass period was William "Frenchie" Marchant. On his release he announced he had forgiven Budgie Allen, the man who betrayed him. In 1987 the IRA shot Marchant dead on the Shankill Road.

UVF leaders still believe the system gave the IRA a golden opportunity to pin-point loyalists: "For loyalists it's always easier to compile information on republicans. There are plenty of UDR and policemen who have information about the IRA and INLA. Republicans have less inroads into loyalist areas. So I believe the Provos after the Supergrass system were simply using the lists of names brought out in the Supergrass trials to target loyalists. The IRA and INLA never had that type of information before. Added to that was the fact that republicans were also meeting our people on the landings of Crumlin Road jail every day. They remembered a few faces. I think that must be the Supergrass system's longest legacy," said one UVF leader who escaped the treachery of the Supergrasses.

During the period that their comrades were held on remand, the UVF outside resorted to desperate measures to thwart the Supergrass system. There was a particularly ghoulish plot to poison several of the "paid perjurers", as they became known. UVF supporters managed to steal chemicals from inside Shorts Aerospace factory in east Belfast. The chemicals were then smuggled into the jail with the intent of lacing food eaten by the Supergrasses with the poison. The plot however was abandoned when UVF prisoners tried the poison out in custard: the dessert turned a sickly green colour, alerting potential informants that they were about to be poisoned.

There were even more bizarre incidents inside Crumlin Road courthouse, directly across from the prison. During Budgie Allen's testimony in the witness box, supporters of the accused threw "Trill" birdseed and made bird noises, clearly a reference to Allen's nickname and the fact that he was singing in canary fashion. Outside the court there were daily protests by loyalist women, which were occasionally brightened by the wife of one of the accused walking up and down the Crumlin Road in a huge chicken costume.

The Supergrass system clearly emasculated the UVF's

capability to wage war, especially in the greater Belfast area. Indeed the number of murders and attempted murders decreased dramatically in that period. There were, though, several high profile attacks by the terror group, one of which has never been made public until now.

On March 14, 1984, Gerry Adams, the Sinn Féin President, was travelling in a car with several party colleagues through Belfast city centre after returning from a court case. Gunmen from the Ulster Freedom Fighters, a cover name for the then legal UDA, ambushed Adams and his comrades. Adams was wounded in the neck during the shooting. Among others who escaped death was Bob Murray, a former US marine, who later broke with Adams to help form Republican Sinn Féin. Ironically, the UFF team responsible for the attack were caught just minutes later by a passing UDR patrol in the city centre.

At the same time a group of UVF men had been waiting in a van parked close to the Westlink roundabout which connects the M1 and M2 motorways. They suspected Adams and his entourage would have to go through the roundabout and slow down before driving up the Grosvenor Road and into their west Belfast heartland. The roundabout was also chosen as the venue for the UVF attack because they could easily escape along the Westlink and be back on the Shankill Road within minutes.

The UVF team had special cutting tools at the ready to open the car door once they had shot off the tyres. Then they planned to kill everyone inside. As they waited for Adam's car to arrive they heard a radio report that the Sinn Féin leader had been wounded in a downtown gun attack. The UVF men could not believe it. They had meticulously planned their own attack and had waited patiently in the van parked only yards away from Grosvenor Road RUC station. But it was all in vain. Their erstwhile comrades in the UDA had inadvertently thwarted their attempt to assassinate Adams.

The aborted murder bid shows the clear lack of co-ordination between the two rival loyalist organisations. The UVF believe that their planned operation would have worked. Privately, many senior UVF men were furious that the UFF had spoiled their chances.

Security policy in the early 1980s was dominated by controversy over an alleged shoot-to-kill strategy by the police and army.

Republicans alleged that RUC specialist units were deliberately targeting and killing republican suspects in disputed circumstances, in particular in the north Armagh area. Many of these cases are widely documented and there is solid evidence to suggest that in many of them the police used excessive force. What is not widely reported is that there have been several incidents throughout the Troubles in which the security forces shot dead loyalists in disputed circumstances. On March 16, 1983, 26-year-old Billy Miller from east Belfast was shot dead by RUC officers while travelling in a stolen car along Elmwood Avenue in Belfast's university area. Miller, a UVF man, was on his way with another man to assassinate a number of people he believed were connected with the INLA. But from the very outset the UVF operation was compromised. UVF sources say the RUC knew that Miller was on his way to murder. His car was followed through the university area by undercover detectives. When his car was stopped by police vehicles, the driver ran off. According to a senior RUC detective who ran the anti-terrorist operation, Miller then drew a gun and was shot dead by one of his officers. The question, however, has to be asked – why was Miller not arrested en route rather than closer to the planned murder scene? Whatever the truth of the Miller shooting, it proved that the RUC's specialist anti-terrorist units were prepared to use the same kind of lethal force against loyalists as they did with republicans. The killing also showed that the police had well-placed informants working with the UVF in Belfast.

From the early to mid 1980s the UVF was in the doldrums. At the start of the decade, the growing entente between Margaret Thatcher and Taoiseach Charles Haughey, coupled with the Hunger Strike crisis, created a sense of foreboding within the loyalist family. The UVF expressed their fears about the development of an Anglo-Irish process. They threatened to crank up their war machine again and even publicly demonstrated some of the new weaponry they had received from Canada. Their violence, however, came in sporadic bursts, most of it directed at the general nationalist population. Only occasionally did they strike directly against republicans.

Two killings in the Bawnmore area of Newtonabbey illustrate the differences between selective attacks and random sectarian killings. On October 29, 1983, a UVF unit from the Rathcoole estate shot dead 26-year-old David Nocher while he was cleaning a shop window on the Mill Road near Bawnmore. Nocher was a former internee but had followed the Workers' Party on their long march away from violent nationalism. Clearly if the UVF were going to target active republicans they had not done their homework. Two months later the same UVF unit turned its guns on another Bawnmore resident. This time they shot dead 26-year-old Joe Craven as he left a social security office in Church Road. Craven was a member of the INLA and was given a full paramilitary style funeral.

The UVF was also beset with a creeping paranoia, exacerbated by the Supergrass system because so many activists were being named in court, and subsequently in the pages of Northern newspapers. Their paranoia reached a crescendo on May 17, 1984, when a UVF unit from north Belfast shot and seriously wounded Jim Campbell, the northern editor of *The Sunday World,* outside his home. Campbell was a tenacious and brave journalist, who never shied away from naming those responsible for sectarian murder and terror in the Province. The UVF took exception to this and tried to murder Campbell. His response was to go on working, even editing the Northern edition from his hospital bed while recovering from his wounds. Today the UVF's political representatives court the media and generally have a good working relationship with journalists. They are generally helpful towards the media. It is all a far cry from ten years ago when some inside the UVF were prepared to murder someone for exercising one of the great freedoms the British have always defended – free speech.

Compared to the 1970s, UVF violence had reached a nadir by the 1980s. But just when the organisation seemed down and out, it came off the ropes lashing out ferociously. The collapse of the Supergrass system and the signing of the Anglo-Irish Agreement sparked off a renewed bout of violence which was to last for a decade and once again almost brought Northern Ireland to the brink of outright civil war.

The sharp growth in loyalist terror during the greatest loss of collective unionist confidence since Stormont collapsed was compounded by other inter-related events. The Provisional IRA's arsenal was significantly boosted by huge arms shipments from the Libyan regime, enabling them to launch a more effective campaign at home and abroad. A new, extremely unpredictable republican splinter group, the Irish People's Liberation Organisation, started to emerge from the chaotic ranks of the INLA. And with hardened paramilitary activists back on the streets after the Supergrass trials collapsed, the conditions were set for a return to war.

In the first uncertain weeks of the Anglo-Irish Agreement the UVF decided to target directly the institutions set up under the accord. One of these was a team of Irish civil servants established in Maryfield on the outskirts of east Belfast, near the suburban coastal town of Holywood. Their job was to monitor complaints and grievances from the nationalist community, ranging from fair employment to British security policy. To loyalists, however, Maryfield, set in a Protestant heartland, was the new nerve centre of nationalist encroachment. A decision was taken to destroy it.

A number of elaborate plans were drawn up to kill members of the civil servant team working in the Anglo-Irish Secretariat. One involved driving a proxy bomb into the building and exploding it near offices used by them. The UVF gathered intelligence from its contacts in east Belfast that a business in the area was delivering milk to the Secretariat every morning. They decided to hijack a milk float and then place a bomb on it, drive it through the gates and cause maximum carnage. The idea was abandoned when the UVF leadership concluded that members of the security forces who were tasked to defend the building might be killed or injured. An alternative plan was hatched, involving a mortar bomb which would be fired over the fence into the Secretariat's office. According to a member of the UVF's Brigade Staff the plan was to put a delayed timer on the rockets which would then explode a short period after impact, thus maximising casualties among the civil servants.

But the UVF faced logistical problems. While they had people with the know-how to construct such a device, it would require a number of test firings and thus weeks, maybe months, before they could put the weapon in place. While the UVF debated the pros and cons of this style of attack they were to be sidetracked down another path.

Within a week of the Agreement being signed the UVF and UDA formed an umbrella group called the Ulster Loyalist Front. The new group organised a mass rally into Belfast city centre, attracting about 5,000 people. Many of those who marched to the City Hall wore combat trousers, army jackets, bush hats and dark glasses. As they marched down Royal Avenue in military fashion the citizens of Belfast thought they were flashing back to the previous decade when the UDA was at its height and thousands of angry loyalists were taking to the streets.

The ULF, however, had little success in bridging the gaps in intelligence and co-operation between the two main loyalist groupings. It was to take another six years before the UVF and UDA acted in real unison. Behind the mask of unity lay serious divisions over strategy, personalities and territory.

What did unite the two loyalist groups and also brought together the majority of unionists in the north was a deep hatred of the Anglo-Irish Agreement. Three weeks after it was signed more than 100,000 people took part in a huge anti-Agreement rally in central Belfast. Effigies of Margaret Thatcher and Irish Tricolours were burned. Bellicose speeches were uttered from the steps of City Hall. The booming cry of "never never never" from DUP leader Ian Paisley echoed across Belfast.

Into this stormy political atmosphere stepped loyalist paramilitaries who thought their time had come again, to recruit and renew. Posters depicting men in uniforms with guns and the title "Organise" started to appear on walls in Protestant areas as the UDA tried to boost its ranks. This mass recruitment campaign was not matched by the UVF. They continued to lurk in the shadows preferring to keep their organisation relatively small tight and secretive, as one UVF leader explained:

"Even though the UDA were trying to recruit everybody we didn't do the same. Our aim was to continue to retain the mystique about the UVF. It was the same policy as the early days – no one could be really sure who was in the organisation."

In the very same month the Agreement came into being there was another less noticed but quite significant development, at least by the standards of the paramilitary underworld. A group calling itself the Protestant Action Force

239

issued a statement in *Combat* warning that they would kill a Sinn Féin member every time a UDR soldier was killed. Everyone in Northern Ireland knew the PAF was merely a UVF mask of convenience.

This statement marked the start of a ruthless campaign of violence directed at Sinn Féin by the UVF which was to last almost a decade.

As Sinn Féin expanded politically, its councillors, party activists and representatives were forced to come more into the open. Now the UVF and others had clearer visible republican targets. The warning in *Combat* was a precursor to a vicious and protracted war between republicans and loyalists. (The use of a cover name was not an innovation exclusive to the UVF. Since the early 1970s the UDA had adopted the nom de guerre of Ulster Freedom Fighters when it carried out violent attacks and murder. Republicans also resorted to this. The Provos and the INLA were involved in a number of blatantly sectarian killings under the disguise of groups like the Irish Freedom Fighters, the Republican Reaction Force and the Catholic Reaction Force.)

As 1986 began the agreement continued to be a source of deep discontent within unionism. But despite the unity of opposition demonstrated in the monster rallies against it, the unionists failed to force Britain to abandon the Accord.

Ironically, in the infant months of the agreements the main force holding the line was the Royal Ulster Constabulary. During riots in Protestant areas on the "Day of Action" and strikes called in protest at the Hillsborough Accord, RUC officers actually came under fire from the UVF. Even worse was to come for the force.

The police were called upon to defend the gates of Maryfield from violent loyalist protesters and later, to implement a number of policies drawn up under the Agreement. At the start of the 1986 marching season, nationalist pressure managed to persuade the British government to reroute a number of traditional loyalist marches from passing through Catholic areas. The main pressure point, the first test of the Agreement's practical effectiveness, came in Portadown. An Apprentice Boys parade was banned from passing down the Catholic Tunnel area of the town on Easter Monday, March 31, 1986. Violent clashes broke out between loyalist marchers and police officers in riot gear blocking the entrance into the area. In two days of rioting a 20-year-old protester, Keith White, was killed by a plastic bullet. His death signalled a campaign of violence directed at the RUC by loyalists, primarily the UVF in mid-Ulster.

By May 2, fifty homes belonging to police officers had been attacked with petrol bombs, stones and in some cases bullets. The attacks were not conducted by the RUC's traditional enemies but by people who were supposedly on their side. Graffiti started to appear in Protestant areas which mimicked a television advertisement at the time for a brand of coal. It stated: "Come home to a real fire – join the RUC".

Even in the early days of the anti-Agreement campaign the UVF had issued a statement challenging members of the Northern Ireland civil service, the UDR and RUC, to "join the resistance". They warned members of the security forces in particular that "if you are not for us then you are against us". Those officers who failed to fall in line with that kind of thinking paid a severe personal price in attacks on them, their families and their homes.

The spring and summer of 1986 marked an interesting sea change in political relationships within the northern Protestant community. Scenes of loyalists attacking police officers from their own community in violent clashes were transmitted around the world. The gap between many in the RUC and those in the wider unionist community widened. UVF leaders to this day believe the carefully orchestrated attacks on police officers' homes in this period produced results. They point to the large number of RUC reservists who resigned from the force in protest at having to implement Anglo-Irish policies they themselves cared little for. It is true in some cases that police officers even stripped off their uniforms in public in open rebellion at what they were being asked to do. Others, however, preferred to do their duty.

Moreover, the implications of loyalist paramilitaries attacking police homes probably proved disastrous to the anti-Agreement campaign. Many middle-class unionists became alienated from the increasingly violent turn of events. Most unionist people in the North are by nature generally law-biding and would think it their moral and civic duty to support "their" police force in a time of crisis. The choice for them was simple – the police or the paramilitaries behind the scene. The vast majority plumped for the former option. This choice illuminates a wider problem for organisations like the UVF. The loyalist paramilitary essentially competes with the policeman or UDR soldier for the support of the general Protestant population. In general, ordinary unionists will normally support the legitimate pro-state forces as opposed to underground armies like the UVF.

But in this critical period for unionism, alienation between the poorer sections of the Protestant community and the security forces deepened. One of the worst black spots was the Ballysillan area of north Belfast. After clashes between the RUC and loyalist youths, the local UVF unit placed a landmine on a road leading into the estate. The fact that the UVF were willing to murder policemen in the same fashion as the Provisional IRA demonstrated the growing hostility between sections of the loyalist population and the police.

But the focus of the Ballysillan UVF was mainly concentrated on the Catholic population of north Belfast. In the months leading up to the Anglo-Irish Agreement the UVF killed two people, both of whom were Protestants, in internal loyalist disputes. However, from a period from mid-January 1986 to late July of that year the UVF went on the rampage, killing seven people, all of them Catholics with the exception of one Protestant woman married to a Catholic. The murder spree started with the death of Catholic nightwatchman Leo Scullion, who was shot dead outside Ligoneil, to the death of 28-year-old taxi driver Martin Duffy outside the Chester Park Hotel on the Antrim Road on July 19. Most of those murdered in these months if not all, had little or no connection to republican organisations. They were killed, it seems, simply because they were soft, available Catholic targets.

The rationale behind this murder campaign was chilling, according to a senior member of the UVF. "It was the old tactic of terrorising the terrorist and his community. By killing Catholics the pressure would be put on the IRA. Ordinary Catholics would realise the Provos could not defend them." This UVF member said he disagreed with this blunt and brutal tactic. He preferred that the organisation selectively choose its targets and go for prestigious republican hits. While this latter strategy may have been the preference of older UVF members, who realised the national and international damage caused by episodes like the Butcher killings, younger elements were going for the first option. Most of the killings in the first half of 1986 were carried out by men described by loyalist sources at the time as having an average age of about twenty. Indeed some of those involved in the north Belfast killing squads were the sons of men convicted of violent loyalist activity in the early 1970s. This new generation of killers was inducted through the loyalist blood and thunder band culture and then into the junior UVF. From there, they "progressed" to full UVF status. This came about due to their willingness to carry out the north Belfast killings. Many of them were instructed not to return without having killed someone, even if they missed their intended republican targets. This policy explained the randomness of the murder campaign. These young men cared little for the politically sophisticated game of armed propaganda.

In this murderous period pressure mounted within nationalist areas of Belfast on republicans to hit back. One chilling piece of graffiti on walls in the New Lodge Road area stated that "We need another Darkley" – a reference to the INLA's killing of three Protestant men at a church hall in the Co Armagh village in 1983, shortly after the UVF shot dead an IRSP member in Armagh city.

By mid-summer 1986 the Provos saw a chance to step in and portray themselves as the defenders of north Belfast nationalists, hitting back directly at the UVF. On Saturday night, September 14, an IRA unit sledgehammered their way into the home of John Bingham in Ballysillan Crescent.

Bingham almost escaped his killers. He ran up his staircase towards a security door fitted onto the upstairs hallway. But just he reached it, the Provos opened fire, hitting him in the back

The Bingham killing was a major coup for the Provisionals. They had just murdered the leader of the Ballysillan UVF, a man centrally involved in the six-month assassination campaign in the city. But the circumstances leading up to Bingham's death were unusual and begged many questions about UVF members' personal security. He was known to have been extremely careful about his movements. He shifted from one house to another and had only returned home from his family's caravan in Millisle on the North Down coast the very same afternoon. UVF leaders were puzzled as to how the Provos had known Bingham was back at home.

One of his close confidants said there were numerous theories as to how the IRA were able to target him that day. "One suggestion was that John's involvement with pigeon fancying might have led to his death. We got an anonymous letter saying he was set up by someone in that fraternity. He only returned, in fact, to Ballysillan Crescent because of his pigeons. But the truth is we never had hard and fast information as to who exactly was involved. When there's a shooting in Belfast of a loyalist or a policeman you would always get a fair bit of information as to who did it. Many of the shootings between the UVF in the Shankill and the IRA in Ardoyne were very personal. You normally got a name to an operation. But with John it was different. The Provos seemed to have kept that very tight."

One theory (or perhaps rumour is a better term) was that a former IRA commander in Ardoyne who spent time in Crumlin Road jail during the Supergrass period carried out the killing. But those in the UVF who investigated the shooting admit to this day that they were never sure who was responsible. They did, of course, try, and one bizarre intelligence-gathering operation illustrated their uncertainty about who killed Bingham.

"We heard that the O/C of the Provos in Ardoyne was signing on at the dole in Belfast City Centre. So I went down with a guy who said he'd spotted him there. He thought he's seen the fellah and pointed him out. Then he wasn't so sure he could make out it was him. I got frustrated and said to the fellah sarcastically 'sure all the taigs look the same anyway.'"

The lack of knowledge didn't discourage Bingham's comrades in Ballysillan from seeking revenge. Two days after Bingham was killed, a UVF unit attacked a couple in the grounds of Holy Cross Catholic Church on the Crumlin Road facing Ardoyne. In a ferocious attack they forced the woman to watch as they beat and then shot 33-year-old Raymond Mooney dead. Mr Mooney and his companion had just left a church meeting. They were innocent victims of blood-thirsty revenge-seekers.

An even more disturbing aspect of this killing was the role

of a democratically-elected politician calling for revenge just hours after John Bingham's death. George Seawright – who was murdered the following year by the IPLO – had a reputation as a loudmouth loyalist firebrand. The independent councillor had been expelled from Dr Paisley's DUP after calling for the incineration of Catholics. The Scots-born rabble-rouser had been on television just after the Anglo-Irish Agreement was signed, jumping on the car belonging to Tom King, the then Secretary of State, at Belfast City Hall. This kind of antic earned Seawright a reputation as a political clown. But there was also a more sinister sectarian side to his politics. By publicly calling for vengeance after Bingham was murdered (the two had been close friends) Seawright created an atmosphere in which elements within the UVF were willing to seek out a victim. Raymond Mooney paid the ultimate price for such dangerous talk.

The death of John Bingham, however, failed to end the sectarian warfare erupting in Belfast. Instead it triggered a mini-war between the UVF and the Provisionals in which the battlegrounds were north and south-east Belfast. This battle would be a series of score-settling operations in which unconnected civilians would be caught up.

One UVF leader believed that the conflict that was emerging with the Provos over the next two years had a wider agenda: "I'm a bit of a conspiracy theorist. We were busy organising ourselves against the Anglo-Irish Agreement. Then suddenly we found ourselves side-tracked in a war with the Provos. It must have been very convenient for the government to have that."

The UVF-IRA conflict continued into the spring of the following year. It was being fought out in an increasingly violent atmosphere. The UDA placed incendiary devices in stores in Co Donegal and Dublin, marking a renewed offensive by the rival loyalist terror group. Meanwhile, the IRA was secretly boosting its arsenal with huge shipments of guns, ammunition, rocket launchers, heavy machine guns, surface-to-air missiles and Semtex explosive. By the end of 1986 the Provos had enough weapons to arm two infantry battalions. During this period the IRA kept up its onslaught not only on the security forces but on judges, their wives and civilian contractors working for the police and army.

While republicans and their sympathisers in the media have always portrayed these attacks, even those on civilians, as not sectarian, loyalists view them very differently. They are seen as simply an attack on the general population of the north. The UVF reciprocated with equal terror.

On April 2, 1987, two UVF members carrying an automatic shot-gun and a Browning pistol went to the house of Larry Marley in Havana Court in Ardoyne. Marley refused to open the door when they knocked, so they fired through the door, killing him instantly. In a terse statement after the killing the UVF said: "Laurence Marley had served a long prison sentence for IRA activities including blackmail, possession of arms and explosives. Upon his release he became re-involved with the organisation and this re-involvement cost him his life."

While the UVF gloated over the death of this north Belfast republican (seen as a direct response to John Bingham's murder a year before) it took time for the organisation to realise just how important Larry Marley was. Up to 6,000 people attended his funeral and many clashed with police officers after the RUC, in an attempt to prevent a paramilitary style funeral, refused to let the coffin leave the Marley home. It was the largest republican funeral since the Hunger Strikes, and it later emerged that Marley had helped to mastermind the Maze breakout and had become a senior figure on the Provos Belfast Brigade. As one UVF commander admitted: "We knew he was a top Provo in Ardoyne but we never realised how respected he was in the movement."

Just over a fortnight after Larry Marley was killed the

conflict widened to west Belfast when the UVF mounted its first serious attack on a Sinn Féin figure in the city after shooting up Alex Maskey's home in Andersonstown. The same day the UDA stole 171 weapons, including sub-machine guns, from a UDR base in Coleraine.

The UVF too benefited from certain UDR soldiers. "Shortly after the Agreement was signed there were loads of offers coming to us from people in the UDR and TA (Territorial Army) who were coming forward with promises of keys to armouries in bases where they worked. Most of the time though these offers of help came to nothing. You had to be careful as well in case you were being set up."

Seeking retaliation for Larry Marley's death, the Provisionals tried to kill the UVF's brigadier general in July. Although a PIRA unit managed to break into his home in the Shankill area, the UVF commander managed to escape injury.

Three weeks later the mini-war claimed another life. The IRA took revenge for Larry Marley by shooting dead William "Frenchie" Marchant outside the Progressive Unionist Party's headquarters on the Shankill Road. Marchant was not a senior figure in the UVF, as some republicans alleged. Close colleagues believe he was probably singled out because he was a known face to the IRA. Marchant, like John Bingham, had spent a considerable period in close proximity to republicans in Crumlin Road jail during the Supergrass trials.

In the following months in 1987 there was a series of attempted killings by both sides in the conflict. In one instance the UVF tried to kill a former IRA prisoner on the Colin Glen Road in west Belfast in June. But already the UVF was starting to turn its attention out of the northern capital towards rural areas. The move from city to country was taken for very simple logistical terrorist reasons. The combined threat of the UVF and a renascent UDA under the leadership of John McMichael put republicans on their guard. Huge sums of money were spent (much of it from the very coffers of the state republicans vowed to destroy) to fortify the homes of IRA and Sinn Féin members. Steel doors were welded onto the bottom of staircases, security cameras were placed strategically outside houses, bullet-proof windows were fixed in place along with a whole range of measures to make paramilitary activists safer in their homes.

One UVF intelligence officer explained the difficulties this posed: "You couldn't lie in Ardoyne in somebody's garden waiting for a Provo to come. In Belfast it would have taken a JCB digger to break into certain Provo homes. But in the country it was easier, their houses were larger, harder to protect, and some of them lived in isolated communities."

The rural UVF campaign, particularly in mid-Ulster, was boosted by gaps in RUC intelligence in the region. Up until the early 1980s the special branch had ran one of the most successful intelligence operations in Northern Ireland. However intensive internal police investigations into the Branch's role in controversial shootings of republicans in the 1980s caused disruption within the force's anti-terrorist units. Paradoxically, then, the very investigations demanded by nationalists indirectly helped loyalists to re-start their violence in mid-Ulster.

This deadly struggle was played out behind a backcloth of wider terror. In November 1987 on Remembrance Sunday the Provos killed eleven civilians at a war memorial in Enniskillen. A month later they killed UDA chief John McMichael by placing a bomb under his car outside his Lisburn home. Despite the worldwide revulsion over the massacre, the IRA plotted to extend their campaign within and without Northern Ireland. At the start of the year it prompted the then RUC Chief Constable Sir Jack Hermon to warn that the Provisionals intended to hike up their violence.

One of their prestige operations was to be a bomb at a British Army band service in Gibraltar. But the three IRA members involved were shot dead by SAS soldiers in controversial circumstances. At the subsequent funerals for the IRA trio a lone loyalist gunman, Michael Stone, attacked mourners. Stone intended to kill leading republicans in a gun and grenade attack. Instead he murdered two civilians and one IRA member. He was later captured in bogland near the M1 motorway by the RUC after escaping from mourners. Stone became a loyalist hero figure. The jacket he wore on the Milltown attack was auctioned, graffiti in Protestant areas praised his deed. The impact of Stone's attack should not be underestimated. His willingness to go into the enemy's heartland, the IRA plot at Milltown on the Falls Road, was admired within the wider loyalist community. Many young loyalists, who were later to become prominent in the UDA, such as Johnny Adair, admitted to the authors that they were inspired by Stone's bravado. (Stone is currently in the Maze prison serving a life sentence.)

Not to be outdone by Stone and the UDA, the UVF continued to organise gun attacks on PIRA activists in Belfast. On May 15, 1987, a UVF unit shot into the Avenue Bar in the city centre close to the *Belfast Telegraph*. The object had been to murder a leading republican from Unity Flats; instead they shot dead three Catholics believed to have been unconnected to the Provisionals. Ironically the UVF almost managed to kill another leading Provo from the same area who was drinking in the bar at the time with the former IRSP councillor, Sean Flynn.

The inter-paramilitary violence between the UVF and PIRA flared up again in June when the Provos shot dead Bobby "Squeak" Seymour at his shop on the Woodstock Road in east Belfast. The killing was the work of an IRA unit drawn from the Markets and Lower Ormeau areas. Shortly after Seymour's death the UVF had hard intelligence as to who pulled the trigger, who gathered the intelligence and who gave the order. Over the summer there were frantic attempts to avenge Seymour's death. He had been a popular figure within loyalist ranks and many UVF members from east Belfast took his death very personally.

An attempt was made on the life of the man who gleaned the information about Seymour outside his home in the Lower Ormeau. Around the same time another leading Provisional who was involved was shot outside a department store in south Belfast but survived. However the UVF were lucky a third time when they went for the IRA's O/C in the area, Brendan "Ruby" Davidson. On the morning of July 25 a UVF unit drove into the Markets area. One of them stepped out of the car and went to Davidson's house in Friendly Way. The UVF man, carrying an AK 47 rifle, was dressed in an RUC uniform. He rapped on Davidson's door and shouted: "It's the Peelers". Given that he was under constant police attention, Davidson believed it was the RUC and opened the safety latch. The UVF member fired several shots striking the Markets IRA O/C in the side of the head, killing him instantly.

A UVF leader who had been close to Seymour explained why Davidson's killer had been dressed as a police officer: "The Markets was a difficult area to get into. There is only one way in and one way out. So the boys dressed up as police officers. The way the UVF got their hands on any police uniform was simple. A peeler would be spotted in a Protestant area handing his uniform into a cleaners. The UVF would then get somebody to steal it or break in and take it. Caps were harder to get. The best way to steal one of them was at a football match or during a riot. Once you had both they were invaluable as the Davidson case proved."

What the UVF didn't know at the time was that the man they had killed was (at least according to senior RUC officers) an important police agent operating for the state within the Belfast IRA. They allege Davidson was working for the security forces at the highest ranks of the Provos. He had been part of an IRA team which launched rocket attacks on RUC vehicles. Republicans, of course, still dismiss this as black propaganda designed to sow mistrust within the ranks of the IRA's Belfast Brigade. They point to Davidson's key role in IRA operations in the city, including his part in a terror unit specialising in rocket attacks on the security forces. But security sources insist Davidson was an important informant for them in the secret war with the IRA.

The UVF are unconcerned as to whether or not Davidson was an informer. They have said they were happy enough to have avenged "Squeak" Seymour's death. One thing is certain, the deaths of Seymour and Davidson illustrate the vindictive and unforgiving nature of the paramilitary world in the north.

After the Anglo-Irish Agreement was introduced, there was little or no political innovation from the ranks of the UVF. They left the political struggle against the Agreement to the established unionist parties. Later they would conclude that the mainstream unionist leaders had let the cause down.

But in the early months of the Agreement the UVF had given considerable help to the Ulster Unionist Party and to a lesser extent the DUP. When the Unionist MPs resigned their seats and fought by-elections which they turned into referendums on the Anglo-Irish Agreement, the UVF lent its logistical support. In a letter published in the March issue of *Combat* the North Belfast MP Cecil Walker thanked the UVF's political wing for their support: "It is with the deepest gratitude and appreciation that I acknowledge your party's wonderful efforts on my behalf during the recent election campaign."

The co-operation between the constitutional and the illegal wings of unionism didn't last long. The UVF, along with the UDA, had been one of the driving forces behind an alliance of loyalist workers founded at the start of 1986. It was known as the '86 Committee and was used for its industrial and paramilitary muscle during the Day of Action on March 3rd that year. UVF leaders involved in the committee realised they were being manipulated during a meeting with the leaders of unionism at the UUP's headquarters in Glengall Street a few days before the strike. As they filed out, one recently elected Unionist MP said to David Ervine "Put a bit of backbone into them men" – meaning get the paramilitary might behind the strike. The '86 Committee knew the unionist parties wanted a general strike but preferred if both Paisley and Molyneaux declared it.

However as they left Glengall Street with an understanding that this support would be given, the media turned up en masse. The next day the headline in the Ulster Newsletter read: "Hard men change minds".

The UVF and PUP members realised they had fallen into a trap. By inviting the media to Unionist headquarters, the constitutional unionist parties were able to say it was the '86 Committee which forced a strike and Day of Action rather than the leadership.

"We were being used," Ervine recalled. "The implication to the media was 'it's not us who are calling this strike . . . it's them hard men. It's not our fault'. That was a way of getting so-called respectable politicians off the hook."

The UDA also became disgruntled with the unionist political leadership. They too had initially preferred to let the politicians take control of political opposition to the Agreement. One interesting by-product of the failure to defeat the accord was the soul-searching within loyalism. Less than two years after the agreement was signed, the UDA produced a discussion paper entitled "Common Sense". The document advocated power-sharing within the context of a devolved government. Its moderate tone brought praise from unusual quarters, including the Catholic Primate of All-Ireland, Tomas O Fiaich. The UVF were less complimentary. They claimed that "Common Sense" virtually replicated a

Progressive Unionist Party paper in 1977 which also argued for a form of power-sharing government.

Regardless of who got there first, both loyalist organisations were willing to call for political arrangements which were regarded as more moderate and generous towards northern nationalists than what was coming from the main unionist political forces.

Throughout the last thirty years a curious contradiction has run through Loyalism. On the one hand these paramilitary groups have been responsible for some of the most blatant and brutal sectarian carnage. On the other, their political representatives have articulated policies that seemed more imaginative than anything coming from the Ulster Unionist Party or the DUP. That is, the UVF and UDA were prepared to support policies such as Power Sharing and a Bill of Rights, ideas which were anathema to many unionist politicians who simply wanted the old Stormont regime to return.

However, as one UVF commander has often said, (borrowing a term from a Peruvian Marxist guerrilla group) "Words divide, actions unite". In the history of loyalist paramilitaries it was the sectarian actions rather than the progressive words which caught the headlines.

David Ervine and others have described the bungled anti-Agreement protest as a "defining moment within unionism". The UVF and PUP had already harboured a mistrust about parties like the DUP ever since the failure of the 1977 Ulster Workers Strike. Now those suspicions were transformed into deep hostility and mistrust. The formation and virtual collapse of Ulster Resistance compounded that feeling within the UVF.

Ulster Resistance's fate is a good example of how established unionist leaders flirted with illegality only to walk away from it when it became politically expedient to do so. The organisation was formed on November 10, 1986, at the Ulster Hall in Belfast. At the foundation ceremony, thousands of ordinary loyalists were told Ulster Resistance would become a force to "take direct action as and when required" to defeat the Anglo-Irish Agreement.

Among those attending were the DUP leader Ian Paisley and his deputy Peter Robinson. They were among many who donned red berets with the Ulster Resistance logo, during what seemed like the foundation of another loyalist paramilitary organisation. The UVF were mistrustful of the new organisation's antecedents but decided to take a look. Just like TARA, almost twenty years before, UVF members were told to attend the rally and infiltrate Ulster Resistance. What they found was mostly disappointing. As with TARA the unionist leadership eventually walked away from Ulster Resistance. After its early promise as a new mass loyalist movement, Ulster Resistance faded away. But an important nucleus of UR activists remained, mainly from the mid-Ulster and north Down areas. Many came from solidly middle-class backgrounds, a few had served in the regular British army, the UDR and the Territorial Army. The UVF was able to draw in a number of UR activists from the remnants of the quasi-legal group and use them to smuggle new weapons into Northern Ireland.

Politically, however, Ulster Resistance's demise marked a turning point in the growing disillusionment between loyalist paramilitaries and the unionist establishment. One UVF leader said the combination of political failure, the transparent attempts by politicians to manipulate loyalist terror groups, and those same political leaders' unwillingness to get their own hands dirty, was of massive significance.

One UVF man said: "The struggle against the Anglo-Irish Agreement was a watershed for loyalists. We had been let down by the leadership of unionism. All those suspicions about their intentions since the 1977 strike were now totally confirmed. We were on our own."

This sense of being let down didn't apply only to the UVF. Prior to this period the UDA had a close working relationship with elements within the DUP. During the early months of opposition to the Agreement, John McMichael had shared platforms in east Belfast with senior DUP figures. UVF leaders said it was fascinating to watch the relationship between the rival loyalist terror group and the DUP break apart.

But that feeling that their own politicians had betrayed them should not be misinterpreted as acceptance for the Agreement. One senior UVF member, reflecting on the period, said the accord left many working-class unionists fearful of Britain's intentions. "Many people thought the Brits weren't just neutral in this conflict anymore. They were working to a nationalist agenda."

In this era of uncertainty over the future, loyalist paramilitary violence continued unabated into the following years as the UVF took its terror onto another plane. Unlike the UDA, the UVF had concentrated its violence solely within Northern Ireland. There were no attacks in the south, especially since the organisation seemed reluctant to re-start the bombing campaign it had abandoned at the end of the seventies. However, a publicity stunt in the same month that Ulster Resistance was founded demonstrated that the UVF was willing to venture south and, if need be, attack targets there. The November issue of *Combat* contained a front page photo of masked UVF men in combat dress laying a wreath at the British War memorial at Goldenbridge in the Inchicore area of Dublin. The wreath spelt out the initials "UVF" and was placed there, according to a statement, to commemorate the 70th anniversary of the Battle of the Somme. The memorial was erected to remember all those, Ulster Protestant and southern Catholic, who were killed in the last two world wars. Although the modern UVF's stunt may have been partially connected with the renewed and growing loyalist interest in the legacy of the Somme for Ulster, another more up-to-date message was being conveyed. As one UVF member described it: "We are not afraid to come down here into the enemy's heartland and take the war to you."

## Nine

## TALKS AMID TERROR

At the end of the 1980s a contradictory process was emerging from within the UVF's ranks. On one hand their campaign of terror, directed at times against republicans but also at the general Catholic population, was intensifying. However at the same time there was a growing collective realisation among the membership that no one would win the war. Many in the organisation were coming to the conclusion that a cessation of violence was inevitable.

This mood was captured by one UVF leader from east Belfast who joined the terror group at the very start of the Troubles: "People in the movement were beginning to think that the war was coming to an end. The Provos just couldn't bomb us into a united Ireland and we couldn't drive our republican enemies into the Irish sea. There was a real feeling that we didn't want to inflict this war on another generation. Within a year or two a public statement from a leading Provo seemed to suggest they were thinking the same way."

Like him, many other senior UVF members had been locked in paramilitary struggle for over two decades. Now quite a number of their own sons were joining up and moving along a path their fathers had once trod from violence to imprisonment. "There were fellahs coming out of prison after doing fifteen or sixteen years. They thought it was all over and then they realised the war was still on. What made it worse was seeing their own kids do the same as they did back in the early seventies."

A clear example of the deeds of the fathers being replicated by their sons was an incident connected to the organisation's Ballysillan unit in north Belfast. In 1986 six young UVF men had been arrested in a flat in Ballysillan Crescent during the height of the murder campaign in the city after the Anglo-Irish Agreement. The RUC found four loaded guns ready for use during the raid. It later emerged that at least two of those arrested (who were on their way to commit murder) had followed in their fathers' footsteps. In the early 1970s their fathers had been arrested and convicted in almost identical circumstances.

Yet at the start of 1989 any movement towards peace seemed a distant dream. The UVF were still very much in the business of war. On January 18 they shot dead 27-year-old Ian Catney in Smithfield shopping complex in central Belfast. The victim had had double misfortune. The previous year he had been wounded in the face during the INLA-IPLO feud. Ian Catney's cousin was Kevin McQuillan, the IRSP spokesman who was a prime target for the IPLO during the bitter conflict. The publicity surrounding the IPLO murder clearly put him in the frame, so far as loyalists were concerned. To this day republicans insist he was not an activist and that the IPLO indirectly set him up for assassination by loyalists. The UVF of course are to this day far from apologetic, claiming that he was an active republican.

None of this, of course, deterred the IPLO themselves from continuing to stoke the fires of sectarianism in greater Belfast. In the aftermath of its feud with former INLA comrades the republican faction went on a series of wildcat attacks on loyalist pubs and clubs. On February 18, 1989, for instance, the IPLO sprayed the Orange Cross Social Club off the Shankill Road with machine-gun fire. One man, Stephen McCrea, a former loyalist prisoner, was killed in the attack and several other drinkers in the bar were wounded. The IPLO claimed they had been after the UVF's brigade staff which was meeting in the club at the time of the attack. The UVF leadership however denied that any of its senior personnel were there. One thing was certain, the UVF now faced a second republican front. In addition to worrying about the callous efficiency of the Provisional IRA, the UVF also had to contend now with a more unstable group in the form of the IPLO. In the coming months and years this volatile republican off-shoot would further poison the political atmosphere, creating fear and paranoia in both communities.

In such a highly charged set of circumstances only a supreme optimist would have suggested that the paramilitaries were slowly inching towards ceasefires. The UVF themselves kept up the pressure on republicans both in Belfast and even more so in the country areas. Four days before the Orange Cross attack, they had shot Sinn Féin councillor, John Joe Davey, in a laneway outside his home at Gulladuff, near Magherafelt. His murder was part of a pattern of terror within rural communities directed at Sinn Féin and republican activists. It had started the previous November with the murder of Phelim McNally, the brother of a Sinn Féin councillor in Coagh. In the period from McNally's death to John Joe Davey's, the UVF carried out three other unsuccessful attacks on Sinn Féin members and their relatives in Cookstown and Moneymore.

The UVF unit responsible for these shootings was extremely secretive. It never made any claims of responsibility through local newspapers or radio stations. It also had access to high grade intelligence emanating from the lower ranks of the RUC and UDR about republican activists in the mid-Ulster area. A month after John Davey's murder, the UVF's south Derry unit shot dead Gerard Casey at his home in Shamrock Park in the Co Antrim village of Rasharkin. It turned out that Casey had been the IRA's commanding officer for the Provos' north Antrim brigade.

259

During the first half of 1989 the terror in Ulster's countryside ran in tandem with ongoing paramilitary score-settling in Belfast. In March, the UVF shot dead two Catholics, one in west Belfast, the other in the north of the city. In response the Provisional started targeting known loyalists. On March 16th they shot dead Jackie "Nigger" Irvine at his home in Skegoneil Avenue in North Belfast. Irvine had been a senior member of the UVF from the 1970s and had gone in search of arms for the organisation abroad. But at the time of his murder the UVF insist he was no longer an active member. This meant little to the Provos who like the loyalists attacked those with former as well as current associations with rival organisations. The IRA also launched two separate attacks in the space of 48 hours on a UVF member in the Tigers Bay area, once at his own home, the other occasion at a friend's house. The Provos, too, proved they had accurate intelligence about their enemies.

The flurry of UVF attacks in this period confounded the pundits, who just twelve months before, predicted the terror group was on its knees. The discovery of a weapons dump on the outskirts of north Belfast the previous year was described at the time as a devastating blow. The RUC certainly scored a temporary coup against the UVF. They uncovered thirty-eight Kalashnikov rifles, fifteen pistols, an RPG rocket launcher with warheads, 100 grenades and 40,000 rounds of ammunition at a hide-out near the Flush Road outside Ligoneil. The arsenal was part of the arms shipment smuggled by three loyalist organisations into Northern Ireland in late 1987.

However on May 15, 1998, the UVF used a weapon which demonstrated they still had access to the guns and ammunition sent from the Middle East. A UVF unit drove into the middle of nationalist Ardoyne, a strongly republican area close to the Shankill Road. The gang got out their van and opened fire on the Sinn Féin advice centre in Brompton

Park with an rocket launcher. Miraculously no one was injured. The attack signalled a new development in the UVF's campaign against the republican movement. The Ardoyne incident was the first time loyalists had used rockets in murder bids against Sinn Féin and the Provisional IRA in Northern Ireland. The UVF had also demonstrated they were willing to use elements in the Lebanese arms shipment which hadn't been put to use before. Over the next few years the UVF and UDA carried out a series of rocket-propelled grenade attacks on Sinn Féin advice centres and pubs where republicans drank.

Unlike the immediate period after the Anglo-Irish Agreement when the UVF's killing campaign was nakedly sectarian, especially in north Belfast, the organisation claim the post-1989 era saw them successfully striking at the Provisionals. Most of the victims in this time, the UVF claims, were connected to the republican struggle. Nationalists however argued that the intensified UVF and UDA campaigns merely showed that loyalists were back to the business of simply killing Catholics.

This charge, according to UVF members, caused extreme frustration within the ranks of both loyalist groupings; as one paramilitary veteran explained: "If we wanted in 1989 and onwards simply to go out there and kill Catholics that would have been easy. All the UVF could have done was set up a sniper to take a position on the Shankill and shoot at anything that moved on the Falls. Or we could have sent out a hit team in a car and just driven by the nearest corner or taxi rank and sprayed the place at random. But we didn't do that. We went out of our way to target selective people. Sometimes we hit the right people, sometimes mistakes were made."

Loyalist frustration over accusations that they were only out to kill ordinary Catholics erupted in the late summer of 1989. On August 25 the UDA shot dead 28-year-old Loughlin

Maginn at his home in Rathfriland in Co Down. After the murder, nationalists claimed Mr Maginn was an innocent victim of sectarian assassins and was picked out just because of his religion.

In response to this the UDA contacted the journalist Chris Moore and provided him with confidential security files, allegedly of Provisional IRA suspects in the Co Down area. The files, which were leaked by a UDR man from Ballykinler army camp on the Down coast, included Loughlin Maginn's name. The logic in handling over the file to the media appeared simple. The UDA wished to prove it had only targeted those it had hard intelligence on. Here, according to his file, was a republican activist. But the UVF suspected their loyalist rivals had built a trap for themselves.

Regardless of their original intention, the UDA's tactic backfired on them. Several leading members of the organisation were arrested and charged with possessing secret security documents. In retaliation the UDA started to leak scores of files to the press, warning the RUC that it had hundreds more sensistive documents. The files started to rain like confetti at a wedding. Journalists' pigeon holes were full of envelopes and parcels containing mugshots of terrorist suspects, files of IRA members and details about other republican suspects. By and large the UVF resisted leaking files. But according to their second-in-command, they too had access to security force documents which he said were "more common than beermats" in certain loyalist premises.

Nationalist outrage over the tide of security files pouring out of the UDA's hands resulted in a special investigation by John Stevens, the Deputy Chief Constable of Cambridgeshire. By September, a number of leading UDA men, including Tommy "Tucker" Lyttle, were in custody after documents were seized at the organisation's east Belfast headquarters. Ironically, Lyttle was a long-term RUC informant within the UDA. Eventually three UDA brigadiers, a company commander and a former brigadier were put behind bars during the Stevens investigation, thus effectively decapitating the organisation's leadership.

The short-term impact of the collusion controversy and John Stevens' endeavours made it harder for loyalists to get access to security files. As one member of the UVF brigade staff put it: "The files just stopped coming through then. A lot of people who would have passed stuff on in the past wouldn't do it anymore."

The reason for the reluctance of rank and file UDR and RUC men to leak files or infomation on republicans was prosaic. As one UVF man put it: "If a republican suspect was stopped at a car a UDR man or RUC man might take his name, age, where the suspect was going, his car registration, car colour and so on. This kind of information was passed to us all the time. Sometimes it was given to us directly or a UVF member picked up through a part-time soldier or cop loose talking in a loyalist bar. But then things started to tighen up after Stevens. They devised a system where if a suspect was stopped and questioned, and if the suspect was later attacked by loyalists, the cops would trace back to see if that person was ever stopped and by whom. People who passed on things before started to get nervous."

The UDA leaks led to a clean-out by the security forces. The old order was removed. Ironically, the long-term impact of the Stevens inquiry was the replacement of older UDA leaders, like Lyttle, with new younger militant members. The very diligence of the RUC in undermining the UDA in the autumn of 1989 resulted in a more determined, ruthless and dedicated organisation emerging from the debris. As the current second-in-command of the UDA in west Belfast, one of those who replaced the older leaders, remarked cynically: "John Stevens did us a favour. He got rid of the touts and gangsters and we replaced them. We should have put up a mural on the Shankill in John Stevens's honour."

While the UDA rebuilt itself, the UVF concerned itself with internal problems of their own, namely a highly-placed informant working within the Belfast brigade. On Saturday September 2 1989 a two-man UVF hit team from the Shankill drove up the Crumlin Road in Belfast on a stolen motorbike. They stopped at a row of shops at the entrance to Ardoyne. Their target was a 43-year-old Catholic, Patrick McKenna. He was shot dead outside the shops. The UVF alleged Mr McKenna was a PIRA member from the Ardoyne but this was strenuously denied by his family.

As Mr McKenna's killer and his accomplice escaped on the bike they were followed down the Crumlin Road by an Astra car. Unknown to them, they were being stalked by an undercover British army unit. As they tried to turn off the Crumlin Road into Camrai Street their motorbike was rammed by the soldiers' car. The UVF men were catapulted into the air. What happened next is matter of dispute. When one of the men, 27-year-old Brian Robinson, fell on the ground, eyewitnesses say he was coldly executed by one of undercover soldiers. They further claim that, but for their arrival on the scene, the driver would have met the same fate.

The witnesses say that among the passengers in the Astra was a woman. It has since emerged that the undercover soldiers were part of a secret army corps known as the 14th Intelligence Unit. This group was involved in covert operations across greater Belfast at the time. Five months after the Robinson shooting, the same unit were responsible for killing three petty criminals at a west Belfast bookmakers which the trio were about to rob.

Brian Robinson's death posed a number of serious questions about secret British army operations in Belfast in the late 1980s. In an obituary for Robinson in October's *Combat* the UVF alleged he had been killed to "counter-balance" nationalists claims that the security forces were aiding and abetting loyalist paramilitaries. The obituary stated: "The Northern Ireland Office has been reeling from adverse media attention due to a revelation concerning a security leak to loyalist paramiltaries by members of the security forces which had resulted in the death of a south Down republican. The political scales had to be balanced."

In addition the question has to be asked that if the undercover unit tracking Robinson and his accomplice knew about the UVF men's mission, why then did they not try and stop them killing Patrick McKenna?

The UVF leadership also became preoccupied with finding out who betrayed Robinson and his comrade. They got the answer to that puzzle five years later but were too late to act upon it, as republicans got to the UVF informant first.

It was ironic that Brian Robinson died at the hands of the British Army. He had been involved with the UVF since he was a teenager but his own family had long-standing connections with the British military. His grandfather Robert had been a war hero. Robert Robinson served in an artillery division and escaped capture during Dunkirk in 1940. After returning from France he served as an anti-aircraft gunner defending London during the Blitz. He died during a German air raid after his battery received a direct hit from a Luftwaffe bomb.

The Brian Robinson killing forced the UVF to enter the collusion row. Until then they had stayed out of it, avoiding the UDA's mistake of leaking security force documents all over the place. A month after Robinson was buried, however, the UVF leaked documents containing sensitive information on the Republic to local newspapers. A cover note with the documents read: "UVF. Some of the material given by former friends who murdered Brian Robinson". Thus the leak was to be the UVF's revenge for Robinson.

The material included names, addresses and phone numbers of twenty-four Dublin judges on the Republic's

Supreme Court and the High Court benches. As well as intelligence on the southern judiciary, there were papers containing military codes and transmission frequencies. There were sheets headed "Office of the Chief of Staff, Army Headquarters, Parkgate, Dublin 8" – the address of the Irish Defence Forces.

Although the Republic's authorities investigated the leak, it was stressed that much of the information was out-of-date and that military codes were changed every week to maintain radio secrecy. Dublin politicians tried desperately to play down the importance of the security breach. Nonetheless, it showed the UVF had access to high-grade material.

Robinson's death didn't deter the UVF from sending out units to continue to attack republican targets. On October 4th 1989 they tried and failed to kill a relative of Sinn Féin councillor, Alex Maskey, in west Belfast. A month later the UVF shifted their focus back onto rural areas where they were to have greater success.

Late in the evening of November 29 a UVF unit burst into the Battery Bar near the village of Coagh in Co Tyrone. They shot dead 33-year-old Michael Devlin and 39-year-old Liam Ryan. While Devlin had no known republican connections, there was no dispute about Liam Ryan. He was a senior Provisional IRA member in Tyrone and had served a prison sentence in the United States for attempting to smuggle detonators and explosives from North America to the Province. Clearly the UVF had scored a major coup. It was part of a campaign which was beginning to inflict serious damage on the Provisionals in mid-Ulster.

In response, the Provos were dragged back into the type of retaliatory action they had not engaged in for some years. Several months after Ryan's death, on March 7, 1990, the Provos killed three Protestant men at a garage in Coagh. The IRA alleged the garage was a UVF meeting place, although this was denied by the murdered men's families and the loyalist terror group. In general republicans see their enemy as the British Army backed up by its local surrogates, the RUC and UDR. The IRA prefers to be attacking Britain and its institutions of power in Northern Ireland. The Provos believe they are fighting an anti-colonial struggle against a foreign occupier. Therefore they are reluctant to get dragged into an ethnic war with Northern Protestants. However by the end of 1989, that was exactly what has happening. The Provos also now faced a second front.

As for Michael Devlin's death in the Battery Bar, the UVF were callously uncompromising. "He was with Ryan at the time," said a UVF Brigade staff member. "For many loyalists that kind of association with known IRA men is enough justification."

This hardnose stance among many in the UVF towards the killing of Catholic civillians is also seen in murders which the loyalist group carried out in direct retaliation for republican actions. The IRA's first victim of the new decade was Harry Dickey, who was blown up outside his home in the Sydenham area of east Belfast. Dickey was a member of the UDA's political wing, the Ulster Democratic Party. Five days later the UVF murdered a Catholic taxi driver in Lurgan, Martin Byrne. He was found dead in his car. In a statement the mid-Ulster UVF said Byrne was killed in direct retaliation for Dickey's death.

In such circumstances it was hard to imagine that the UVF was contemplating ending the conflict. The attacks on republicans went on through the first quarter of the year. On March 7 the mid-Ulster UVF, in particular its Portadown unit, shot dead Sam Marshall as he walked with Colin Duffy and Sinn Féin councillor Brendan Curran from Lurgan's social security office. Curran was wounded in the arm. The UVF intended to kill all three men, who were active republicans in the North Armagh area. Duffy was charged with the murder of a UDR man in Lurgan three years later.

(The key witness in the case was Lindsay Robb, a UVF member, who was later found guilty of gun-running in Scotland. With Robb now a discredited witness, Duffy won an appeal against his conviction and was released in September 1996).

Over the next three months the mid-Ulster UVF killed three more people, two Catholics and a Protestant mistaken for a Catholic. One of their victims was 60-year-old Patrick Boyle who was killed at his home on June 4. In a statement admitting responsibility the UVF said Mr Boyle had not been their intended target. They meant to kill his two sons, who were wounded in the shooting. In the midst of their murder campaign, the UVF brigade said that it wished to "reiterate to the general Catholic population that they have nothing to fear."

This did not instil any confidence among the Catholic community, as the Portadown UVF were hardly true to their word. On September 23, 22-year-old Colin McCullough was shot dead in front of his girlfriend by the IRA as they sat in their car at Oxford island on the shores of Lough Neagh, a renowned beauty spot favoured by bird watchers and wild fowlers. The Provos targeted McCullough because he was an off-duty member of the UDR. In republican eyes the victim served in a British regiment, wore a uniform, had combatant status and was consequently a legitimate target. To Protestants, however, the killings was a simple sectarian act. To them, McCullough was singled out just because he was a young Protestant spending the day with his girlfriend.

Just under a fortnight later the UVF in Portadown responded by replicating the Provos' mode of murder. On October 6, 19-year-old Denis Carville was sitting in a car with his girlfriend at the same spot where McCullough died. The UVF singled him out and shot Carville in front of the woman.

Later the same month the IRA shot dead a Protestant taxi

driver in the grounds of the Royal Hospital for Sick Children off the Falls Road. Just a day later the mid-Ulster UVF responded by shooting dead a Catholic taxi driver near Moy in Co Tyrone.

So now, two clear and distinct patterns were developing from within the UVF. The first was the direct targeting of known members of the republican movement. Coupled with this was a more reactive tactic in which the UVF would respond to PIRA, INLA and IPLO attacks across the north with equal if not deeper ferocity. The thinking was crude and brutal but some, including the Portadown UVF leader King Rat, still believe it was brutally effective. "If a Prod taxi driver gets killed, then stiff a Taig one. If they kill someone working for the security forces, then kill Catholics working in Protestant areas."

In 1989 and 1990 loyalist murders and attacks continued to increase. Yet the combined killing power of the UDA and UVF still didn't match the death toll caused by republicans.

1991 however was to mark a turning point in Ulster's terror. By the end of the year loyalists had been responsible for almost the same number of deaths as the IRA, INLA and IPLO together. And eventually loyalists would outkill republicans. This upturn in UVF and UDA activity happened in the face of an ongoing tenacious campaign of violence by the Provisional IRA. In the first few weeks of 1991 the UVF killed one person, a Lurgan Catholic. It was the only action in January 1991. Yet in the same month the IRA launched 14 separate attacks across the north on the security forces.

The increased loyalist violence was only one pivotal change in the political landscape. The other development in 1991 saw the three loyalist groupings merging closer together than ever before. This coming-together would help produce a temporary ceasefire.

But before any move to peace the UVF were still busy

targeting their republican enemies. The previous November the organisation had killed one of the Provisional's most important members in Tyrone. Now they returned to the same area where Liam Ryan had been gunned down, to wipe out an entire Provo unit.

On Sunday evening March 3, 1991, two UVF units from east Tyrone travelled to Cappagh village near Lough Neagh. One of the units took up a position at the outskirts of the village. The other waited for the arrival of a car which they knew contained Provisional IRA volunteers. When the car arrived at Boyle's bar the UVF unit opened fire with automatic weapons. All three men in the car were killed. Then the UVF team moved into the pub, firing from the doorway into the pub. Inside, another man was shot dead.

The trio killed in the car park were John Quinn (23), Dwayne O'Donnell (17) and Malcolm Nugent (20). All three were active IRA members in the county. The fourth man kiled was 50-year-old Thomas Armstrong, who was not connected to the Provos. He had been caught in gunfire as the UVF unit tried to kill Brian Arthurs. He escaped death by shielding himself behind the bar. Arthurs was later convicted for IRA offences and became the Provos' commanding officer in the Maze for a short time. His brother Declan had been killed by the SAS at Loughgall in 1987.

The UVF gloated over their success in striking at the IRA in such an active republian area. Yet in a statement the UVF also qualified their jubilation with a challenge. "We conclude by saying that if the Provisional IRA were to cease its campaign of terror, the Ulster Volunteer Force would no longer deem it necessary to continue with their military operations." In other words – you stop, we stop.

The Cappagh shootings according to senior UVF members, were a massive morale boost for the organisation. One brigade staff member desribed the attack as "one of the best things we did militarily in thirty years. We proved we could take the war to the Provos in one of their strongest areas."

Another by-product of Cappagh was the spread of a new loyalist mythology. The media in particular became fixated on the Portadown UVF leader, King Rat. He became the loyalist bogeyman who got blamed for every operation the mid-Ulster UVF carried out. However the UVF's leadership insist that King Rat was not involved in the Cappagh operation. Rather it was units from areas outside Portadown. Indeed it would be wrong to imagine that the mid-Ulster UVF simply means Portadown. The organisation draws members from Dungannon, South Derry, Armagh City, Cookstown, Lurgan and smaller rural parts of mid-Ulster. UVF leaders in Belfast admit that they even encouraged the King Rat myth regarding incidents like Cappagh, to take the pressure off those actually involved. Moreover the mid-Ulster UVF doesn't recruit from working-class loyalists in larger towns like Portadown. Its membership consists of well to do farmers and businessmen, many of whom are regarded as pillars of their local communities. In the Cappagh killings, for instance, a wealthy UVF supporter who has a business in south Belfast helped the terror group to buy the cars used in the attack at auctions in the city.

While the UVF's rural base stretches as far west as the Clogher valley, it has virtually no organisation in Co Fermanagh. This may be surprising to informed observers of the northern conflict. To Ulster Protestants, Fermanagh is the front line. Hundreds of Protestants, some of whom were off-duty policemen and soldiers, have been killed by the Provos in that county. Loyalists have consistently alleged that in Fermanagh, in particular, the IRA is locked in a land war with its Protestant neighbours. By killing the head of Protestant households republicans are able to drive unionists out of areas, with the result that the land falls into nationalist hands. Since the Bosnian war Europe has become used to the

271

phrase "ethnic cleansing". Protestants and unionists firmly believe that in border regions they too are subject to a low level form of ethnic cleansing aimed at pushing them further to the east of the Province.

Given this perception one would imagine that Fermanagh would be fertile ground for loyalist paramilitaries. Yet the experience of the UVF and UDA in the border county proves the opposite is true. Unionists in this region are by far the most law-abiding in Northern Ireland. They prefer to see the UDR, RUC and British Army as their true defenders, at least for the present.

There is only a trickle of support for outlawed loyalist groupings in Fermanagh. A senior UVF member pointed out that even at times of great moral outrage among Protestant Fermanagh, his organisation still made few inroads. For instance, the IRA's west Fermanagh brigade shot dead 21-year-old Gillian Johnston, a Protestant riddled with bullets outside her home in Leggs near the Donegal border. The UVF went into the area afterwards and offered assistance to any unionists hell bent on revenge. Their efforts proved fruitless as the UVF's second in command recalled: "Even though the Prods were taking a hammering down there the UVF was not successful in building a base. Most Prods wouldn't support us at any cost even though we made offers of help all the time."

The lack of UVF activity in Fermanagh was in sharp contrast to the murderous activities of its mid-Ulster brigade, especially the Portadown unit led by King Rat. Once again the Portadown UVF took it into its hands to avenge the deaths of Protestants killed by the IRA in other parts of the Province. The response was as always disproportionate. On March 28 a UVF unit tried to kill a republican in a mobile shop on a Catholic housing estate in Craigavon. Instead they shot dead two teenage girls, Eileen Duffy and Katrian Rennie, along with 29-year-old Brian Frizzell, who had no connections to the republican movement. The man responsible for murdering the young women in cold blood at point blank range was one of King Rat's close associates in Portadown, who is still often seen associating with the loyalist leader at rallies and marches in the town. The mobile shop shooting happened after the IRA shot and seriously injured a Protestant woman who had been working for the security forces. She was the widow of an RUC officer previously killed by the Provisionals.

Regardless of the circumstances leading up to the triple murder in Craigavon, the killings were in themselves nothing more than a frenzied sectarian attack. The UVF may have insisted their men had gone after a republican target in the shop. Yet when that target didn't appear, why then did King Rat's right-hand man feel it necessary to gun down two young women?

It should never be forgotten that, while the UVF leadership protest that they do not see the general Catholic population as their enemy, many of the rank and file, especially in polarised areas like Portadown, simply hate Catholics. A few of them would have no problem "stiffing a taig". There is ample evidence to show that in many UVF attacks if their units failed to find a republican target then the nearest Catholic would be killed to satisfy their blood lust. It is also worth pointing out that the UVF is a loose alliance of people from various unionist viewpoints, ranging from the outright bigoted anti-Catholics to those who want historic compromise with nationalists and who quite genuinely abhor sectarianism. Portadown and Belfast offer illuminating contrasts here. The mid-Ulster town is a citadel of loyalism, a narrow bigoted place where a large number of people have short vision but long memories. Many of those involved in Portadown came originally from areas that were once mixed and are now exclusively Catholic and strongly republican. King Rat himself comes from south Armagh and has had to bury many relatives who were killed at the hands of the Provisionals in the early 1970s. In Belfast, however, there is some evidence to suggest the UVF tried to go out of its way, at least in the post-1989 period, to target republicans and try to leave the Catholic population alone. UVF men in the city have had more experience of the other side's point of view. Some senior members even have Catholic relatives in republican strongholds like Ardoyne. This is not to underplay the virulent sectarianism in Belfast but to show at least that in the city, a deeper neutral civil society exists and this has partly diluted bigotry.

The modern UVF straddles two worlds – sectarianism and political innovation. At times the organisation can swing from one extreme to another. This dualism is also reflected within the Provisionals. There are clearly many Provos who equally loathe sectarianism and would be personally horrified at accusations that they are sectarian. But there are other Provos, especially in areas like north Belfast and Tyrone, who simply hate unionists and would be happy to expel them all from Ireland to Britain. The tension between the two strands of thinking appeared to be working its way through both organisations at the start of the 1990s, though on the surface it seemed unlikely that the anti-sectarian, innovative strand was winning through.

Yet even at the height of the UVF's murder campaign, moves were being put in place to bring all loyalist violence to a halt. Since the start of 1991 both main loyalist groups joined forces to form a politico-military front. The relationship of course between the UVF and UDA has always been a fraught one. At times the two organisations have gone to war against each other in a kind of regimental rivalry contest. As was illustrated by the bungled attempt to assassinate Gerry Adams, the lack of co-ordination between the UVF and UDA could even hinder loyalist goals. This finally seemed to have dawned on loyalist leaders who recognised the need for some form of united front. The prospect of inter-party talks on Northern Ireland's future, kick-started by the secretary of state Peter Brooke, prompted loyalists to think that a ceasefire might just provide the chance of political dialogue succeeding.

In the spring the UDA, the UVF and its satellite Red Hand Commando formed the Combined Loyalist Military Command. The body was to have two functions. One component part dealt with the basics of terror and became known as the Combined Loyalist Military Alliance. The other part had a loose discursive role which would draft political statements. Each of the three groups picked liason officers. The UDA's LO on the military side was its south Belfast brigadier, Alex Kerr, who later fell out of favour with the organisation. The UVF's LO was the terror group's second in command. He was later to claim that the UVF made most of the running and by and large wrote the CLMC's script. He said:

"The CLMC seemed the logical thing to do at the time. By then all the talk was about moving towards peace. We could see an end in sight. One suggestion was that loyalists should now work together. I know this might sound elitist but we basically ran the show. It was our idea and the UDA simply came on board."

Naturally this version of the CLMC's genesis is angrily disputed by the UDA. The organisation's south Antrim brigadier believe Ray Smallwoods, a former prisoner who served a sentence for attempting to kill Bernadette McAliskey, played a pivotal role. The UDA leader insisted that their resurgence was frightening not only the nationalist population but also the UVF. Senior members of the UVF admit the UDA's renewed activity was causing some problems for them in certain areas of Belfast. In the Lower Shankill, for instance, scores of young loyalist teenagers were flocking to join the UDA and its junior wing, the Ulster Young Militants. Like King Rat, the UDA had cultivated a new legendary figure of its own in greater Belfast. Johnny

Adair, from Hazelfield Street, rose through the UDA's ranks and eventually became a member of the Inner Council. He was centrally involved in the UDA's terror campaign in North and West Belfast for a four-year period starting from 1990. Adair became a hero figure for young loyalists and a symbol of hatred for nationalists. He acquired a reputation as a loyalist scarlet pimpernel escaping death at the hands of the IRA, INLA and British Army. There were sightings of him everywhere. On one occasion the RUC arrested him as he walked through the nationalist New Lodge Road area in north Belfast. At the time Adair (a fanatical Rangers supporter) was wearing a Glasgow Celtic shirt as camouflage as he scouted the New Lodge for republican targets.

The UVF leadership admit they were worried about Adair and his team in the UDA's so-called 2nd battalion. They felt this unit was unstable and out of control. The older loyalist organisation concluded that the UDA had to be brought into line if any joint response to the Brooke talks was going to work.

Those involved in setting up the CLMC believe its formation sent political shockwaves into the nationalist system. The UVF's liaison officer on the military alliance reflected that the innovation proved loyalists could be as politically sophisticated as republicans: "We confounded the pundits who always said we were just mindless sectarian killers and nothing else. We showed we could exercise control over our troops."

The military alliance, however, was a volatile one. The UDA and UVF could still operate independently of each other. Mutual suspicion also coloured the CLMC. The UVF believed they were the superior force, capable of striking directly at republicans whereas the UDA's targets were more random and sectarian. The UDA countered this by accusing the UVF of elitism and of being as guilty of sectarianism as they were.

The CLMC's formation attracted the attention of a wide range of mainstream political and church leaders. Several members of the CLMC held discussions with Archbishop Robin Eames, the Church of Ireland Primate, to discuss the possibility of a loyalist ceasefire. The loyalists leadership also crossed the divide to speak to the priests in Clonard Monastery in west Belfast, Frs. Alec Reid and Gerry Reynolds. The purpose of the latter discussions was to guage the IRA's views on declaring a similar ceasefire.

When the wrangling and cajoling finally paid off, the main political parties in Northern Ireland (with the exception of Sinn Féin) agreed to talks by the end of April. The CLMC met in Belfast to respond to the Brooke initiative. The loyalist leadership agreed to suspend their violence on a temporary basis.

On April 22 they laid out their views: "In the light of impending political dialogue and in common with a sincere and genuine desire to see a peaceful and acceptable solution to our political differences, the Combined Loyalist Military Command shall order a universal suspension of aggressive operational hostilities commencing midnight preceding the political summit." The statement continued by pointing out that "The timescale of such a suspension will be dependent upon the positive outcome of the respective stages through which the political stages may pass." There was also a sting in the tail of the CLMC declaration: "Republican forces will probably attempt to disrupt this important and constructive political dialogue . . . let them therefore be warned that the Combined Command will order defence and, where fitting, retaliatory action if so required."

The CLMC said they had called their temporary ceasefire in order to give the talks a chance. Those directly involved in the alliance have stressed that had the talks succeeded and the IRA followed suit, the ceasefire would have become permanent. The desire for peace was genuine, according to the UVF, and had widespread support, including from within the prisons. A second statement was issued from both UVF and UDA inmates in the Maze. It welcomed the ceasefire and urged political leaders to reach an agreement which would "command the consent and support of the majority of the electorate in Northern Ireland."

Clearly the CLMC ceasefire was some sort of breakthrough. The underground shifts within loyalism appeared to be paying off. The key question, however, was would republicans follow the same path?

The ceasefire statement had warned of republican provocation during the talks. The IRA was fearful and suspicious about the talks which they saw as a means of imposing an internal, partitionist solution on Northern Ireland. The period of the Brooke talks and the loyalist ceasefire saw an intensification of IRA activity rather than any creeping moves towards a cessation of violence.

In May the Provos killed two RUC men and a former police officer in a series of attacks in Belfast and Co Fermanagh. The IRA also shot dead Wallace McVeigh, a Protestant businessman, in Belfast's Balmoral market. His "crime" was simply that he supplied fruit and vegetables to army bases. The Provisionals left huge bombs in Protestant towns and villages such as Richill in Co Armagh. Those loyalists who went along with but were still sceptical about a ceasefire saw the increased IRA violence as evidence that the Provos were not interested in peace. They decided something had to be done in response.

The CLMC statement contained an important qualification which many failed to notice in the giddy euphoria over the ceasefire. It had been headed "Combined Loyalist Military Command – Northern Ireland." The use of the words "Northern Ireland" was very significant. The UDA had insisted that the terms of the cessation should only apply to the Province. The UVF agreed to this. Attacks therefore outside the North, that is in the Republic, were to be permitted. Thus on May 25 a UDA unit travelled across Lough Foyle in a boat to Donegal. Once on the Republic's side of the Lough they were picked up by an elderly farmer, a Donegal Protestant who supported the loyalist cause. The UDA men were driven to the home, of Sinn Féin councillor Eddie Fullerton in Buncrana. After breaking into his home the UDA unit shot the Sinn Féin councillor dead and returned back to Northern Ireland.

Eddie Fullerton's murder demonstrated that the UDA could carry out terror attacks across the border and had hard intelligence on republican activists living in what was once regarded as a safe haven. The killing also underlined the fact that the CLMC was an extremely loose arrangement. The UVF's representative on the military side of the alliance confessed that they had had no idea what the UDA were up to during the ceasefire. As a result, the UVF decided to keep their plans within their own circle.

The murder did not rupture the CLMC's unity. Each side always accepted the autonomy of the other. The real test of the CLMC's resolve was continued IRA violence and the bickering going on at Stormont between the parties at the Brooke talks. In June with the loyalists still on ceasefire within Northern Ireland the Provos kept up their onslaught. They killed five people including a British soldier, a policeman and three UDR men during that month.

Under extreme pressure and with the Brooke talks breaking down in acrimony, the CLMC decided it was time to go back to war. Those who set the alliance up said there was a deep sense of gloom and disillusionment that their efforts seemed to be in vain. The parties couldn't agree, the Provos wouldn't stop. Yet in the long run the CLMC's formation and the loyalist willingness to shut down their violence planted the seeds of a longer-lasting peace.

When they announced the end of their temporary

ceasefire at midnight on July 4, the CLMC stated: "We have proven that we have a desire for peace which can be seen as genuine, and have no vested interests in the continuation of violence." The message again to republicans was simple – you stop, we stop.

The UVF ended their truce with the murder of Thomas Hughes, a Catholic taxi driver who was shot dead on July 19. At the time the UVF alleged Hughes was an IRA activist, a claim denied by his family. Shortly after he was killed several Sinn Féin members from the Lower Falls area were stopped and questioned by the RUC on their way to bring back Thomas Hughes' body at the city morgue on the outskirts of Belfast. For the UVF that was good enough confirmation that Thomas Hughes had republican connections. For nationalists, this was no justification.

Within the space of the next five months the UVF murdered eight people and tried to kill scores more. One of their prime targets had been the commander of the IPLO in Belfast, Martin "Rook" O'Prey. He was known to have carried out the machine-gun attack on the Orange Cross social club and to have played a part in George Seawright's murder. O'Prey had a long history of paramilitary involvement stretching back to September 1981 when, along with Gerard "Doctor Death" Steenson, he shot a UDR soldier at a west Belfast factory. Both men were then still in the INLA.

O'Prey's name became infamous within loyalist circles, especially on the Shankill. As one UVF member put it: "When the Catholic kids rioted with kids from the Shankill along the peace line they used to shout at the Prods 'We'll get Rook for ya'. O'Prey was an enemy celebrity on the Shankill."

On Friday August 16, 1991, two UVF men entered the back of O'Prey's house in Ardmoulin Terrace under the shadow of Divis Tower off the Falls Road. When they reached the living room they found O'Prey, along with his daughter and another man. The UVF unit opened fire, killing O'Prey as he lay on a sofa in the room. The other man was lucky not to have been killed as well. According to the UVF brigade staff who were briefed about the shooting afterwards, the gunman couldn't make out at the time whether or not the other adult in the room was a man or woman. As the UVF unit were instructed not to shoot at anyone else unless they could identify them, they fled the house and escaped in a car which was later found burnt out in the Shankill.

O'Prey's own comrades have always insisted he was set up. In the aftermath of his death, the IPLO suspected one of their own members had passed on information which led the UVF to O'Prey's home. The alleged traitor was then eventually picked up and interrogated in a flat in the Grosvenor Road area. Fortunately for him, the suspected traitor managed to escape by leaping from a window of the flat. Later the IPLO said this man had met loyalists in Belfast during drug deals in a city centre bar. A businessman connected to the IPLO was alleged to have been the conduit to the UVF. He was offered £30,000 to set O'Prey up, according to the IPLO leader's best friend and comrade. However the UVF deny this web of intrigue ever existed. They simply kept watch on his home for three weeks and monitored his movements. In fact O'Prey only moved into Ardmoulin Terrace about a month prior to his death. The UVF received a tip-off from a part-time UDR soldier that O'Prey had moved house. Their second-in-command said one of the reasons for his downfall was that O'Prey hadn't been more security conscious.

"In the paramilitary mind many involved think that when they move house their whereabouts aren't known by the opposition for some time. It takes a while for one organisation to find where a rival operator has moved to from his or her old address. In the first few weeks living in his new house O'Prey might have felt a bit safer. Who knows?"

The one thing certain about O'Prey's death was that it marked the end of the IPLO. Within a year of his death the IPLO imploded into factionalism as former comrades went to war with each other over the spoils of drug dealing and bitter personality clashes. The UVF contributed more than they might have imagined at the time to the IPLO's demise.

After O'Prey's death, the UVF killed a further three people over the next three months, two of them republican activists. Inevitably increasing attacks on the republican movement by the UDA and UVF had to bring about an IRA response. In the space of a couple of hours on November 13 the Provos launched a wave of shootings aimed, they said, at leading loyalists. In fact they killed four Protestants who were all unconnected to loyalist terror groups. In one of the incidents, the IRA shot dead two brothers, Stephen and Kenneth Lynn, who were renovating a house on the Upper Crumlin Road. The pair had the misfortune to work at the home of a prominent loyalist who had previously owned the house.

The IRA offensive drew a depressingly familiar reaction from the UVF in Mid-Ulster less than 24 hours later. The Portadown unit, again led by the man involved in the mobile shop murders, shot dead three people as they left the Heyster forklift factory in Lurgan. Their target had been a Sinn Féin member who worked there. Instead they gunned down three workers, including a Protestant, all of whom were unconnected to republican paramiltiaries.

Yet even in the midst of the UVF campaign in mid-Ulster the organisation once more issued another "You stop-we stop" challenge to the Provisionals. This time it was sent out by King Rat himself. At the end of November the notorious loyalist paramilitary said he was prepared to lay down his arms if the Provos did the same. In a bizarre statement the Portadown man admitted that nationalists regarded him as the devil. He also accepted that some of the UVF's victims were shot simply because they were Catholics, although he added that all such murders were in direct response to the IRA murdering Protestants. King Rat pleaded for peace: "The aggressor is the IRA. We have asked the IRA to quit on numerous occasions and have said the UVF would quit." It seemed that the dualism of waging war but promising peace even extended to the Portadown unit, arguably the most openly sectarian element within the loyalist terror group.

The tension and violence on the outside was mirrored behind the walls of Belfast's Crumlin Road jail. During the Supergrass period republicans and loyalists lived within spitting distance of each other while on remand on the word of informers. Even when the Supergrass system collapsed, the government continued with its policy of forcing integration on prisoners who were deadly enemies. From the late 1980s republicans and loyalists ran campaigns to demand segregation from each other. They wished to be held on the same lines as their comrades in the Maze, where different blocks were the exclusive territory of rival paramiltaries.

In Crumlin Road there were daily clashes between loyalists and republicans. Sometimes rival paramilitaries, who were on remand accused of trying to kill their rivals, were held in cells along the same landings. As far back as 1989 the UVF, through *Combat* magazine, predicted that lives would be lost if the policy of integration continued. Their warning proved correct.

On November 24 an IRA Semtex bomb exploded in the canteen area where loyalists were having their evening meal. Two prisoners, 27-year-old UDA man Robert Skey and 23-year-old Robert Caldwell, a UVF prisoner, were killed in the blast.

Before the explosion the clashes between loyalists and republicans were limited to fist fights and scaldings with hot water and tea. The UVF leaders were astonished that the Provos had gone one massive step further and decided to kill fellow prisoners. The UVF believed there was an understanding that no inmate would be killed by the other side even though that was fair game on the outside. They could only conclude that Provos from outside Belfast, who were less concerned about the silent code of conduct in Ulster's jails set up by Belfast men, were responsible for placing the bomb. One factor might have been the UVF attacks on nationalists in rural areas. Indeed the men who made the bomb came from Co Tyrone. The UVF were to "pay them back" several months later by murdering one of the men's relatives.

Regardless of what prompted the Tyrone Provos to leave the bomb in the jail, the deaths of Skey and Caldwell resulted in an unique display of UDA-UVF unity. Less than a fortnight later loyalists fired an RPG 7 rocket at a window of the prison from a vantage point along the Crumlin Road. Miraculously the rocket bounced off the grill on a window of the jail's canteen. At the time republican prisoners were having their evening meal.

The rocket attack was claimed in the name of the Combined Loyalist Military Comand, the only terrorist operation ever declared by the alliance. It was the only example of loyalist military unity. At the start of 1992 the UDA and UVF were still working independently of each other; and once again one of the loyalist groups was to get in the way of the other.

On February 5, 1992, a UDA unit carrying assault rifles sprayed Sean Graham's bookmakers on the Lower Ormeau Road in south Belfast. They killed five men, ranging in age from a fifteen-year-old schoolboy to a pensioner. The scene inside the betting shop afterwards was harrowing as local women ran to the premises to see if their husbands, lovers and brothers were among the victims. As the victims lay dying inside, race commentary still blared out of televisions and loudspeakers.

The UDA said the slaughter was in direct retaliation for the murder of eight Protestant workers who were blown up in an IRA landmine at Teebane crossroads after returning from work at an army base in Omagh in Co Tyrone.

The betting shop massacre had been ordered by the UDA's commander in the Upper Ormeau area, Joe Bratty, who was well known to Catholic residents living in south Belfast. (Bratty was later shot dead by the IRA.)

Unknown to either the UDA or the people of the Lower Ormeau, the murders prevented the UVF from attacking a Sinn Féin member on the same day at almost the same time. The UVF had intelligence that the republican always returned home at a specific time. On the day of the bookies shooting, a UVF unit was in place ready to shoot the Sinn Féin activist at his home. The guns to be used in the attack were buried in a dump across the bridge straddling the river Lagan. As the UVF men were about to collect the weapons, they heard shooting coming from the other side of the bridge. When they saw police landrovers and ambulances speeding down the Ormeau Road they realised they had to call their attack off. The UVF's second-in-command said his men were furious that they had been denied the chance to shoot a leading republican by the actions of the UDA. As with the Gerry Adams assassination bid, the lack of military co-ordination between the UDA and UVF hindered basic loyalist goals.

By the end of 1992 loyalist paramilitaries had outkilled the IRA, the first time ever in the history of the modern Troubles. The rivalry between the two loyalist organisations continued. The UVF regarded the UDA campaign as ludicrous and openly sectarian. One UVF member was contemptuous about the UDA's actions: "We kept asking ourselves what these people were doing. We were never impressed by them. Aside from the killings, many of which were very dubious, all they ever did was break windows and let car tyres down."

The UDA however stated confidently that it was they who dictated the agenda. The organisation's south Antrim brigadier pointed out that UDA killings in 1992 were almost double those of the UVF. He scoffed at the UVF's charge that the UDA were always more prone to kill any available Catholic. The UDA commander pointed to the murder of Anne Marie Smyth, a young Catholic woman from Armagh who fell in with a group of young loyalists at a social club in east Belfast. Afterwards, at a party fuelled by drink and drugs, she was severely beaten and then brought to wasteground off the Ravenhill Road where her throat was cut. Those responsible were young UVF members. So much for the UVF's claim to be anti-sectarian, the UDA leader said.

There was also a glaring contrast between the UVF and UDA regarding the media. For an organisation deeply involved in terror, the UDA was extremely transparent. The Inner Council gave scores of interviews to journalists during this most bloody year. On one memorable occasion one of the authors arrived at the UDA's headquarters on the Shankill Road above Frizzell's fish shop. He was forced to queue up along the staircase behind a line of reporters who were also seeking interviews with the UDA leadership. While waiting for an audience with the Inner Council the journalists were offered tea, baps, fish and chips. The UDA might have been embroiled in murder but their underlings were extremely courteous to the press.

The atmosphere during these interviews was a mixture of menace and bizarre hilarity. One minute the UDA leaders would be excusing murders or threatening to take the war to Dublin or asking about this or that republican. Yet in the next breath they would chat about football, women and whether or not a journalist could get them a ticket for the next Northern Ireland-Republic of Ireland World Cup clash.

The UVF did not follow their counterparts "up the road" on the Shankill. The older loyalist terror group retained its secrecy, particularly since many of its leaders had an inherent mistrust of the media. A UVF brigade staff member tried to explain the difference in attitudes to the media at this time: "The UDA were image-building. They had suffered from all the bad publicity over racketeering and so on. So they had to portray themselves in a different light."

To a certain extent, though, this image-building paid off. The UDA's recruitment soared in direct proportion to their violence. In Belfast the UDA taunted the UVF over an alleged labelling of the older loyalist group as "the peace people."

The jibe seemed inaccurate. Combined with the UDA, the UVF terror group killed twelve people in the space of two months in the middle of 1992. The UVF kept up its pressure on the IPLO, which itself was engaged in a series of blatantly sectarian attacks on pubs and clubs in loyalist areas. On April 29 the UVF shot dead Conor Maguire at his workplace in the Ligoneil area of North Belfast. Maguire was an IPLO gunman who had been involved in a series of shootings in the north of the city, including the murder of a 17-year-old Protestant at a video store on the Upper Crumlin Road. When Maguire was killed he was wearing a flak jacket which in the end offered him little protection. More lives were almost lost several days later at his funeral when crowds of loyalists attacked mourners, including leading IPLO members such as Jimmy Brown, when the cortege passed by the Protestant part of Ligoneil.

For some time the UVF had also been gathering intelligence on republican activists at Queen's University Belfast. The university had attracted large numbers of republicans, especially prisoners recently freed from the Maze. IRA woman Mairead Farrell was still a Queen's student when she was shot dead by the SAS in Gibraltar. The Provos had a secret unit operating in Queen's for a considerable period of time. They were activated only once though, when they shot dead university lecturer and unionist politician

Edgar Graham in University Square in December 1983. The cell went underground after that, spending most of its time compiling intelligence on security force members and unionists at the university.

The UVF discovered that a prominent north Armagh republican was attending Queen's and regularly drank in the York Hotel in nearby Botanic Avenue. Sheena Campbell stood for Sinn Féin in the general election earlier that year. She was the girlfriend of party councillor Brendan Curran, whom the UVF had shot and wounded two years earlier.

On the evening of Thursday, October 19, a young UVF man walked into the York Hotel. He was wearing a baseball cap and had a scarf wrapped around his neck. He spotted Sheena Campbell drinking with friends in the bar and shot her dead at point-blank range.

The Campbell murder fitted into the UVF's strategy of terrorising Sinn Féin members and/or their families. Two months later they killed Martin Lavery at his home on the Crumlin Road. Lavery's brother, Bobby, is a prominent Sinn Féin councillor in north Belfast and has been the target of repeated loyalist murder bids.

Yet while the UVF was killing Sinn Féin members, the loyalist leadership was at the same time searching for a chink of light which might indicate if republicans wanted an end to the carnage. The absurdity of waging war but promising peace was demonstrated by the UVF's attitude to a speech by a prominent Sinn Féin member at Bodenstown in June. During his address to the republican faithful at Wolfe Tone's graveside, Jim Gibney, a key strategist for the party, said the conflict had gone on long enough. Gibney added that it was time to move forward in a peaceful way and that a "sustained period of peace" was needed before any British withdrawal from the North.

The UVF were genuinely impressed by what Gibney had to say. Within forty-eight hours of the Bodenstown address, the

UVF replied by stating again that it would "act positively" if the Provos declared a ceasefire. In a rare statement to the natonalist Irish News, the UVF leadership welcomed what it called Sinn Féin's departure from "simplistic republican dogma". The UVF issued a challenge to republicans: "Now that we have entered the real world, the next logical step is for Sinn Féin to persuade the IRA and its acolytes to cease their primary and futile violence, which in turn, will bring a positive response from this force."

Jim Gibney may not have realised it but in nailing up the staging post towards an IRA cessation in just over two years' time, he also helped to prompt the loyalists towards their own ceasefire. The signals sent out from the grave of republicanism's founding father gave cause for hope in the UVF's heartland hundreds of miles away on the Shankill. These were the strange contradictions of making war but preparing for peace in the early 1990s.

Gibney's speech and the UVF response to it seemed to suggest that beneath the surface there was a way out of the darkness. The 1991 loyalist ceasefire also showed that the UVF and the UDA wanted the violence to end. But there was still a long and bloody road to travel before republican and loyalist guns would fall silent.

*Ten*

# THE OTHER PEACE PROCESS

It was a supreme irony that die-hard republicans totally opposed to Gerry Adams's attempt to bring about an IRA ceasefire were the ones who indirectly helped to bring together the UVF and the Dublin government in the spring of 1993. This accidental meeting boosted an alternative peace process that was running parallel to the Hume-Adams initiative, and helped push loyalists towards their own ceasefire.

Indeed, the whole story of the road to the ceasefires has so far only been half-told. The impression created by nationalist-orientated journalists is that the peace process was the sole property of Irish nationalism: Gerry Adams, John Hume and Albert Reynolds. However another process was underway, a key component of which was the growing rapprochement between loyalists and Dublin.

On March 29, 1993, the rejectionist Republican Sinn Féin helped to organise a public meeting in the Republic's capital to discuss the possibility of working-class Protestants and Catholics uniting in the North. The meeting was held in McKinley House on the quays and drew the usual audience of far leftists and republicans. They included the veteran communist, Michael O'Riordan, as well as various Dublin Trotskyites who spend most of their time ideologically point-scoring amongst each other. Through a network of community workers in Dublin and Belfast, several Shankill road men also attended the debate. Unknown to the southern audience, a number of the Shankill men were senior UVF members. After the meeting, which the UVF men said was full of far left fantasies, everyone adjourned to Boss Croker's pub on Aston Quay, around the corner from Republican Sinn Féin's headquarters.

Over a pint the UVF men were introduced to Chris Hudson, a Dublin trade unionist and spokesman for the Peace Train Organisation which campaigned against IRA attacks on the Belfast-Dublin rail link. Hudson was keen to engage with northern working-class Protestants, especially those from loyalism's heartland.

There was a double irony to this first chance meeting. Hudson had very personal reasons to mistrust and abhor the UVF. He had been a good friend of Fran O'Toole, the Miami showband member murdered in south Armagh by the UVF almost twenty years before. Hudson had played in a band called The Chosen Few with O'Toole in the 1960s when both men lived in Dun Laoghaire. When Hudson's contacts with the UVF became more formalised in the following months he was to remind them of his friend whom their organisation had slain. Hudson's own family background was strongly republican. His uncle had been executed by Free State forces during the Civil War. In homage to him the local council named a road in Dun Laoghaire in Co Dublin after the republican veteran.

Reflecting back on the first meeting, Hudson said he was simply curious to talk with real-life loyalists. At that time he had no brief from either the Irish government or any southern political party. Hudson's curiosity paid off. He was later invited to Belfast by the Progressive Unionist Party's David Ervine, a former UVF prisoner, who was now fast becoming one of loyalism's most articulate spokesmen.

In this period it seemed paradoxical that the UVF and its political allies wanted to open up lines of communication with Dublin. Only a few weeks after Hudson was invited to meet the UVF leadership, the terror group issued a statement warning that they would kill southern politicians if IRA and INLA violence escalated. They also vowed that if joint authority was imposed through strong cross-border institutions, they would kill the Irish civil servants tasked to run such bodies.

On June 9 – the same day the Opsahl report, a citizens' inquiry into political moves forward in the north, was launched in Belfast – Chris Hudson travelled north. He met David Ervine at Duke's Hotel in University Street. From there he was driven to the UVF's headquarters on the Shankill Road where he was to speak to the organisation's leader and its second-in-command. The meeting lasted about one and a half hours. It was punctuated with threats that the UVF were prepared to bomb Dublin.

Hudson remembered the atmosphere as fraught. "I remember feeling very apprehensive during that first meeting. It was held in the Shankill Historical Society offices. I started out by condemning the violence of the UVF. Afterwards outside I said to David Ervine, to break the ice a bit, 'I hope those guys in there don't think I'm some sort of quiche-eating peacenik.' Eventually that line became a standing joke between David Ervine and myself."

As well as developing his contacts with the UVF, Hudson also maintained his relationship with mainstream liberal unionists which he had forged during the Peace Train campaigns in the late 1980s. He was particularly friendly with Chris and Michael McGimpsey, the brothers who took the Irish government to the Supreme Court in order to prove the south's territorial claim was illegal. Shortly after his meeting in Belfast, Hudson organised a dinner party at his Blackrock home. Chris McGimpsey was invited down and among the other guests was Fergus Finlay, Dick Spring's special adviser on foreign affairs. During the meal McGimpsey mentioned that Hudson had held a meeting with the UVF. Finlay expressed interest in the contact. In the course of the evening

Hudson agreed to keep Finlay briefed about anything the loyalists had to say in relation to Dublin. At this point Hudson stressed that the contacts were extremely loose, with no official sanction from the Irish government.

Nonetheless the June meeting had opened a line of communication between Dublin and the UVF which had not existed before. It was all the more important given that the UVF was making truculent noises towards the Republic over its sponsorship of northern nationalism. What was even more contradictory was the fact that the UVF was intensifying its violence and contemplating shifting its focus to the south.

In the period between the meeting in Boss Croker's and the discussions on the Shankill Road, the UVF killed six people and launched scores of other murder bids in the north. The onslaught began with the murders of Patrick and Diarmuid Shields at their shop in Lesnagleer near Dungannon in Co Tyrone. From that point the UVF started to catch up with the UDA's violence. They carried out a series of ferocious attacks. Among the victims was a woman, 27-year-old Sharon McKenna. She was shot dead at an elderly woman's flat in the loyalist Mount Vernon area of north Belfast, where she had visited on a regular basis. The UVF alleged she was in the area simply to spy on behalf of the INLA. This was vehemently denied by her family and the republican terror group as well as the RUC.

UVF shootings and bombings spanned across counties Derry, Armagh, Tyrone and Greater Belfast. It was a frantic time for both loyalist groupings. The UDA also continued its murder campaign, targetting both Catholics and Sinn Féin activists. At times they killed both on the same day. In Castlerock on the north Antrim coast the UDA shot dead four workmen renovating a house. Three were Catholics unconnected to the republican movement. The fourth victim, James Kelly, was an IRA member from South Derry.

But loyalists were not only engaged in the business of terror. The UVF's political wing was trying to emerge from the margins. While the UVF became the paramilitary counter-weight to the IRA, the Progressive Unionist Party tried to match Sinn Féin on the propaganda front. The PUP received a massive publicity boost on June 1 when their sole councillor in Belfast, the veteran Shankill representative Hugh Smyth, was elected Lord Mayor of Belfast. The fledgling loyalist party now had a new platform to promote itself. In addition, David Ervine and Billy Hutchinson, another ex-UVF prisoner, were fast becoming plausible advocates of the loyalist cause. Ervine in particular rapidly became a telegenic spokesman for the PUP. Both he and Hutchinson had certainly learned from Sinn Féin's example in trying to use the media to articulate their viewpoint. However, at the ground level many PUP and UVF members were less adept at handling journalists. There was and still is a deep suspicion of the press and broadcasters. Indeed many ultra-unionists who hark back to Stormont blamed the media focus on the old regime in the late 1960s for bringing down their beloved state.

A frightening illustration of loyalist paranoia towards the media was seen in the aftermath of the death of a loyalist during rioting on the Shankill on June 29. Robert "Herbie" McCallum died after a grenade he was holding exploded in his hand. He was part of a UVF security team guarding an Orange march which the RUC had re-routed away from Catholic homes along the Springfield Road. McCallum's courage could not be questioned. Instead of dropping the grenade and running away, he tried to carry it to wasteground for fear of it exploding near fellow loyalists beside him. McCallum didn't die of his injuries right away (he passed away three days later) but the explosion set off a highly charged situation. Riots broke out between the RUC and loyalist demonstrators. In their frustration the loyalists turned against camera crews and journalists at the scene. Several news crews and reporters had to flee for their lives from the Shankill that afternoon.

The hostility towards the media was in sharp contrast to the attitude republicans adopted towards the press. During Sinn Féin marches or IRA funerals, republicans bent over backwards to help journalists. There were even occasions when Sinn Féin workers constructed wooden platforms just to help cameramen and photographers get better pictures of their rallies.

This, of course, is not to imply that the media is in cahoots with republicanism, as some more irrational loyalists believe. Sinn Féin and the IRA simply realise they can best sell their message around the world by being nice to those who carry that message. This elementary fact about the modern media was not lost on the likes of Ervine and Hutchinson, though among the loyalist grassroots there was and still remains a sullen mistrust of the reporter with the notebook or the microphone.

Such grassroots loyalists would therefore appreciate even less the need for contacts with Dublin over the summer of 1993. Chris Hudson didn't meet the UVF face to face until mid-November, but contact was kept up. For security reasons Hudson established a coded language between himself and David Ervine. In their phonespeak, the UVF became "The Cricket Team", the Combined Loyalist Military Command was known as "The Full Cricket Team". Hudson would convey some of the thinking within the Irish cabinet to Ervine, particularly the views of Fergus Finlay, and indirectly Dick Spring. In their code Spring was "The Grocer" and Finlay "The Grocer's Assistant".

Hudson decided it would be politic to be totally up-front with Finlay about his contacts. He even told him that the UVF called him "The Grocer's Assistant". Finlay suggested that maybe they should change the code to describe him as

"The Sorcerer's Apprentice". Spring's adviser also quipped to Hudson that maybe the Irish government should authorise a tap on his phone. Hudson tartly replied that he wouldn't be surprised or worried if they were already listening in.

The interregnum between Hudson's first meeting with the UVF leadership and his next one was one of the most violent periods in the history of the modern troubles. In this five-month period the UVF killed six people, including five Catholic civilians and a prison officer. In contrast the UDA seemed to be completely out of control. In the same time frame they killed twenty people. By the end of 1993 both loyalist organisations had again outkilled republicans. There seemed no end in sight to the terror.

Pressure on republicans was mounting. The UVF started sending letter bombs to the homes of Sinn Féin activists in Belfast and South Down. In one incident a bomb was posted to the home of the girlfriend of the Sinn Féin activist in Down, James Murnan. It exploded in the kitchen injuring Murnan in the legs and chest. Murnan's girlfriend was Maureen Maginn, the widow of Loughlin Maginn whose murder at the UDA's hands had sparked off the collusion controversy in 1989.

For the first time since the early 1970s the UDA started to direct their terror back on constitutional nationalism. In 1993 the UDA attacked fifteen members of the SDLP. Most of the incidents seemed half-hearted attempts to scare rather than kill or maim. As one UDA inner council member put it: "We weren't seriously out to kill the likes of Joe Hendron or any of the rest of them. The aim was simply to show them that they would pay a real price if their party leader forged a pan-nationalist front with Gerry Adams and Sinn Féin."

While the UVF had no problem about targetting republicans, Irish civil servants or the occasional Dublin minister, they drew the line at the SDLP, which they saw as a bulwark against Sinn Féin in the Catholic community. The

UVF publicly stated they would not attack the party regardless of what the UDA was doing.

The UVF took a different attitude towards the Irish government. In the first week of October 1993 they sent a parcel bomb to Dick Spring. The device was discovered at the main postal sorting office in Belfast. British army bomb disposal experts defused the device, which had been sent to Spring via the the Anglo-Irish secretariat in Maryfield. This was despite the fact that the UVF's political wing was still seeking a meeting with Spring's right-hand man Fergus Finlay. These were the contradictions of working for peace while waging war.

However, the bulk of loyalist violence in this period was concentrated in working-class areas of Greater Belfast. The conflict in the north of the city was personified by two young men who had risen through rival republican and loyalist paramilitaries to assume positions of leadership. Johnny Adair's emergence coincided with an upsurge in UDA attacks in north and west Belfast. At the same another young man was coming to prominence within the Provisional IRA in Ardoyne. The security forces regarded both individuals as unstable and unpredictable. The two fought out a bitter and sometimes very personal feud in the city throughout 1993. It climaxed on Saturday, October 23, when an IRA bomb prematurely exploded in Frizzell's fish shop underneath the UDA's Shankill Road headquarters. Nine people, including two children, were killed in the blast. The bomber, Thomas Begley, also died in the explosion. The IRA's target had been Adair and the rest of the UDA's inner council whom the Provisionals believed were meeting at that venue. They were far off the mark. Within minutes of the explosion, Johnny Adair was seen strolling down the Shankill. Other inner council members such as Ray Smallwoods were at home when the explosion happened.

The Shankill bomb shook Northern Ireland to its foundations. In the coming days there was wild talk that the province was teetering on the brink of civil war. Just a week later the UDA shot dead six people in a pub in Greysteel near Derry city. The massacre in the small Catholic village marked the end of the most bloody month in Northern Ireland for seventeen years.

Behind this bloody picture, however, moves continued to bring the carnage to an end. Chris Hudson was asked to go to a meeting with the UVF on Wednesday, November 10, 1993. He travelled to the north with his wife Isabella and met David Ervine in Belfast. Despite the terrible events of the previous month, Ervine told him that the UVF still wanted peace. Hudson went alone to meet the UVF first- and second-in-command on the Shankill. At the meeting he was astonished to discovered that the UVF leaders had a message for Dublin. During the discourse Hudson took notes and then transcribed them onto the headed notepaper of his own union, the Communication Workers.

The authors have obtained the minutes of the meeting which were then passed to Fergus Finlay and Dick Spring. The UVF sent down a number of points to Dublin which indicated they were willing to call a ceasefire. They were:

* They (the UVF) maintain they have pulled the UFF (UDA) back to the original position that if the IRA call a ceasefire loyalist paramilitaries will cease their activities.

* There is some doubt that even if there is a ceasefire then paramilitaries will be reluctant to give up all their arms.

* The UVF may consider an initiative of their own in calling a ceasefire.

* If a PIRA member should present himself/herself as a target at present they will have a go at their target.

* A cautious welcome for Spring's six points, need clarification?

* The UVF would see paramilitaries talking to paramilitaries and feeding back into main political talks.

* The UVF have sent signals to the PIRA but have not received positive response.

*They (the UVF) will consider making a public statement giving some welcome to the Spring proposals.

At the very end of the minutes, which had an optimistic tone to them, the UVF inserted a warning to Dublin:

*If joint authority is imposed on Northern Ireland the loyalist Paramilitaries will make Northern Ireland ungovernable. Also they, the paramilitaries, will cause destruction in the Republic."

After the November meeting Hudson again spoke to Ervine, who requested a meeting with Fergus Finlay. Hudson said he thought this was unlikely as the Irish government would not meet Sinn Féin while the PIRA campaign went on. Given the UVF's continued violence, Dublin had to be consistent. Ervine then added that the UVF might be able to deliver a "very big prize". When asked what that was, the loyalist representative replied: "Peace".

Even without the face-to-face meeting, the Irish government still had a direct channel of communication with the UVF and a clear picture of their thinking at the end of 1993. Finlay encouraged Hudson to continue his contacts with the loyalists. The government's special adviser said he regarded the communications between Hudson and the UVF as "useful feedback". He also confirmed that Dick Spring was kept informed of Hudson's dealing with the loyalist terror group's leadership. The UVF man described how the contacts were important. "At least we were getting a sense of the fear that Hume/Adams was inspiring amongst loyalist paramilitaries. Spring was made aware of this although we never asked Chris Hudson directly to open the talks with the loyalists."

The UVF on the other hand regarded Hudson as a vital conduit between themselves and their enemies in Dublin.

For them the trade unionist was a lightning conductor who transmitted the anger and energies of loyalism to the Irish Cabinet.

The contacts undoubtedly gave Dublin an alternative perspective on unfolding events north of the border. At that time John Hume and Gerry Adams were involved in their initiative under the approving eyes of Taoiseach Albert Reynolds. By late autumn gushing euphoria in the southern media over Hume-Adams and the promise of peace from republicans reached such an orgasmic state that unrealistic and dangerous proposals were being floated. One of the most ludicrous was the suggestion that an IRA ceasefire should be coupled with a British initiative in which John Major's government would act as "persuaders". That is, to persuade the unionists that their best long term option was to accept the union was going, so that the unionists should cut a deal with nationalist as they would soon be on their own. Such naive thinking missed the entire point of unionist history throughout the 20th century. Unionists have always suspected that influential sections of the British ruling class wanted out of Ireland. The UVF owes its genesis to the Home Rule crisis when unionist mistrust in Britain pushed Ireland towards civil war. After Stormont collapsed, the British continued to stress their neutrality in the North. This was rubber-stamped when the Thatcher government signed the Anglo-Irish Agreement. Later both Peter Brooke and Sir Patrick Mayhew made keynote speeches underlining that Britain had no selfish, strategic or economic reason to remain in Ireland.

Had the British fallen into the trap and gone further by actively persuading the unionists to join in an imagined "agreed Ireland," the province really would have been pushed to the brink of outright war again. Such a statement would have been seen as the green light to withdrawal. Thus the signals transmitted via Hudson from the UVF to Dublin seemed to give some elements in the Irish government a more realistic understanding of reality north of the border.

Dick Spring had already taken some of this on board when he launched his "six principles" on October 27. Among them was the promise that there would be no change to Northern Ireland's constitutional status unless there was consent. That principle was underpinned when John Major and Albert Reynolds announced the Downing Street declaration on December 15.

A further meeting between Hudson and Ervine took place three days later. It was held in Belfast's Central Station and lasted for about one and a half hours. Hudson recalled that it had been fairly positive, with Ervine conveying that the UVF felt reasonably unconcerned about the Downing Street declaration. However, he stressed that the UVF would not make any public pronouncements on the declaration until the Provos did.

Another meeting was arranged for the New Year. This time the venue was Dublin. Ervine travelled down with the UVF's second-in-command. Hudson held the discussion at the home of the former Workers Party strategist and *The Sunday Times* columnist Eoghan Harris in Blackrock. The encounter took a theatrical turn when the mercurial Harris produced a sword which had belonged to his grandfather, an IRA veteran from Co Cork. To calm his loyalist guests, Harris told them it was a UVF ceremonial sword which had been given to his grandfather by a Belfast Protestant in the 1920s. Harris offered it to them as a present. After this bizarre interlude, Hudson got down to business with the loyalist representatives. They told him that there was a greater possibility of a loyalist ceasefire. They also said that they were "cautiously impressed" by Dick Spring's attitude and still wanted to have that elusive meeting with Fergus Finlay. Yet while the loyalists kept promising peace, Hudson reminded them of the ongoing UVF violence.

That violent campaign re-started twenty days after the Dublin meeting when the UVF shot dead Cormac McDermott at his home in Ballymena. They said they targeted him because he had been selling *An Phoblacht/Republican News* in the north Antrim area. During the gun attack they also shot his wife in the face, but she survived.

The loyalist group has also vastly improved its bomb-making skills with the help of a number of former British soldiers. On January 4 they sent two parcel bombs to the Dublin offices of Sinn Féin in Parnell Square. An Irish army bomb disposal expert lost a thumb trying to defuse one of the devices, which was hidden in a video box. Twenty days later the UVF sent another letter bomb from Belfast to a house in Craigavon. Again they intended to injure or kill republicans. This time the device exploded after a young boy opened it, injuring him and his mother. Meanwhile, the mid-Ulster UVF also started using bombs again. On March 11 a booby trap device hidden in a hollow concrete block killed Francis Brown outside his brother's house in the nationalist Obins Street area of Portadown. In a statement the UVF said the brother had been the target.

While the UVF campaign against nationalists intensified in the first half of 1994, the leadership were side-tracked into investigating a sordid affair which exposed the organisation to accusations of drug dealing and gangsterism. A young Protestant woman from the Shankill area, Margaret Wright, was brutally beaten, shot in the head and then her body dumped in a wheelie bin after an orgy of drugs and drink in a loyalist band hall in the Village area of south Belfast. Ms Wright had had the misfortune to turn up at the illegal drinking den run by the inaptly named Pride of the Village Flute band. Many in the hall were drunk or high on drugs during a rave party. As the atmosphere turned nasty, some of the women in the shebeen suspected that Margaret Wright was a Catholic. On their word the young woman was taken to a room, tortured and then murdered.

When her body was found the whole sordid story of her death unravelled. Local people living in the Village called for the band hall to be destroyed and the UVF to take measures against those involved, some of whom were members of the organisation and its satellite, the Red Hand Commando. Five days after Ms Wright's murder the UVF abducted one of their own members, 21-year-old Ian Hamilton from the Woodvale area. After an interrogation, the brutality of which can only be imagined, Hamilton confessed that he shot Margaret Wright. The UVF internal security team, which questioned him then murdered their captive.

The damage to the reputation of the UVF and the RHC in working class loyalist areas was immense. There were revelations that some UVF members were taking drugs and involving themselves in the torture of young women. Nationalists saw the Wright case as double standards. The UVF second-in-command insists that even if Margaret Wright had been a Catholic they would have taken the same action against Ian Hamilton and others who were later discovered to have been involved in her murder. Yet nationalists point to the inaction of the UVF over the murderers of Anne Marie Smyth. Ms Smyth was Catholic who fell into the hands of young loyalists at a party in the Ravenhill area of east Belfast. She was also tortured and then murdered by her captors. No action was taken against those responsible. Moreover, two of those charged with Ms Smyth's murder are still held on UVF wings in the Maze prison, although many UVF prisoners have objected to their presence. As one UVF leader put it: "The presence of those who killed Anne Marie Smyth on our wings is still a source of controversy today."

The sectarian ferocity of some young UVF members in Belfast was equally matched by their comrades in mid-Ulster.

On May 8, a UVF unit targeted a former republican prisoner living at an isolated farmhouse outside Dungannon. Under cover of darkness they fired a volley of shots into the house. Instead of killing their target they shot dead 76-year-old Roseanne Mallon. Her nephew, the intended target, wasn't even in the house at the time. Shortly after the murder the UVF's mid-Ulster Brigade gave an interview in the small Scottish loyalist magazine *The Red Hand*. They said they regretted killing Mrs Mallon but added that her nephew was still a target. The killing was compounded by controversy when it later emerged that British army surveillance cameras were found in fields overlooking the Mallons' house. This discovery sparked off a fresh round of allegations that the security forces had colluded with the UVF in the murder.

The mid-Ulster brigade also extended its area of operations to include parts of the region it hadn't been busy in before. In Armagh, under the cloak of the Ulster Protestant Militia, the UVF shot dead two young men in a taxi office in the city centre. The UVF started to carry out attacks outside its traditional killing zones of mid-Ulster and greater Belfast.

A unit had been re-activatated in Antrim town following the release of a loyalist prisoner who came originally from the Tiger's Bay area of Belfast but had settled in the town. His group was responsible for a series of attacks on republicans and ordinary Catholics in Antrim over a twelve-month period. The Antrim UVF had access to some security force material on IRA and INLA suspects in Toomebridge, south Derry and east Tyrone as well as Antrim. They even leaked a number of the files to local newspapers in the Antrim area, put bombs under the cars of republican activists and tried to assassinate several Sinn Féin members. However those who suffered most at their hands were ordinary Catholics. The Antrim UVF's last victim was Gerard Brady who was found dead in his taxi cab after he had picked up a fare at local restaraunt and driven to Carrickfergus on June 17. Mr Brady's common-law wife Michelle Kincaid was a Protestant and she spoke out strongly against those responsible for his death, labelling his killers as "Scum". After his murder Michelle, along with Gerard's two young sons and her father, had to flee the Antrim UVF's wrath. They had taken exception to her condemnation. In fact it wasn't until two years later that Michelle and her family felt safe enough to return to Antrim. This individual tragedy illustrates the deep strain of sectarianism within some of the UVF's rank and file who after killing Gerard Brady still felt they had the right to expel his wife and family, for condemning his murder. The killing shone a light into the chasm between the progressive intent of the UVF leadership in the middle of 1994 and the mentality of some of its grassroots members, who were still knee-deep in terror.

That terror could have ended in the middle of 1994. The UVF leadership had known for some time that the IRA was preparing to call a ceasefire. Through their discussions with churchmen and Southern politicians, including emissaries of Albert Reynolds, the UVF were informed of the Provisional's intentions. The loyalist leaders made it clear to the various go-betweens that they too were prepared to call a ceasefire. One of the key contacts between the UVF and the British government at this time was the Church of Ireland primate Robin Eames. Dr Eames, who had spoken to the UVF before, deeply impressed the man representing the loyalist organisation in the discussions. One of the UVF leaders who met Eames during this period said of the Archbishop: "If you were sitting in a dark room listening to this man you could be forgiven for thinking he was a lawyer and not a churchman."

In response to various pleas for peace, the UVF considered declaring a ceasefire before the Provisionals. Two UVF representatives have confirmed that they were ready to call a unilateral end to their violence in March 1994. They said this almost happened, but was scuppered by the threat of PIRA attacks on loyalists. During their discussions with nationalist mediators, in particular two churchmen from west Belfast, the UVF men were told to prepare for an IRA onslaught on loyalists. This, the UVF were informed, was to be the Provos' parting shot before they called their ceasefire.

"We were told to batten down the hatches," one UVF leader recalled. "The tone of the messages passed to us from nationalists seemed to suggest we should just roll over and accept whatever the Provos would throw at us. Ironically, the people telling us this were the same ones who urged us to call our ceasefire there and then regardless of what the Provos did to us. There was no way loyalists were not going to respond if the IRA hit us hard. That ended any chance of an early ceasefire."

Tragically, this message ended an early unilateral loyalist ceasefire and indirectly led to more people losing their lives up until the end of the summer.

Throughout this crucial period Chris Hudson maintained his telephone contact with political representatives of the UVF. The tone of their conversations became increasingly bellicose. Hudson was so alarmed that he sought a meeting with Fergus Finlay. In Iveagh House on April 7 Hudson told Finlay that the UVF's language in relation to Dublin was dangerous.

His warning proved prophetic. For some time the UVF had been trying to attack prestigious republican targets south of the border. In the end their intelligence department only had to scan the back pages of *An Phoblacht/Republican News* to find what they were looking for. A social night was planned in Dublin to celebrate the release of IRA prisoners, including the leading Belfast republican Bobby Storey. The function was held in the Widow Scallans pub in Pearse Street and entertainment was provided by the folk band, the Irish Brigade. The event coincided with a Billy Joel concert in

Dublin's Point Theatre. It was a perfect cover for the UVF. They could travel down posing as Billy Joel fans travelling from the North that Saturday for the gig in the Point. The three-man team selected for the attack came from East Belfast. After entering the downstairs part of the pub, the UVF team placed the device beside a pillar. The aim was to blow it up and thus bring down the roof causing massive casualties. But as they were leaving the men were tackled by a doorman, Martin Doherty from the Finglas area of Dubin. In the fracas one of the UVF men shot Doherty dead. They then escaped in a car across the Liffey and then after changing into another vehicle, the UVF men set fire to the car they used to take them to Widow Scallans.

Martin Doherty was a member of the Provisional IRA's Dublin Brigade. He was given a paramilitary funeral, with his coffin flanked by unmasked men in black berets. In a statement the UVF said a "detonation problem" had prevented the bomb at the Widow Scallans from exploding. At the very least the organisation demonstrated it was prepared to go all the way to Dublin to attack republicans and their supporters, although it should not be forgotten that many ordinary Dubliners who were not attending the Irish Brigade function could have been killed in the attack.

The ballistics reports into the weapon which killed Martin Doherty raised some interesting questions. It concluded that the gun, a nine millimetre pistol, was the same one which had been used to murder the UDA leader and racketeer Jimmy Craig back in 1988. The same gun was also used in the same year Craig was shot dead in a murder bid on an IRA man who himself played a part in killing Bobby "Squeak" Seymour. Senior UVF commanders still refuse to discuss exactly how the gun that killed Craig ended up being the same one at Widow Scallans six years later. Either the UVF stole the gun from the east Belfast UDA, or the UVF themselves played a role in Craig's assassination.

A day after the Dublin attack, the UVF's mid-Ulster brigade left a bomb at the Sinn Féin offices in Newry. The bomb failed to explode due to a faulty timing device. Twenty-four hours after the Newry bombing, the UVF turned its attention to Sinn Féin councillors in Belfast. A remote controlled bomb with a listening device was left on a window ledge at City Hall outside Sinn Féin's offices in the council chamber. The bomb was set off by a UVF man across the road in Wellington Place. It exploded while no one was in the room although the blast injured several Protestant workmen who were restoring the front of the City Hall building. The device went off minutes after the IRA shot dead a young Protestant man just yards away, at the back of the old Anderson and McAuley building in Royal Avenue. The UVF's renewed bombing campaign in the late spring of 1994 also extended to Derry, an area where the UDA rather than the older loyalist group were traditionally stronger. A pipe bomb was left at the home of a Sinn Féin member in the city, although no one was injured in the attack. In the space of three days the UVF had launched four separate bomb attacks on Sinn Féin. The explosions on both sides of the border marked a significant escalation in the UVF campaign against republicans.

After such a brazen attempt to wipe out IRA and Sinn Féin members in Dublin, the UVF expected the Provisionals to hit back. Instead the other active republican terror group, the INLA, went back on the offensive, attacking the UVF in its heartland. On the afternoon of June 16 Trevor King, Colin "Crazy" Craig and Derek Hamilton were standing on the Shankill Road near the Co-Op store. Hamilton was showing King and Craig some pictures of an album of loyalist murals when a car pulled up beside them. Out of it stepped a gunman who at point-blank range shot each of the trio in the head. Craig died almost instantly. Hamilton clung to life for twenty-four hours before dying. King survived on a life support machine for more than three weeks. According to close friends King, while lapsing in and out of consciousness, requested that the machine be turned off.

King's death was a major blow to the UVF. He had joined the organisation in the early 1970s and was one of the gunmen during the Battle of Springmartin. King had been held on the word of Supergrasses in Crumlin Road jail and when released rose through the UVF's ranks to become its director of operations. Hamilton on the other hand had no direct involvement. He was a businessman who owned an electrical shop on the Shankill. Although Colin Craig received a paramilitary funeral during which camera crews and journalists were threatened, the UVF started to brief journalists about their slain comrade's chequered past within days of his funeral. Senior members of the UVF's brigade staff insisted that Craig had been working as an agent for RUC special branch. The absurdity of his death was that prior to the INLA shooting, the UVF leadership had decided to pick up and interrogate Craig about his alleged work for the security forces.

One UVF commander accused Craig of treason: "Colin Craig was about to be taken out by the UVF but the INLA got there first. We had been building a file on him for some time. We knew, for instance, that he helped provide the information which led to Brian Robinson being killed in 1989."

He went on to allege that Craig's handler was a detective from Tennent Street RUC station off the Crumlin Road. Indeed, within minutes of the Shankill shooting this detective was spotted by UVF supporters on the road. It should be noted however that many UVF supporters and friends of Craig dispute the leadership's assertion that he was an informer. In November 1995, for instance, one of the authors was in the home of a UVF supporter in Edinburgh. On the wall of his son's bedroom, alongside framed photographs of Gusty Spence, was a picture of Colin Craig at a loyalist prisoners' welfare fund-raising function. The owner of the house, a member of the Independent Orange Order, referred to Craig as a "hero" and refused to accept that he had been working for RUC special branch.

The INLA gunman responsible for the triple killing is known to the UVF. He is an experienced killer who was involved in the murder of Gerard "Doctor Death" Steenson during the INLA-IPLO feud in 1987. The other INLA member involved was Geno Gallagher. When Gallagher was shot dead by a breakaway faction of the INLA two years later the UVF on the Shankill were jubilant. One of the authors telephoned a leading UVF man after Gallagher was killed and was told: "Don't bother me now, we're all away to the pub to celebrate".

Throughout the UVF's history there have been two contradictory lines of strategic thought. One follows the argument that it is always better to target known republicans and leave ordinary Catholics alone. The other, more visceral, attitude is that when republicans attack loyalists or Protestants, then the UVF should respond by terrorising the entire Catholic population in an effort to force the IRA and INLA to stop. The dominance of these two positions depends on the circumstances. In the aftermath of the Shankill shooting many loyalists took the latter option and went for irrational revenge.

That "revenge" was exacted on June 18, 1994, at O'Toole's bar in the tiny village of Loughinisland in Co Down. A UVF unit clinically singled out and then shot dead six men drinking in the pub who at the time were watching the Republic of Ireland's opening game against Italy in the World Cup. Five others were badly wounded. The murdered men had no republican connections. Among the dead was one of the oldest victims of the Troubles, 87-year-old Barney Green.

310

His story was particularly touching. A harmless, deeply religious man, Mr Green was known to say a decade of the rosary before being picked up at his home in Ballynahinch whenever he wanted to go to O'Toole's pub for an evening. The murder of Barney Green seemed to encapsulate the futile and naked savagery of those behind the massacre.

A few days after Loughinisland one of the authors was summoned to a meeting with two senior UVF members in east Belfast. During a heated conversation the two men stressed over and over again that the massacre was "definitely not policy". They went on to say that those involved carried out the killing on their own without first checking with the leadership. Later one of the UVF leaders explained that his organisation, while tight at the centre, had a loose federal structure which allowed individual units to carry out their own operations. Essentially that was what had happened at Loughinisland in the aftermath of the Shankill shooting. None of this fails to excuse the slaughter of six men whose only crime was their religion and who happened to be in the wrong place at the wrong time.

Yet despite the slaughter, Chris Hudson decided it was worthwhile to pursue his contacts with the UVF and their political representatives. He held another meeting in Belfast shortly after Loughinisland and discussed the way ahead. It turned to be one of his more negative encounters with the loyalists. It ended with the UVF telling him that some in the leadership were ready to strike at Dublin again. One chilling idea proposed that the UVF should shoot dead an American tourist in Dublin as a simple, brutal means of damaging the Republic's tourist industry.

The UVF had also revised plans to destabilise the south which had first been devised after the Anglo-Irish Agreement. Armed now with the high-powered explosive, Powergel, the UVF had been improving its bomb-making skills. They had also devised a bombing strategy. A hit list of potential economic and tourist targets was drawn up. They included a chemical works in Drogheda, harbours, forests and even historical interpretative centres.

UVF thinking ran close to that of the IRA at the start of the 1990s. The Provos had struck at prestigious targets like the Baltic Exchange in the City of London. The aim of this was to cost the British exchequer millions of pounds and press home the republican case in the heart of the UK. The UVF saw there was plenty of evidence to suggest that the Republic's vital tourist industry was extremely volatile. During the second World War, in which the Republic played no part, transatlantic tourism to Ireland dropped dramatically as American tourists imagined that in anywhere in Europe they might be a target. One UVF member said it would have been easy to scare off Americans from the south: "A few shots at a tourist bus full of Yanks would have sent them packing back to America. That would hurt the south alright."

The UVF leadership also kept one eye on IRA strategy over the weeks running up to the Provo ceasefire. The loyalists suspected that republicans would have preferred to see the UVF and UDA still killing while Sinn Féin basked in the glory of an IRA cessation. Progressive Unionist Party politicians pointed to what they believed was "a summer of provocation" by the IRA against loyalists. It started on July 11, when an IRA unit led by the organisation's O/C in Belfast shot dead Ray Smallwoods outside his home in Lisburn. Smallwoods had been one of the main voices within the UDA calling for a ceasefire. David Ervine said the killing was a "totally cynical exercise", pointing out that Smallwoods had been in constant touch with the two priests in Clonard Monastery, Frs Alec Reid and Gerry Reynolds. Through the clerics Smallwoods had conveyed to republicans that loyalists wanted peace. Of course republicans allege that Smallwoods played a key role in the UDA's terror campaign, acting as the organisation's politico-military strategist. In their eyes he was a legitimate target.

During the summer the Provisionals also resorted to a tactic not employed since the mid-1970s. Their units placed bombs at four pubs in north and south Belfast which were frequented by loyalists. In addition to this the IRA also shot dead UDA south Belfast leader Joe Bratty and his colleague Raymond Elder on the Ormeau Road. The UVF claims this was further evidence of provocation aimed at torpedoing any chance of a loyalist ceasefire. David Ervine believed the IRA summer offensive was not simply a matter of the Provos settling old scores before the cessation. In his mind the Provisionals were working to a more sophisticated agenda than pure revenge.

"Adams and McGuinness wanted to swan the world stage while the Prods continued to kill Taigs. A loyalist ceasefire would, of course, screw all that up."

But the 1994 "summer of provocation" was not totally one-sided. Violent UVF activity went on throughout July and August. On Saturday, August 20, the UVF was responsible for two bomb attacks on republican targets. In Newcastle, Co Down they placed a bomb on a trailer at the home of a leading republican. The UVF failed to detonate the device by remote control because women and children were in the area at the time. The device used was similar in design to the bomb placed at the Sinn Féin office in Belfast City Hall. Several hours after the aborted attack in Newcastle, the UVF placed a bomb outside the Trocadero Pub in Belfast's Cromac Street. No one was injured in the explosion.

Four days after the bombings, the UVF in mid-Ulster carried out a callous act of brutality. In the early hours of Sunday morning a UVF unit broke into a house near Omagh. They were unable to find the owner of the house, Patrick O'Hagan, who as a former IRA prisoner served a sentence for possessing explosives. So instead they murdered his wife

Kathleen who was heavily pregnant at the time. Mrs O'Hagan was chased around the house by her killers while her children screamed in horror. When they caught up with her a gunman shot her dead in front of the children.

Shortly afterwards the UVF said they had intended to kill Kathleen O'Hagan as well as her husband. Yet they added that they would have spared her had they known she was pregnant at the time. Her husband escaped death because he was at a party nearby, organised to celebrate the return of a relative from the United States. The UVF's explanation for the slaying of a pregnant woman was that it was in retaliation for the Teebane massacre four years before. The murder demonstrated once and for all the ferocious nature of sectarian hatred and memory in mid-Ulster. Kathleen O'Hagan's killing would not have been out of place in Bosnia at the height of ethnic cleansing.

The IRA "ended" their war on August 31, 1994. While all of nationalist Ireland as well as the "Irish diaspora" celebrated, most unionists were initially deeply suspicious. Many thought the Provisionals would not have halted their campaign unless Britain had struck a secret deal with them. Those still engaged in dialogue with the UDA and UVF gave repeated assurances that no deals had been concocted.

Three days after the IRA cessation Chris Hudson travelled up to Belfast with a message from the Irish government to the UVF. Hudson met Gusty Spence and David Ervine. Dublin had three points it wished to pass on. Firstly, that there were no secret deals between the two governments and the IRA. Secondly, there was no hidden agenda. Finally, Hudson told Spence and Ervine that the Taoiseach Albert Reynolds had insisted in the run-up to the IRA ceasefire that he would only tolerate a total cessation of violence and wasn't interested in temporary or tactical delays in violence. Hudson added that within days Gerry Adams would be standing on the steps of Government Buildings in Dublin holding hánds in a new love-in with Albert Reynolds and John Hume. This photo-call, Hudson said, was not the start of a new pan-nationalist coalition. To the Irish government, the handshake on the steps was merely a symbolic pay-back to Adams for helping to bring about the IRA ceasefire. This information, according to both Hudson and Ervine, seemed to settle nerves within the UVF camp. Hudson was himself determined to check that the Irish government's assurances were genuine. A few days after his Belfast meeting Hudson went to see Fine Gael Senator Maurice Manning in Dublin. Hudson regarded Manning as a man of honour and when the Senator assured him he wasn't being hoodwinked he accepted the government's bona fides.

The UVF themselves were busy lowering the temperature in their strongholds after the IRA ceasefire. On the first night of the Provo cessation the UVF organised a march along the Shankill Road, mainly comprised of women, which was billed as a celebration of the Provisionals' "surrender". The marchers held up banners proclaiming "25 years and still British" and one rather amusing poster "Gerry the Brit". Fresh slogans were painted up on gable walls declaring that "On behalf of the loyalist people of the Shankill Road we accept the unconditional surrender of the IRA – signed UVF." The paradox, of course, was that just hours earlier republicans had held their own cavalcade to celebrate an IRA victory. They too believed their side had won. In every sense the two opposing rallies in Belfast pointed the way ahead for eighteen months of relative peace, a period of political illusions and peddled half-truths. An era in which everyone won and nobody lost. All the circles seemed to have been squared.

Privately UVF leaders admitted that there had been no surrender by republicans. Rather they saw the situation in later summer of 1994 as a point of mutual exhaustion. David Ervine said the object of the Shankill march and the triumphant graffiti was to instil communal confidence in loyalists who thought there might be another British sell-out around the corner.

None of this loyalist confidence, real or apparent, prevented the UVF from continuing its attacks on republicans or the Irish Republic. On September 1, with the IRA ceasefire still only hours old, the UVF tried to kill a top Provo who was drinking inside the Beaten Docket pub in central Belfast. Only for the weapon jamming, their target would have been killed in front of scores of customers.

Throughout the summer months the UVF had experienced technical problems with their bombs. Three days after the Beaten Docket attack they concluded they now had the ability to explode a large device and perhaps kill a large number of republicans. An attack was planned on a prestigious republican target in west Belfast on the night of September 4. At the last minute the original attack was inexplicably abandoned. Instead the UVF hijacked a car on the Shankill and drove it to Sinn Féin's press centre in Sevastapol Street off the Falls Road. A Sinn Féin rally had just ended at the time and enough warning was given to the media for the area to be cleared. The bomb exploded, causing some damage to the party's offices. It demonstrated once and for all that the UVF had perfected its bomb-making capabilities. Indeed senior UVF members insist there was going to be no loyalist ceasefire until they were able to prove they could cause large scale carnage with their bombs.

The "other peace process" developed while loyalists were still engaged in violence. A vital component in the drive towards a ceasefire was the thaw in relations between the UVF and Dublin. Yet the last weeks of violence were riddled with contradictions.

A UVF unit managed to break into the house of the INLA chief of staff, Hugh Torney, in the Lower Falls area. Their aim was to kill Torney in retaliation for Trevor King's death in June.

Torney though was careful about his personal security and failed to turn up at the house. The UVF men left his family whom they'd held hostage and fled the area. A few days later on September 12 the organisation placed a bomb underneath a seat on the Belfast to Dublin train. As the train pulled into Connolly Station a warning was telephoned from the North that a bomb was on board. Although the bomb went off, the explosive did not detonate and passengers were sprayed with unexploded Powergel. The station was cleared and fifteen minutes later the device exploded. The UVF later said it was placed there "as a warning to the southern government that the Ulster people will not be engulfed in a united Ireland, either by coercion, persuasion, force or political stealth."

The bomb was a major embarrassment for Chris Hudson. His enemies, through the pages of *An Phoblacht* and *Phoenix* magazine, delighted in the irony of Hudson, the voice of the Peace Train organisation, talking to a terror group that was putting rail passengers' lives at risk with bombs on trains.

"I remember ringing up the PUP in Belfast and shouting down the phone at them 'a bomb on a fucking train, thanks very much.' After all my work with the Peace Train it was extremely embarrassing. But I knew I had to go on," Hudson recalled.

The Connolly Station attack pointed up the uncertainties within the UVF rank and file about moving towards a ceasefire. The unit responsible for the bombing consisted of some of those behind the Loughinisland massacre. With people like this, the UVF leadership had a lot of convincing to do before the ceasefire could be called.

That caution was reflected across the entire spectrum of loyalist paramilitarism. At the end of September the Combined Loyalist Military Command met to discuss their next move. The CLMC laid out six points they said had to be addressed if a ceasefire was to happen. The statement showed the unease about ending the campaign. The points were:

*We have yet to ascertain the bona fides of the permanence of the IRA "Ceasefire".

*The intent of the INLA is yet to be established.

*To be convinced that no secret deals have been concocted between HMG and the IRA.

*That our constitutional position as a partner within the United Kingdom is assured.

*To assess the implications of the joint Governmental "Framework document" as soon as possible.

*It is incumbent on the British government to ensure that there is no change or erosion within Northern Ireland, to facilitate the illusion of IRA "victory". Change, if any, can only be honourable after dialogue and agreement." In conclusion the joint statement called for the same patience to be given to loyalists as was granted the IRA in the run-up to their cessation.

Privately, the UVF leadership had been given assurances that there were no secret deals or sell-outs. To create the climate in which a ceasefire would be easier to call, the organisation set out on a propaganda campaign, mainly through the pages of *Combat* magazine, to allay fears in their own ranks that their ceasefire could be construed as surrender.

In September's *Combat,* in an article entitled "Just what are the fears and hopes of the Loyalists", a former life sentence prisoner argued the case for a ceasefire. While recognising loyalist suspicions about the IRA cessation, the ex-prisoner urged his community to seek confidence in itself. "It is felt by some that the current ceasefire called by the IRA is the result of the SDLP, USA senators and Irish and British governments convincing Sinn Féin that the United Ireland objectives of the IRA by using the bomb and bullets tactic are unwelcome, unrealistic and unobtainable," he argued. "In short loyalists could be celebrating a victory because the IRA have called a ceasefire without having achieved the objectives they set out to achieve."

As well as convincing their constituency on the outside, the UVF leadership also had to persuade their prisoners in the Maze that there were no sell-outs and that a ceasefire would benefit them. The UDA faced the same problem but spent considerably longer talking to their inmates than the UVF. This difference illustrates the contrast in the way the two loyalist groupings regard their prisoners. For the UVF, the one hundred or so inmates under their control are simply another battalion of the organisation. While their views were and are taken on board, they must as a UVF battalion ultimately act in accordance with the leadership's wishes. The UDA, however, admitted that its ceasefire was predicated on the support of their prisoners. In the fortnight running up to the loyalist cessation the Northern Ireland Office allowed the UDA leadership to meet their inmates on a regular basis inside the Maze. Ironically Johnny Adair, who had been sentenced to 16 years a few months earlier for directing acts of terrorism, became a critical voice in support of the UDA calling a ceasefire. John White, the man who killed Senator Paddy Wilson and Irene Andrews, was another key player for the UDA. Since he had only been released from the Maze two years before, White knew most of the UDA life and long-term prisoners. He also persuaded them to back the leadership's support for a ceasefire. Indeed the prison view was so vital that some UDA men wanted to declare the ceasefire from the car park of the Maze a few days before the CLMC called their violence to a halt.

Another difficulty for the UVF at this time was the fresh stocks of explosives in their arsenal. Many middle rankers argued that the UVF should use up more Powergel and let off a few more bombs in the Republic before declaring a ceasefire. They argued that for the first time in decades the loyalists now had the ability to match Provo terror in every field, including explosions. These sceptical voices argued that if there was going to be a ceasefire then it should come with a bang.

But the primacy of politics as opposed to cold logistics won the day. Gusty Spence argued tirelessly among the UVF battalions that the organisation should move towards a cessation. The support of the UVF's commanding officer for the ceasefire was equally crucial. He had the respect of many ordinary members who were uncertain about the uncharted political waters their organisation was wading into. Along with him and Spence, David Ervine and Billy Hutchinson were able to convince the membership that the union was indeed safe. Even unpredictable UVF figures like King Rat in Portadown swung behind the idea of a cessation.

Their confidence was not näive. In contrast to the loyalist project, republican goals seemed a lot less attainable in the autumn of 1994. Essentially the IRA volunteer's task is a revolutionary one. His organisation has to overturn the entire constitutional position of a state against the wishes of the majority of its citizens. Republicans face a mammoth talks given that they have to radically transform not only Northern Ireland but also the Irish Republic in order to obtain the 32-county socialist unitary dream. The UVF member's task is much simpler, at least in the short to medium historical term. He or she is defending the status quo, maintaining things as they are. This was beginning to dawn on the leaders and members of violent loyalist groups. Their thirty years of violence was about to come to an end.

Chris Hudson, who had helped build bridges of confidence between Dublin and the UVF, would not be there in person to see it. He was scheduled to go to Pakistan as part of his work for the Oxfam charity. A few days before he flew east, he telephoned David Ervine and Gusty Spence. He pressed them on when the ceasefire was coming, they told him to be patient.

"I kept asking them for the date. I was so excited that everything was almost in place. David and Gusty kept saying to me 'It's coming Chris, it's coming soon.' I wanted to leap for joy."

## Eleven

## PREPARED FOR PEACE, READY FOR WAR

About an hour before the loyalist ceasefire was finally declared, Gusty Spence, the man who embodies the beginning and the end of modern UVF violence, sat in his car looking out at the trees and green spaces around Fernhill House estate in the Upper Shankill. As he puffed on his pipe he said, in a reflective mood, quite deliberately, out loud: "I'm looking at history".

The setting could not have been a more appropriate place for the announcement of the end of three decades of loyalist terror. It was here, after all, that the original UVF in Belfast trained and prepared for war against the British government and nationalist Ireland at the start of the 20th century.

The press photographers gathering at Fernhill on October 13, 1994, asked Spence if he meant that history was being made on that hopeful day. The former UVF commander replied in the negative, pointing out that there had been 30,000 men in Fernhill's grounds eighty years before. Spence was grasping at the historical connection between Carson's army and the militia he helped to rejuvenate in the mid-1960s.

On that bright autumn morning Spence seemed to sense some sort of historic and personal achievement. It was he who had been chosen to read out the document which sealed the end of the armed campaigns of the UVF and UDA. Spence was after all the alpha and the omega man of violent loyalism. He was there at the start and he would see it come to an end.

Joining him on a table inside the house were all the shades of loyalist paramilitarism. John White, a former UDA prisoner who had served a sentence for murdering SDLP Senator Paddy Wilson and his friend Irene Andrews, Spence's colleague David Ervine and the spokesman for UVF prisoners, Jim McDonald, were among those at the top table.

Camera bulbs flashed, tape recorders clicked and long fat cables fed the images of the loyalist leadership, bringing their violence to a halt across the planet. Spence told the world that all loyalist hostilities would cease at midnight. The permanence of their ceasefire would be "dependent upon the cessation of all Nationalist/Republican violence. The sole responsibility for a return to war lies with them."

Spence made two salient points contained within the ceasefire document, which also paid tribute to the loyalist groupings. He boldly asserted that "The union is safe" and therefore the UVF, UDA and Red Hand Commando members killed in the conflict did not die in vain.

Unlike the IRA statement of August 31 the Combined Loyalist Military Command offered an apology to the victims of loyalist violence. Spence told the assembled media that the CLMC showed "abject and true remorse" to the loved ones of innocent victims.

The claim that the union was still secure was a fateful statement. It would be thrown up in the faces of Spence and other loyalist leaders over the next two years, especially by cynics in the Protestant-unionist community.

Meanwhile, thousands of miles away in Pakistan, Chris Hudson watched the unfolding events at Fernhill House. Hudson sat in his hotel bedroom in Islamabad watching live coverage of the CLMC announcement on BBC World Service television. He was euphoric gazing at the screen as the loyalists entered the global village as peacemakers. He poured himself a celebratory drink.

The euphoria was infectious. It even spread to hardline

areas of Northern Ireland like Portadown. Billy Wright described October 13 as the "happiest day of my life". The UVF leadership in Belfast tried to temper the celebrations. The final hours before the midnight peace announcement were remarkably quiet in UVF strongholds such as the Shankill Road. The organisation's leadership had appealed to grassroots supporters not to act in a triumphant fashion.

Their advice was generally accepted, although a small number of fringe loyalist supporters including quite a number of women marched from the Lower Newtonards Road in east Belfast to the City Hall. About one hundred of them, many quite drunk, arrived there just before midnight while peace campaigners who were holding a vigil counted out what was meant to be the final seconds of the Troubles. The peaceniks sang "Oh Danny Boy". The loyalists chanted the "Sash". A quarter of a mile away in the city's docks area, camera crews trained their lenses on the hands of the Albert Clock as they moved to the midnight peace hour. It was a surreal end to an incredible day.

After the celebrations came the hard questions. Who if anyone had won the war? Had the British government done a deal with the IRA? Had the republican leadership sold out and if so, could it survive a damaging split?

Even before the loyalist ceasefire the Democratic Unionist Party was convinced that the peace process was a sham and that the British were preparing to hatch a deal behind Ulster's back. David Ervine recalls that a few weeks before the cessation a prominent DUP member expressed surprise when told that the UVF was preparing to call a ceasefire. "He told me we should keep going, that we had the IRA on the run and there was no point giving up now," Ervine said.

Over the next few months relations between the DUP and the UVF's political representatives deteriorated. The PUP accused the DUP of being afraid of the new force in loyalist politics. Charges of sell-out and surrender were mere ploys by the DUP to strangle fledgling loyalist parties from developing a wider electoral base. The DUP countered by arguing that both the PUP and the UDA-aligned Ulster Democratic Party were dupes of a perfidious British government. Paisley's party pointed to exploratory talks held between the British government and loyalists at Stormont. These talks with loyalists were just paving the way for Sinn Féin to gain entry into the corridors of power at Stormont. Then the real bargaining would begin and Ulster would be sold out.

The attitude of the loyalist political representatives towards the first official talks with the government was somewhat more benign. David Ervine, Billy Hutchinson, Gary McMichael and others believed loyalism should stride confidently across the world and not be afraid to put its case anywhere. After their meeting at Stormont the PUP delegation claimed that they had been assured " . . . the future of Northern Ireland will be founded on democracy and consent". Interestingly, the PUP envoys to the first round of talks included Lindsay Robb, who, within less than a year, would be serving a prison sentence for arms offences on behalf of the UVF in Scotland. Another of the delegates was Jackie Mahood, a North Belfast businessman who later fell out of favour with the PUP leadership.

Loyalists had indeed broken new ground in their first round of talks with Government. Only a year before, their military wings had been denounced as murderers and thugs by some of the same Stormont ministers they later shook hands and took tea with. Despite the bonhomie between the loyalists and Government officials, however, they refused to give ground on the issue of the decommissioning of terrorist weapons. This became a central demand both of the British and the established Unionist parties. For the UVF and UDA decommissioning was an unrealistic proposal while the IRA and INLA maintained their arsenals.

The first major post-ceasefire test for the PUP came with

the publication of the Framework Document by both the British and Irish governments. The document outlined a three-stranded approach to governing Northern Ireland in an atmosphere of peace. The sticking point for most unionists appeared to be a number of proposed cross-border institutions in fields such as tourism and agriculture. The PUP and UDP did not appear to be hung up on the cross-border bodies. While they expressed serious misgivings about the nature of such institutions (mainly if they had executive powers) they noted that the bedrock of any agreement would be the wishes of the greater number of people in Northern Ireland.

In contrast, the DUP took a more apocalyptic view of the Framework proposals. The party pasted posters across the Province claiming that it was another "piece in the process". The graphic poster design, showing Northern Ireland being lifted out of the UK, demonstrated that the process was moving towards a United Ireland. In DUP eyes the Framework Document was the first reward to the IRA for ending its campaign. Within days of the document's launch in Belfast by John Major and John Bruton, mocking graffiti appeared in the east of the city. "The Union is Safe – Ha Ha Ha" it read, a clear reference back to the CLMC's bold assertion on the day of the ceasefire.

Unlike the leaders in the Unionist parties, loyalists such as Billy Hutchinson were willing to engage in debate with nationalists and republicans. Hutchinson, for instance, took part in a discussion in Pilot's Row community hall on the nationalist Bogside area of Derry about "Unionist/Loyalist Perspectives on the Peace Process". Hutchinson told republicans gathered there that the war was over and that a new unionism could be forged free from religious bigotry and reaction. He repeated a CLMC statement issued just before the IRA cessation which recognised the right of anyone to seek constitutional change as long as it was by democratic and peaceful means. Loyalists also supported a written constitution and a Bill of Rights as well as some non-executive cross-border bodies.

Among those on the platform with Hutchinson was Robin Perceval, an English-born republican activist in Derry. Hutchinson's visit to the lion's den included a photograph of him and Perceval along with the unionist mayor of Derry, Richard Dallas. This was reported in full in *Combat*. The UVF magazine failed to mention Perceval's Sinn Féin connection. Perhaps that was still a bit too much for some *Combat* readers.

Despite the jibes of sell-out (mostly from the DUP) the UVF ceasefire held firm throughout the first half of 1995. Most volunteers seemed happy to accept the leadership's assurances that their fears were unfounded. This, however, did not produce a totally peaceful atmosphere, either on the streets or in the prisons. On May 14, 1995, around 150 UVF prisoners rioted in the Maze after searches were conducted for mobile phones and other electronic equipment. The inmates managed to fight their way onto the roof of their H-Block and posed for the media in prison warders' hats they had taken during the fracas with officers. One UVF man even brandished a replica Armalite rifle for the cameras. Ostensibly, the cause of the riot was the prisoners' objection to the searches on their wings. In reality, UVF commanders admit the violence and the destruction were also due to the pent-up frustration many loyalist inmates felt over the abscence of any prospects that they might be freed as part of a post-ceasefire deal with the Government.

Outside, so-called punishment attacks by both republican and loyalist paramilitaries continued. Human Rights organisations such as FAIT questioned the legitimacy of the ceasefires while these abuses went on.

Some of those targeted in a wave of post-ceasefire punishment attacks were labelled as drug dealers. Many of the victims of paramilitary justice and politicians regarded this as sheer hypocrisy. Even before the ceasefire the UDA and UVF were accused of dabbling in drug-dealing. The head of the RUC's Drug Squad even linked loyalists to republican splinter groups such as the IPLO, alleging they colluded to carve up the drugs trade in Northern Ireland. Both the UDA and UVF leaderships strenuously denied they were involved in drugs or, much worse, colluding with republicans in the business.

The RUC accept that the UVF's Brigade Staff are opposed to drug-dealing. However there have been several instances of individual UVF and UDA members being caught with large quantities of drugs, particularly Ecstasy. Areas such as Antrim, Ballymena and Portadown are cited as places where UVF members have linked up with criminals to control the Ecstasy trade. But the extent of UVF involvement in drugs contrasts sharply with that of the UDA. Senior RUC officers believe top UDA personnel are key players in the drugs trade, although several other members of the Inner Council oppose any involvement in dealing.

The drugs issue in post-ceasefire Northern Ireland became the new spectre haunting society once the terrorist campaigns ended. It further damaged relations between the UDA and UVF. The latter organisation took a truculent stance against drug dealers, issuing threats through the local media and on the walls of the Shankill Road that those involved in the business would be shot.

In the spring of 1995 a propaganda war broke out between the two loyalist terror groups over which one of them was more anti-drugs. The CLMC had been planning to issue a joint statement condemning drug-dealers and threatening to expel any loyalist involved in it. Instead on May 11 the UDA issued a unilateral statement denying connections to the trade. Down the road on the Shankill, the UVF leadership reacted furiously and issued their own statement the same day also stating their opposition to drugs. Moreover, the UVF briefed journalists about senior UDA men they claimed were drug-dealing. The UDA countered that everyone knew elements within the mid-Ulster UVF, namely in Portadown, were also dealing in drugs. The squabble heightened tensions within the loyalist community.

On the fringes of loyalism the small Red Hand Commando grouping was also trying to clean up its image. It had been severely tarnished by the Margaret Wright murder and the subsequent allegations that several RHC and UVF members were high on drugs when Ms Wright was murdered. The Red Hand, a satellite group of the UVF, decided to take direct action against those involved. It murdered Billy Elliot, the RHC's second-in-command and the man responsible for the gang which killed Ms Wright. Elliot, who had been involved in dealing Ecstasy in Belfast and Bangor, was murdered outside his home in the Co Down town. He was actually shot dead on the orders of the the RHC's leader, a dedicated former loyalist prisoner, who was also strongly opposed to drug dealing. RHC comrades had cynically lured Elliot to his death, sharing a cup of tea with him minutes before the assassination.

After Elliot's death the RHC issued an ultimatum to those arrested for Margaret Wright's murder: they must all plead guilty or else they themselves would be killed, either in jail or out of it. In the trials that followed a bizarre scenario emerged. All but one of the defendants in the murder trial at Belfast Crown Court, including Elliot's wife Alison, pleaded guilty. The judge, however, refused to accept their pleas given the RHC threat to their lives. In the same courtroom sat the Red Hand's leader. In fact he remained in the public gallery for the duration of the trial, which finally got underway after most of the defendants managed to convince the judge they wished to put in a guilty plea. Journalists in the press box joked as to who the real judge was during the

Wright trial – the man in the wig sitting in front of the defendants and the lawyers, or the man in the public gallery making personally sure they made the right plea?

The IRA also took a keen interest in the growing drugs trade. The Provos set up a bogus group known as Direct Action Against Drugs. DAAD started a campaign of murder and intimidation against drug dealers, small and big. In total, between mid-1995 to early 1996, the IRA shot dead eight of those it alleged were known drug barons. They included Mickey "Moneybags" Mooney, who had probably signed his own death warrant not by drug-dealing but by beating up republicans who crossed him. The murder squad worked under the direction of a senior IRA/Sinn Féin member who was later arrested for serious terrorist offences. One of the chief killers in the DAAD anti-drugs purge was a Markets man who used the murders to boost his reputation within the Provisionals. This man later became the IRA's Commanding Officer in Belfast.

DAAD's campaign had twin objectives. As well as killing suspected drug dealers, it also kept IRA volunteers busy targeting and executing operations. The squalid murders, mainly of low level dealers and users, sent a chilling signal to both the government and the loyalists that the IRA, in Gerry Adams' words, hadn't gone away. In this period the UVF was particularly worried that the IRA might use the DAAD flag of convenience to assassinate loyalists. The UVF's Brigade Staff sent out warnings to the IRA not to use their anti-drugs purge to attack loyalists, even those involved in dealing Ecstasy.

Their warning reflected deeper concerns about the real intent of the Provisionals in the second half of 1995. Many in the UVF suspected the DAAD killings were a dress rehearsal for a renewed IRA campaign. Both the UVF and UDA claimed that the IRA was again targeting their members. IRA activists were seen driving through loyalist areas and openly flaunting their presence there in a bid to wind up grassroots loyalists. Sinn Féin was also winding up the marching issue, organising, behind the scenes, many of the nationalist residents' groups who opposed Orange parades in areas like the Lower Ormeau in south Belfast and Garvaghy Road in Portadown. The UVF believed that republicans were seeking to create street violence and thus provide some sort of pretext for a return to IRA violence. The street protests through the marching season reached their climax during the first Drumcree stand-off in 1995, which ended when a deal between Garvaghy Road residents and Orangemen allowed a small Orange parade to pass the nationalist area. It seemed, at least at that stage, that both sides had managed to draw back from the brink – just.

The UVF leadership back in Belfast had little to do with the first Drumcree protest. In mid-Ulster however local UVF units, especially the Portadown group, were deeply involved in the stand-off between Orange marchers and the RUC. Billy Wright played a central role in the organisation of loyalists at the siege of Drumcree. He was regarded as such a pivotal figure that even the Irish government sought his views prior to the 1995 marching season. Fergus Finlay, Dick Spring's special adviser, was asked to meet Wright by Fr. Brian Lennon, a Portadown-based Jesuit, who wanted to resolve the Garvaghy Road issue. Finlay recalled his first ever meeting with the Portadown loyalist leader.

"It was just before the first siege of Drumcree. I remember Wright's house was the closest thing I have ever seen to a brothel. There were purple carpets and white leather settees. The security on the house was amazing. There was a huge oak door and behind it a steel cage. Wright was there with his bodyguard. The meeting lasted about two and a half hours. Fr Lennon had been worried that Wright was unstable and might pose a threat to the loyalist ceasefire. But Wright pledged undying loyalty to the likes of David Ervine and insisted he was committed to peace."

Wright insisted throughout the meeting that loyalist views must be respected by the Irish government or there would inevitably be trouble. Reflecting back on the encounter, Finlay believed it was prudent to meet Wright given his important position in mid-Ulster, even though he failed to produce a compromise over the Garvaghy Road march. At that stage Wright was still loyal to the PUP leadership in Belfast. However, the marching issue and the emerging political stance of the PUP's socialist representatives put the solidarity between Portadown and Belfast under severe strain.

During Drumcree Mark I the CLMC publicly questioned whether the IRA were intent on maintaining their ceasefire. A month later, on August 25, the CLMC issued a more detailed statement which included an important challenge to republicans. The two terror groups stated: "The CLMC remains firmly committed to the defence of the Ulster people from militant Republicanism and, while the IRA's commitment to peace remains questionable, Loyalists must remain prepared. The CLMC wish to re-assure the people of Northern Ireland that provided their rights are upheld the CLMC will not initiate a return to war. There shall be no first strike."

The "No first strike" promise was a pivotal statement. It was a clear challenge to the IRA to follow suit and help solidify both ceasefires. The CLMC was to be disappointed, as the IRA failed to make a similar promise. Had they done so, that really would have been the end of the IRA's campaign. But to do so would have undermined the basic tenets of Irish Republican ideology. For almost three decades the Provos have waged a war on the Irish people's behalf without seeking the Irish people's consent. They have argued that as the true holders of the republican legacy they are the real army and government of Ireland. This near theological conviction has kept their fanatical campaign going. To suddenly declare a "No First Strike" Policy would be to

331

ideologically undermine their historical right to wage war on behalf of the Irish people. Taking that step in republican eyes is the road to surrender.

The UVF and other loyalists' commitment to violence seems more pragmatic than theocratic. Many of those who set up the UVF and UDA embarked on their terror campaigns because they believed, rightly or wrongly, that the security forces were not being allowed to do their job and suppress armed republicanism. If the union was safe and/or the army and police were allowed to take robust action against the IRA, there would be no need for loyalist violence.

Given the IRA's refusal to accept "No First Strike" and also, therefore, disarmament, there was and still is little prospect of the UVF decommissioning its arms. The CLMC said the retention of its war materials was a "purely defensive measure" and that it was inconceivable that loyalists would decommission "with a fully operational heavily armed Republican war machine intact and refusing to relinquish their arsenals."

After the summer of 1995, the UVF recommenced its own campaign of targeting and gathering intelligence on republican suspects. It also strengthened its bomb-making skills, manufacturing several large bombs from commercial mix which is still held in cold storage in the event of a full return to war. The RUC believe the UVF brought back one of its key bomb-makers from Scotland. He came originally from east Belfast and helped to train others in the black art of building bombs. The UDA was naturally doing the same thing. In the absence of goodwill and mutual trust, from the autumn of 1995 until the following year, both terror groups engaged in a game of shadow boxing – with their republican opponents.

Despite this, the UVF's political wing continued to hold talks with the British and Irish governments. Contact with the Irish cabinet was maintained via Chris Hudson. There were also informal discussions with Irish politicians, including Dick Spring who held a meeting with Gusty Spence on October 23, 1995, while on a visit to Belfast. The tone of these meetings was generally cordial, despite growing suspicions within loyalism that the IRA was planning to return to war. Spence gave assurances that the ceasefire was still solid on the loyalist side.

There had been considerable embarrassment for the PUP the previous month at the arrest in Scotland of Lindsay Robb, one of their representatives at the first Stormont talks. Robb was arrested in a pub in Falkirk, allegedly on a mission to buy guns for the UVF. There was, however, something dubious about the entire police operation. Robb was taken to an isolation unit in Barlinnie prison in a cell designed to hold the Libyan agents accused of the Lockerbie air bomb disaster, if they are ever apprehended. The PUP alleged Robb had been set up in an MI5 sting operation involving Scottish and English informants. They also deny, as he does, that he was on a mission to buy guns in Scotland for a new UVF campaign. At the same time Billy Wright was also arrested and charged with intimidation. It is interesting to note that *Combat,* the official voice of the UVF, championed Wright and Robb's case together. They referred to the two men as "Loyalist Hostages". Indeed, the author of the *Combat* article even claimed that it was Wright's trenchant criticism of the Irish government, whom he said had broken promises to loyalists, which led to his arrest. Within a year, *Combat* was singing a different tune altogether about Billy Wright.

It is clear that towards the end of 1995 the Provisional IRA's leadership had decided to resume their armed campaign. The bomb at Canary Wharf which shattered eighteen months of relative peace was actually constructed by the south Armagh Provisionals in November. This was at a time of orgasmic optimism about the peace process which climaxed with the

333

visit to Northern Ireland of US President Bill Clinton and his wife Hilary.

Why did the Provos turn the clock back? Nationalist-orientated journalists who worship at the altar of John Hume claim it was simply British obstructionism during the ceasefires. They point to lack of movement over the release of prisoners, the demand for decommissioning and ultimately the refusal to allow Sinn Féin entry into talks as the reasons for the republican movement calling off their ceasefire. John Major's alleged "binning" of the Mitchell Report and his acquiescence to unionist demands for elections to a talks body were the final straws.

This argument is entirely flawed. It fails to appreciate or understand the historical path of Irish republicanism. The real rationale behind renewed IRA violence was the preservation of Provo unity. As the ceasefires developed, it must have dawned on the IRA that their imagined strategy of tying nationalist Ireland and the United States into a political pincer movement against the British and Unionists was not going to work. They simply could not force by political will the Unionist parties and people from following a nationalist agenda. Nor could they force the British government, any British government, to in turn push the Unionists in that direction. The "Tactical Use of Armed Struggle" strategy was as chimerical as the armed struggle. The best they could hope for was an internal settlement with a few cross-border bodies. In the words of one republican sceptic who is critical of the Adams-McGuinness line: "That would have been to accept that Bobby Sands and the rest of the martyrs died for a Foyle Fisheries Commission and a cross-border milk marketing board."

Rather than risk splitting the movement the IRA Army council opted to return to war, albeit in a piecemeal half-hearted fashion. The Provos had adopted the old Catholic adage about prayer cementing a family together, only in their world it was the republican family which slays together that stays together.

None of this was lost on the UVF leadership who predicted there would be some sort of return to republican violence. Possibly they believed at the time this would be sub-contracted out to the INLA. This seemed unlikely, however, given the action replay of internal feuding and fratricidal brutality which dogged the INLA throughout 1996, much to the delight of loyalists.

Even with dark clouds gathering on the political horizon, loyalist leaders were still offering compromise within Northern Ireland. On January 29, 1996, Gusty Spence said: "Never mind the objections of nationalists, we are not going down the road to correct the regimes of the past." In other words there would be no return to the days of gerrymandering and blatant discrimination under the old Stormont government.

Talks also continued with the Irish government. These were held in secret, normally through the work of Chris Hudson. However the Irish government clearly misunderstood the mood within the general unionist population at the turn of the year. Many of the architects of Northern policy in Iveagh House imagined that the new emerging loyalist parties were the real voice of Ulster Unionism. This miscalculation led to an incident which at best caused massive embarrassment to the PUP leadership and at worst almost fatally undermined the position of the pro-ceasefire elements within the CLMC.

On February 6, 1996, David Ervine travelled along with the UVF's second in command to Dublin for a dinner date with Dick Spring and John Bruton at Iveagh House. The meeting was a convivial affair with the loyalists and the Irish side discussing their personal lives, particularly their children, as well as the political situation. Ervine said he felt uncomfortable when the Irish started to rail against David Trimble, the Ulster Unionist Party leader, for his implacable opposition to Sinn Féin entering talks while the IRA refused to disarm. "The Irish kept saying that Trimble would have to accept that Sinn Féin would be there. He would just have to lump it. The way they talked it seemed to me they thought we were in agreement with them. It was as if we were already on board." The PUP were not dogmatically opposed to Sinn Féin getting into talks. They took the position that loyalists should have the confidence to challenge them once they got there. Ervine predicted that the Sinn Féin's "United Ireland/Brits Out" stance would "founder on the rock of consent" once all-party talks got underway. Yet to expect loyalists, who might have shared a different analysis from Trimble, to go one step further and join in the condemnation of the Ulster Unionist leader was wishful thinking.

There was worse to come for the PUP and the UVF representative present in Iveagh House. When they returned to Belfast the following day, Ervine was met with a barrage of questions from the media about Dick Spring's proposal for Dayton-style peace talks to solve the Northern Ireland conflict. Surely Ervine would have been briefed about Spring's suggestion, given that he had just held a meeting with him in Dublin?

Ervine was nonplussed. No one at the Iveagh House gathering had told the loyalists about the Dayton plan, named after the Ohio town where the United States had forced the warring Bosnian factions to hammer out a tentative peace agreement. In Dayton all the parties negotiated in separate rooms from each other and the ultimate say in discussions was made by their respective sponsors. In the case of the Bosnian Serbs, for instance, the real bargaining was done by the leader of Greater Serbia, Slobodan Milosevic. Following a meeting with Sir Patrick Mayhew the same day Ervine and his comrade returned from Dublin, Spring had floated the idea that Dayton-style negotiations might work in the North.

The UVF leadership was furious. The failure to brief Ervine and his colleagues left them in a very difficult position, given the generally hostile reaction Spring's plan received from most shades of unionism. Within twenty-four hours malcontents, either from the DUP or inside the UVF, or both, daubed graffiti in North and East Belfast claiming that: "Ervine doesn't speak for the men on the ground". A general whispering game started, with sceptical loyalists posing the question – what on earth was Ervine talking to the Irish Government for if they were planning such things behind Ulster's back? News that the PUP were wined and dined in Dublin while Dick Spring planned an unacceptable talks formula was music to the ears of hardline loyalists opposed to the direction the PUP was taking.

The Iveagh House meeting and the Dayton proposal damaged the UVF/PUP leadership. The UVF decided to break off official meetings with the Irish Government. There was deep anger and a sense that they had been duped by the mandarins of the Republic's Department of Foreign Affairs.

To be fair, the Irish side did not see it that way. Fergus Finlay insists they acted in good faith with the loyalist leadership at all times. His recollection of the Iveagh House meeting is somewhat more positive.

"I never understood it. It was a peculiar situation. We had put the idea of proximity talks to the British government. They talks might be on the same line as those of Dayton and the Bosnian situation. The British asked us not to disclose this at the time while they studied our proposals. In that same week we met the SDLP and Sinn Féin. None of these parties were informed either about the Dayton-style talks. The PUP came back to Belfast the next morning when the story broke. They were very offended that they had been caught on the hop. I never fully understood why that offence lasted so long. The Iveagh House gathering had been a most pleasant evening. It was almost a social occasion with us finding a lot of common ground."

Perhaps that was precisely the problem; the Irish government appeared to have been carried away with the conviviality. They failed to remember where these men came from and the kind of pressures they faced in their own constituency. At best Spring and others were guilty of a benign miscalculation. Ervine and the rest of the PUP leadership could afford to be politically one step ahead of mainstream unionism, but still only one step ahead.

Despite the breakdown in relations between the UVF/PUP and the Irish Government, Dublin ministers and their advisers continued to heap praise on the loyalist leadership. Fergus Finlay said he believed from his contacts with the PUP that it seemed loyalists were more ready for peace than republicans. "Ervine and Spence seemed genuinely against violence while the Sinn Féin leadership saw violence had simply run its course." Unlike the loyalists, Finlay added, Sinn Féin took a "Jesuitical view" towards the principle of consent and democracy in Northern Ireland.

If the Iveagh House meeting and its aftermath was embarrassing, worse was still to come. Two days later on Friday, January 9, the IRA exploded a huge bomb in London's docklands, killing two men in a shop nearby. The entire world waited for a loyalist response. None came. Ervine appeared on television and appealed for the UVF and UDA not to retaliate. Gary McMichael reciprocated on the UDP side. It seemed for a while that the loyalist political leadership could hold the line.

Holding that line would have been much easier if only sections of the Irish media and nationalist politicians had resisted laying some of the blame for the IRA ceasefire collapse at the door of Number 10 Downing Street. Loyalist leaders were angry that Irish politicians seemed to hint that John Major had some part in pushing the Provos over the edge. One UVF leader summed up the frustration caused by the attitude of parts of the Republic's political elite: "We were trying to convince people in the CLMC to hold back and not be provoked. Then it seemed it was all John Major's fault if you listened to nationalists. There was a joke in the UVF at the time that we should recruit John Major into the movement because he was so good at planting bombs."

It was this carping from Irish nationalism which partly resulted in the UVF bomb scare at Dublin Airport on March 3. One phone call and an abandoned car caused massive disruption to flights in and out of the capital. The actions was carried out on behalf of the UVF's Mid-Ulster Brigade which although acting independently from the Belfast leadership had widespread support throughout the organisation. The airport scare was a shot across the bows – a warning that if the IRA opted to blow London's economic heartland apart, the UVF would do the same in Dublin.

The loyalist mood turned more bellicose with a CLMC statement the following week. Referring to the IRA's renewed campaign in England, the CLMC said: "From a position of confidence, strength and sophistication, we have withstood the recent provocation of IRA bombs on the mainland which have killed our innocent British fellow citizens.

"These atrocities cannot be permitted to continue without a telling response from this source. We are poised and ready to strike to effect. We will give blow for blow. As in the past, whatever the cost, we will gladly pay it."

Both loyalist terror groups maintained the ceasefire but the pressure of the IRA's bombs in England created a growing band of dissidents within the two organisations. When the IRA bombed Manchester during the Euro '96 football championship, the PUP urged both governments to get tough with the Provisionals. A series of arrests in the Republic and the relative success of the security services in England against IRA units helped to calm things in the loyalist community. Privately UVF leaders were happy that the two governments were taking a more robust line against the IRA, which hardened significantly after the Provisionals murdered Garda Gerry McCabe in June.

Two political events dominated the summer and tested the resolve of the UVF command. The first was the elections to All Party Talks and the Forum, which John Major had promised at the start of the year. The elections were the primary test of PUP and UDP post-ceasefire electoral support. The UVF-aligned party did better than the UDP, polling 3.5 per cent of the vote as opposed to the UDA-linked party's 2.2 per cent. The PUP did particularly well in Belfast, where it put up high-profile candidates like David Ervine, Hugh Smyth and Billy Hutchinson. The party failed to win a seat from an individual constituency to the Forum but entered the talks because it had enough votes overall in Northern Ireland to reach the required quota. If this performance was repeated in local government elections, the PUP would win at least four seats in Belfast, including two in the east of the city.

Loyalist representation at City Hall might be even greater if the PUP and UDP co-operated together to form an electoral pact. But this seems highly unlikely. Both parties say there is little chance of a transfer votes deal given the deep historical differences over the last 25 years. The failure to hammer out such an alliance illuminates the continued divisions and mutual mistrust between the two wings of loyalism. One UDA leader when asked if he saw any chance of an electoral pact with the PUP replied incredulously: "What, do a deal with them blackneck bastards?" ("Blacknecks" is the nickname UDA members give to the UVF and their political allies, the "black" being a reference to the dark uniforms worn by UVF men on parade. The UVF used to call the UDA "Japs" because in the 1970s there were thousands of them!)

The deep suspicions are the result of bitterness over a series of savage street feuds between the UVF and UDA. Several paramilitaries were killed in faction fighting and many in each of the terror groups have long memories.

There were and are important political disagreements between the two ends of loyalism which also make an electoral deal difficult. While the PUP (at least in Belfast) is avowedly socialist, the UDP is reluctant to commit itself to any right-left definition. The UDA is an even more loosely based, federal-type organisation than the UVF, with members sharing political views from the extreme right to the centre left. The two parties also differ in their approach to the Constitutional question. Both are naturally pro-union, but the PUP is less enamoured of the idea of an independent Ulster than the UDP. The UDA in the late 1970s advocated independence for the Province as an alternative to the union, if Britain was going to sell Ulster out.

"On the Twelfth you can still work out which house is a UDA man's and which is a UVF man's. The UDA man will be flying the Ulster Flag while the UVF man will always fly the union jack," said one east Belfast UVF man, succinctly describing the subtle differences between the two loyalist groupings.

Much of the mistrust between the UDA and UVF is down to territorial battles over who controls, or is strongest, in certain Protestant areas. The situation in east Belfast is particularly interesting. In the early 1970s this was the UDA's stronghold where their headquarters was situated and their Supreme Commander, Andy Tyrie, lived. Today the UVF is the dominant force in the east. As one veteran UVF member said: "In the early days there were 8,000 of them in the east and about 80 of us. Now the boot's on the other foot and they don't like it."

It is worth comparing the combined vote of loyalist parties to that of mainstream unionist parties, particularly the DUP. Pundits have predicted that Ian Paisley's party would suffer at the polls for its sceptical approach to the peace process and its hostility to the loyalist parties. In fact the DUP got 18.8 per cent, more than three times the size of the PUP and

UDP votes put together. The DUP's support indicated that a sizeable tranche of the Unionist population did not think the Union was safe.

The resilient vote for Paisley's party should also have been an indicator that there was a core of hardline loyalists opposed to giving ground on issues such as Sinn Féin's entry to talks and compromise over the marching dispute. A sign of things to come perhaps in the next few weeks and months.

Sir Hugh Annesley, the former RUC Chief Constable, banned the Orange march along the Garvaghy Road. His decision brought thousands of Orangemen to Drumcree in defiance of Sir Hugh's decision. The police had opted initially to ban the parade from passing along the disputed route because they knew there would be serious violence from the nationalist side if the march went through. Within a matter of days, the RUC was forced into a humiliating U-turn. The numbers of Orangemen and loyalists facing the thin lines of RUC officers in fields overlooking the Garvaghy Road swelled. The force were advised that the only way to hold the line would be to use troops. That meant the British Army would have to retain the option of using live rounds on the protesting Orangemen to hold them back.

The prospect of a possible Orange Bloody Sunday was too much for the authorities, who reversed the decision and allowed the march to pass. In the middle of the stand-off, Orangemen and some unionist politicians took part in a co-ordinated campaign of mass disruption across the Province. Roads were blocked, ports shut down, rural towns cordoned off and police officers attacked in various parts of Northern Ireland, with the object of stretching RUC resources to the limit.

Surprisingly, neither the UVF leadership in Belfast or the UDA took any part in the Northern-wide campaign to put pressure on the RUC. It was clear the organisation for the protests, particularly in rural areas, was the work of middle-ranking members of the Ulster Unionist Party, the DUP, Orange Order and grassroots unionists fed up with what they saw as territorial reverses in favour of nationalism. In the middle of the siege at Drumcree, Ian Paisley and Robert McCartney visited the protesters to show solidarity. David Trimble, the local MP, was also present, and found himself in the centre of a political controversy when it was revealed he spoke with Billy Wright about the stand-off.

Wright defied the UVF Brigade Staff and played a central role in the confrontation at the church grounds. There were rumours that his supporters had even confiscated a tractor which could spray out petrol and be used as a flamethrower on wheels to break through police lines. He was joined at the Drumcree lines by Alex Kerr, a former senior UDA man, who had broken with the UDP and Gary McMichael earlier in the year. Kerr, an articulate but fervent hardliner, believed like the DUP that the loyalist parties were dupes of the British government. They had been used as Trojan Horses to bring Sinn Féin into the gates of Stormont. Kerr and Wright became the rejectionist double act of loyalism at Drumcreee. They had strong support on the ground among young loyalists, who attacked police officers throughout the siege.

Back in Belfast the UVF leadership were alarmed. Many of them privately felt that the marching controversy was a side issue and that loyalists were falling into a political trap set by Sinn Féin and the IRA. To underpin their concern about Drumcree, the CLMC met in emergency session to discuss what was happening in Portadown. While supporting the Orange Order's right to march along the route, the CLMC appealed to young loyalists not to be drawn into street violence. The tone of the CLMC declaration was remarkably moderate during this highly charged period.

"The CLMC are not the sinister element that public luminaries keep referring to since we have played no part in the recent disturbances in connection with the entire parade issue and we will not permit ourselves to be scapegoats.

"At this point the Loyalist ceasefire is intact but, if for reasons beyond our control, we are unwillingly drawn into this developing situation we wish to make it crystal clear that it will not be of our making. We do not want it."

The CLMC's claim that it was not orchestrating the street violence seemed justified. UVF strongholds like the Shankill were remarkably quiet during the Drumcree siege. The UDA also refused to put men on the streets. There was a wave of rioting in east and North Belfast, but this died down once the CLMC appealed for an end to trouble in the city. Indeed the one lesson to learn from Drumcree Mark II was that Ulster's loyalists were only driving their protest in second gear. Had the paramilitaries really weighed in behind "respectable" unionist politicians and Orangemen that week, Northern Ireland might have been plunged into total chaos.

UVF commanders felt that unionists who were outraged over Drumcree were drawing themselves into the republican movement's game plan. The July CLMC statement made this explicit. "We see the overall picture in relation to our common enemy, the IRA, and an escalation into sectarian civil disorder will given them 'on a platter' the excuse to go back to violence in this Province by portraying themselves as defenders of the Catholic people. This could have disastrous consequences."

They pointed to the behaviour of Sinn Féin in North Belfast during Drumcree week as a glaring example of this strategy. While there were genuine fears and blatant examples of intimidation against Catholic families, it is also true that republicans grossly exaggerated the situation and thus exploited it. In streets off Glandore Avenue, which links the mainly Catholic Antrim Road to the loyalist Shore Road, Sinn Féin supporters arrived in bus loads from Ardoyne to "evacuate" beleaguered nationalists. Only a handful of families living in this area, some of whom had relations in Ardoyne, wanted out. Other Catholics there refused Sinn Féin's offers of help and denied there was a danger of pogroms by Protestants from the lower end of Glandore Avenue. One Catholic resident even angrily remonstrated with Sinn Féin politicians, accusing them of hyping up fears in the area.

While most areas of Belfast were relatively quiet, the small mainly Protestant enclave of Torrens, between the Cliftonville and Oldpark Roads, was a powder keg waiting to explode.

Catholic families claimed they were being intimidated from their homes by loyalists. Protestant residents, however, denied this, and accused republicans from nearby Ardoyne of inflaming the situation. An ugly-stand off ensued, with hundreds of republicans arriving in the area to "rescue" Catholics living there. Protestants in Torrens felt under threat and members of the local UVF went to an arms dump for weapons to defend their area. Shortly afterwards the UVF produced an AK47 rifle and threatened to use it against Ardoyne republicans. Billy Hutchinson was informed of the escalating danger in Torrens and arrived there from the Shankill. Hutchinson persuaded the local UVF men not to open fire on republicans and actually stood in front of the man holding the Kalashnikov. This action forced the local UVF to back off and the weapon was taken out of the area. This incident, more than any other during Drumcree week, marks the closest loyalists came to breaking their ceasefire in the city. Hutchinson's presence in Torrens prevented a slide towards outright sectarian warfare in North Belfast, and probably did more to preserve the UVF cessation than anything else in the long, hot summer of 1996.

In Portadown, however, the UVF were unwilling to listen to the arguments of the Belfast-based leadership. On July 7, in the middle of the Drumcree siege, the Portadown unit murdered Michael McGoldrick, a Catholic taxi driver who had just graduated from Queen's University. Mr McGoldrick was found dead in his car after picking up a fare in Portadown. The weapon used to kill him had never been fired before. The method of his murder was like so many others in the early 1990s when loyalists targeted Catholic taxi drivers. No one claimed responsibility but it was obvious to everyone that the Portadown UVF, no doubt wanting to flex their muscles with this squalid and vindictive killing, were the culprits.

The UVF leadership viewed the killing as a direct challenge to their authority and that of the CLMC. On August 2 the terror group's leadership held a "press conference" in Belfast. They presented seven men wearing balaclavas and black head to toe uniforms. Four of them carried Kalashnikov rifles and stood over three other hooded men, who sat at a table draped with the UVF flag. On the table was an assortment of guns, including Ingram sub-machine guns. One man read from a text headed "Ulster Volunteer Force Command Staff. It said: "As a result of a preliminary investigation into a Portadown unit attached to the mid-Ulster Brigade of the Ulster Volunteer Force, a decision has been taken by the Command Staff of the UVF to disband this unit as from August 2, 1996. There will be ongoing investigations by the Internal Affairs Section of the Ulster Volunteer Force into the activities of this particular unit."

The suspension of the Portadown Unit was the start of a new war of words between loyalists in the mid-Ulster town, particularly Billy Wright and the Belfast UVF. However, the decision to disband the Portadown unit also had the support of other units in rural parts of Northern Ireland, including the rest of mid-Ulster. Central UVF players in mid-Ulster, including the Jackal and the man who acted as a go-between between Dublin criminals, the UVF and English arms dealers, remained loyal to the leadership.

UVF units in Lurgan, Richill, Donaghcloney, Banbridge and other towns and villages in mid-Ulster also toed the leadership line. Several weeks later on September 2, after the disbandment of the Portadown unit, other mid-Ulster UVF members publicly demonstrated their loyalty to the Command staff. During a march to commemorate the death of Brian Robinson, the UVF man shot dead by undercover British soldiers, a member of the mid-Ulster Brigade dressed in black and wearing a balaclava, read out a brief statement beside a loyalist mural on the Shankill Road:

"I would commence by saying that we are very conscious of what this parade is about and have no desire to take away from the dignity of the occasion," he told a crowd at the commemoration. "The current situation pertaining to the Portadown unit of our Brigade is not about freedom of speech, it is about internal discipline within the UVF, a code of discipline that all Volunteers have lived by for the past twenty-seven years. That code was broken. No one person is bigger than this force nor this code. We pledge our full support to the Military Command of the Ulster Volunteer Force in all decisions made on this issue."

The UVF was also coming under pressure within the CLMC to act against its dissidents. The UDA pointed out that it had expelled Alex Kerr and those around him for their insubordination. They even sent a hit team out to assassinate Kerr at his home in Cookstown, although this was foiled by the RUC. UDA leaders insisted that the UVF must also take a firm stance against loyalists in their strongholds who criticised the ceasefire.

The two groups embarked on a joint strategy under the auspices of the CLMC, which issued a statement ordering Billy Wright to leave Northern Ireland by midnight September 1, 1996, or else be killed. This threat also extended to Alex Kerr.

Wright, though, remained defiant. Hours before the

deadline, Wright was greeted as a hero by hundreds of supporters in Portadown gathered there for a march by the Royal Black Preceptory. Many of the Blackmen, including some from lodges in the Republic, waved to Wright in Portadown town centre and give him the thumbs-up sign. After the march Wright was mobbed by enthusiastic followers at a function for UVF prisoners at a social club on the loyalist Corcrain estate. His henchmen in the Portadown unit predicted there would be "an awful feud" within the UVF if the death threat was carried out. Wright was clapped and cheered during the function as he denounced the leadership of the Progressive Unionist Party. He said the UVF command was also totally out of step with grassroots loyalist opinion.

"The IRA tried to kill me and I stood up to them. What guts me are that so-called loyalists are also trying to kill me for speaking my mind." Wright claimed he had received messages of support from within the UVF across Northern Ireland, including a number of men from the Shankill Road. He also got the backing of Billy Lowry, a Scottish loyalist, who had actually stood as a PUP candidate for the Forum elections in June.

Several days later a rally was called in support of Wright in the middle of Portadown attended by at least five thousand loyalists. It was addressed by local Orangemen and the mid-Ulster MP, the Rev William McCrea, who condemned the CLMC threat to Wright. McCrea also singled out David Ervine and Billy Hutchinson for stinging criticism. The DUP MP defended Wright's freedom to speak out against the PUP/UVF leadership line and said he too would not leave Northern Ireland if he was threatened. His presence on the platform with Wright sickened nationalists and provoked a political storm. McCrea protested that he was simply defending the right of free speech within the unionist community. But nationalist politicians saw this as hypocrisy, given Wright's reputation. The DUP was willing to stand beside Billy Wright but unwilling to allow elected Sinn Féin representatives into all-party talks.

A year before, Billy Wright had been a "loyalist hostage" after his arrest in Scotland. Now in the autumn of 1996, he was the UVF's public enemy number one. In September's *Combat* the UVF leadership counter-attacked with an article penned by a "true Ulster Volunteer". The author accused Wright of acting as a dupe for Paisley's party, who were determined to stop the PUP becoming an influential political force in loyalism. He referred back to the mid-1970s when other established unionists tried to wound the PUP under Ken Gibson with charges of communism and socialism.

"The reds under the beds, the lefties and the card-carrying phraseology was used in 1974 by other unionist politicians (but especially John Taylor and Martin Smyth) as well as elements within the UVF at that time, namely Joe Bennett and his ilk.

"The politicians and the scurrilous incantations are still the same but there has emerged Billy Wright, his fellow travellers and his DUP fundamentalist friends. It remains to be seen whose agenda Billy Wright is following and to whom he truly owes allegiance."

The UVF also opened up a propaganda front against the DUP and Robert McCartney's UK Unionists, who were clamouring for decommissioning of loyalist guns and doing their utmost to get the PUP and UDP ejected from the talks.

In the same streets where unionist rejectionists wrote "The Union is Safe – ha, ha, ha," UVF supporters went on the propaganda offensive against Ian Paisley and Robert McCartney. "1912 UVF Clyde Valley Arms, 1996 Paisley and McCartney say surrender guns – Some Carsons," one slogan said. Another accused the two leaders of wanting to leave loyalists defenceless through their insistence on decommissioning while the IRA still held on to their arsenal.

The Carson jibe was meant for Paisley in particular, who in the early 1980s styled his own anti-Anglo Irish protest campaign on the political rallies held by Carson in opposition to Home Rule. The UVF's graffiti campaign was also aimed indirectly at Billy Wright.

"Here was Billy Wright aligning himself with the DUP who wanted the UVF to give up all their guns. By his association Wright was supporting the idea of unilateral loyalist decommissioning even though he was portraying himself as a super-loyalist," one UVF commander remarked.

While the UVF command could point to the contradictions within Wright's alliance with DUP fundamentalists, Wright himself highlighted the loose political allegiances inside the loyalist terror group. In Belfast, the PUP claimed to be a democratic socialist party, Wright said, but this philosophy was absolutely alien to many other UVF supporters outside the city and even some in it. Wright correctly noted that the UVF was an alliance with people of both left and right, working for the one objective, defence of the Union. In areas like Portadown, the UVF was more likely to be made up of right-wing unionists and Evangelical Protestants than jail-educated urban socialists. Indeed many UVF supporters didn't even both to vote for the PUP in rural areas and instead gave their allegiance to the DUP.

Wright still contends that Ervine, Hutchinson and Spence have made the fundamental mistake of imposing socialist ideology on a heterogeneous political movement. Moreover, PUP leaders like Hutchinson have shared platforms with Sinn Féin members and supported the Irish language, things which were anathema to grassroots loyalists, according to Wright.

His prescription was a return to basics and defend Ulster, quietly forgetting the socialist rhetoric espoused by the likes of Hutchinson and Ervine. Many of Wright's young supporters in Portadown take this view. They will say they continue to support the UVF while loathing the PUP. In fact, on the day the Black demonstration took place in their town, several of Wright's friend wore UVF mid-Ulster Brigade t-shirts even thought they spat venom about the movement's command in Belfast.

The death threat still hangs over Billy Wright, who has remained defiant throughout. It is clear he does have considerable support inside Portadown although the picture is less clear in other parts of mid-Ulster. He also has some sneaking-regarders within Belfast, who for now have kept their heads down and failed to challenge the UVF command.

Wright is now in prison serving an eight-year sentence for intimidating witnesses who wanted to give evidence against UVF men who carried a so-called punishment attack in Portadown. When he was sentenced, Wright accused the judiciary of imposing a form of internment on loyalists who opposed the ceasefire. They were, Wright argued, ensuring dissident loyalism would be silenced. Without such a charismatic figure to rally around, those who support Wright's line have no proper organisation or leadership.

For the UVF leadership, however, the Billy Wright issue had been overtaken by other more serious developments. The IRA decision to resume terror attacks inside Northern Ireland following a series of disastrous setbacks in its England campaign has put the loyalist ceasefire under incredible pressure. The IRA bomb at Army headquarters in Lisburn on October 7, 1996, almost tipped the balance towards a resumption of loyalist terror. The CLMC met in emergency session a day after the bomb. At that stage, miraculously, no one had died. UVF sources insist that the fact that there were no fatalities at that stage prevented the CLMC from ending the ceasefire. It was a cruel irony that Jim Bradwell, the soldier who eventually died from the bomb, had clung to life for four days. In that period the CLMC had no early pretext to strike back.

351

In the early autumn the clamour for loyalists to hit back came from inside the UVF rather than the UDA. Less than a week after Thiepval, some UVF battalions were actually taking votes on whether or not to retaliate. On the day Jim Bradwell died, the UVF's west Belfast battalion narrowly voted in favour of keeping their guns silent at a meeting in a hall on the Shankill Road. The UDA watched on with some amusement. They had always been regarded as the more unstable element within the CLMC, the group more likely to break the peace. Now instead it was the UVF, which prided itself on stern military-style discipline and a stable central leadership, who were wobbling on the ceasefire question.

This picture altered radically when the IRA attempted to shoot a bodyguard of DUP politician, Nigel Dodds, while he was visiting his ill son in the Royal Hospital for Sick Children in Belfast on December 21, 1996. Amazingly, no one was killed or seriously injured. The sight of bullet holes in an infant's incubator and the risk of maximum carnage inside the children's ward was too much for some loyalists. Their anger was compounded by the fact that earlier that day UDA inmates had met John Hume in the Maze. The meeting was a cordial affair, with Hume stressing that there were no hidden agendas or backroom deals being hatched in his talks with Gerry Adams. UDA prisoners, including Johnny Adair, accepted that Hume was sincere, although they wondered if he was a dupe of the republican movement.

Following the Children's Hospital attack, UDA leaders warned that violence was inevitable and that their ceasefire could not hold. Twenty-four hours later a bomb exploded under a car belonging to Eddie Copeland, a leading republican from Ardoyne. Copeland, a hate figure among loyalists, was badly injured but still survived the blast.

The UVF played no part in the Copeland attack. It was the work of two UDA men from North Belfast who were aided by dissident members of the Red Hand Commando. The RHC had provided the bomb-making skills to build the under-car booby trap device and the UDA men placed it below Copeland's car. Despite this, the UDA never officially said it was responsible. Loyalist politicians like Gary McMichael protested that the loyalist ceasefire was intact but failed to explain adequately how this statement squared with the attack in Ardoyne.

By now the CLMC was riven with internal divisions, with one section of the UDA arguing that the only way forward was to bring the Province to levels of violence not seen since the early 1970s. Those advocating this chilling scenario believed that the nationalist population should pay a heavy price for resumed IRA violence so that, in the end, exhaustion within northern nationalism would force the Provos to call another ceasefire. Moves, however, for a full resumption of violence have been robustly opposed by the UVF. They feel that loyalism should not be goaded back into war and thus provide the IRA with the pretext of acting as defenders of the nationalist people. They are also heartened by the ongoing success of the security forces in apprehending IRA men and materials following Provo attacks at the start of 1997.

"We shouldn't do what our enemy wants," said one UVF member, reflecting what seemed to be the majority view on the brigade staff at the beginning of the year. The former IRA commander turned informer, Sean O'Callaghan, has made the point that had loyalists not gone on the offensive in the early 1970s, the RUC, British Army and Irish security forces could have dealt more effectively with the IRA. UVF and UDA violence was a distraction and helped to give the Provos breathing space, he contends. O'Callaghan's analysis is shared by many in the RUC who fear that a resumption of loyalist terror would tie up resources which could otherwise be deployed against the IRA. This line has been undermined, though, by recent sightings of known IRA activists in loyalist areas, the offices and homes of PUP and UDP members. Paranoia and the expectation of an IRA purge is at frightening levels within loyalism at present.

Following Canary Wharf there was a growing view within the UVF that Dublin should be a target if the IRA continued to bomb England. This argument was bolstered by the attitudes of some Dublin politicians who lay part of the blame for the IRA ceasefire breakdown on John Major. In the first half of 1997, the demand for a full-scale attack on Dublin waned, particularly after the Irish government toughened its stance towards Sinn Féin. The UVF was far less hostile to the Rainbow Coalition than to Albert Reynolds' administration. They are not enamoured though of the prospect of Fianna Fail returning to power, especially under Bertie Ahern. Loyalist leaders view Mr Ahern's statements on the North in opposition with alarm, given, at times, his stridently nationalist approach. There is some comfort, nevertheless, in the possibility of Mary Harney's Progressive Democrats entering a coalition with Ahern, given her implacable opposition to Sinn Féin and the IRA.

As 1997 opened, Northern Ireland was holding its breath. The nationalist community was particularly worried that loyalist gunmen would return to their streets and that their communities would be plunged back into the dark days of the early 1990s. All the people in the North seemed to be living in a penumbral state between peace and war.

The Provos have turned their violence on and off like a water tap. They suffered a series of setbacks in Belfast when the security forces foiled a series of murder bids against police and troops. The IRA hit back in south Armagh by killing a young soldier in Bessbrook. The UVF replied by sending a deadly signal to the Provisionals that they too could turn the war back on again. The loyalist terror group placed a huge bomb containing twenty-six sticks of gelignite

354

in a holdall outside Sinn Féin's offices in Monaghan town. An Irish army bomb disposal officer said there was enough explosive power in the device to wipe out half the street, let alone the Sinn Féin premises. Amazingly the bomb failed to explode because someone the night before found the holdall in the street and threw it up an alleyway. By disturbing the wiring system inside the bomb this man probably prevented the first explosion in the Republic since the ceasefire.

In this uncertain time it was time to return to Fernhill House. On the museum's balcony on a bone-chilling morning the winter sun was burning off the early mist to reveal the Belfast skyline. Apart from the odd modernist construct like the security tower in nearby nationalist Ardoyne, or the handful of sky-scrapers in the city centre, the view from the museum has not changed since the days of the old UVF at the start of this century.

Staff inside the house once used as a UVF training ground were planning a new exhibition. It will focus on the last thirty years of sectarian slaughter and political upheaval. Among the artifacts Fernhill House will put on display will be memorabilia from ceasefire day, October 13, 1994. These include the actual paper Gusty Spence read from to announce an end to almost three decades of loyalist terror. The signatures of the men at the table that day will also be on show for the general public as well as library television footage of the historic event.

Two murals painted in the city during the ceasefires seem to sum up the attitude of the modern UVF to the Northern Ireland question at the end of the 20th century. One of them, a few miles from Fernhill House down the Shankill Road on a gable wall, shows three UVF men smashing in a door with a sledgehammer, guns at the ready. The slogan above it reads: "Compromise or Conflict." (The house is actually modelled on the Lower Falls home of Hugh Torney, the INLA leader. It depicts an attack on Torney's home just before the loyalist ceasefire. The republican leader escaped death but was later killed by his own comrades.)

Across the city, another huge mural was drawn at the end of flats off the Shore Road. It is two hooded UVF men, their menacing eyes bulging out of their balaclavas, holding Ingram sub-machine guns. On top is a warning: "Preparing for Peace, Ready for War."

At the time of writing we cannot say for sure which of these two options the UVF is to take. The signs look ominous. While the UVF leadership has preferred not to enter back into conflict again, the pressures on them to resume violence are becoming irresistible by the day. This year at Drumcree, the UVF may intervene to back up the Orangemen's right to parade down the Garvaghy Road. This U-turn in policy may be in part due to the preservation of support within the UVF's own constituency. In addition the UVF may be reacting to what they see as increased interference on the part of the Irish government, especially Dick Spring, in an internal Northern Ireland matter. Whatever their motivation, it is clear that Spring and his advisers at the Department of Foreign Affairs are courting disaster if they follow the lines laid down by Sinn Féin/IRA-run residents' groups.

One thing is certain. Soon, very soon, we will know whether the artifacts of the loyalist ceasefire held at Fernhill are still part of a living, developing peace process, or simply museum pieces reflecting a time of short-lived hope that is now past.

# INDEX